Just Authority?

What does it mean to trust the police? What makes the police legitimate in the eyes of the policed? What builds trust, legitimacy and cooperation, and what undermines the bond between police and the public? These questions are central to current debates concerning the relationship between the British police and the public it serves. But, in the context of British policing they are seldom asked explicitly, still less examined in depth.

Drawing on psychological and sociological explanatory paradigms, *Just Authority* presents a cutting-edge empirical study into public trust, police legitimacy and people's readiness to cooperate with officers. It represents, first, the most detailed test to date of Tom Tyler's procedural justice model attempted outside the United States. Second, it uncovers the social ecology of trust and legitimacy and, third, it describes the relationships between trust, legitimacy and cooperation.

This book contains many important lessons for practitioners, policy-makers and academics. As elsewhere, the dominant vision of policing in Great Britain continues to stress instrumental effectiveness: the 'fight against crime' will be won by pro-active and even aggressive policing. In line with work from the United States and elsewhere, *Just Authority* casts significant doubt on such claims. When people find policing to be unfair, disrespectful and careless of human dignity, not only is trust lost, but legitimacy is also damaged, and cooperation is withdrawn as a result. Absent such public support, the job of the police is made harder and the avowed objectives of less crime and disorder placed ever further from reach.

Jonathan Jackson is Senior Lecturer in Research Methodology at the LSE, and member of the LSE's Mannheim Centre for Criminology.

Ben Bradford is a Career Development Fellow in the Centre for Criminology at the University of Oxford.

Betsy Stanko is Honorary Professor of Criminology at Royal Holloway, University of London.

Katrin Hohl is a Research Fellow in the Methodology Institute at the LSE.

Just Authority?

Trust in the police in England and Wales

**Jonathan Jackson, Ben Bradford,
Betsy Stanko and Katrin Hohl**

Routledge
Taylor & Francis Group

LONDON AND NEW YORK

First published 2013
by Routledge
2 Park Square, Milton Park, Abingdon, Oxon, OX14 4RN

Simultaneously published in the USA and Canada
by Routledge
711 Third Avenue, New York, NY 10017

Routledge is an imprint of the Taylor & Francis Group, an informa business

© 2013 Jonathan Jackson, Ben Bradford, Betsy Stanko, Katrin Hohl

The right of Jonathan Jackson, Ben Bradford, Betsy Stanko and Katrin
Hohl to be identified as authors of this work has been asserted by them in
accordance with sections 77 and 78 of the Copyright, Designs and Patents
Act 1988.

All rights reserved. No part of this book may be reprinted or reproduced or
utilised in any form or by any electronic, mechanical, or other means, now
known or hereafter invented, including photocopying and recording, or in
any information storage or retrieval system, without permission in writing
from the publishers.

Trademark notice: Product or corporate names may be trademarks or
registered trademarks, and are used only for identification and explanation
without intent to infringe.

British Library Cataloguing in Publication Data
A catalogue record for this book is available from the British Library

Library of Congress Cataloging in Publication Data
Just authority : trust in the police in England and Wales / Jonathan Jackson
... [etal.]. -- 1st ed.
    p. cm.
    1. Police--Wales. 2. Police--England. 3. Police psychology--Wales.
    4. Police psychology--England. 5. Police-community relations--Wales.
    6. Police-community relations--England. I. Jackson, Jonathan, 1974–
    HV8196.A2T78 2012   363.20942--dc23
    2012004981

ISBN: 978–1–84392–848–5 (hbk)
ISBN: 978–0–415–62346–9 (pbk)
ISBN: 978–0–203–10561–0 (ebk)

Typeset in Times New Roman
by Bookcraft Ltd, Stroud, Gloucestershire

Contents

Figures

Tables

Foreword

This well written and engaging volume articulates and empirically supports a new and innovative approach to policing based upon the goal of creating and maintaining the belief among members of the public that police authority is legitimate. In so doing, the authors are providing a new framework for thinking about the goals of policing, one that emphasises how police policies and practices are experienced within policed communities. Rather than concentrating authority over policing decisions within higher level policing authorities, rather than evaluating police effectiveness in terms of success in combating particular forms of crime defined by police professionals, this approach suggests that the community needs to play a strong role in defining its problems and in determining how the police should address those problems.

This approach builds upon what the authors identify as a central element in the ability of the police to be successful: a view among members of the public that there is a moral alignment between the public and the police, which leads the police to be pursuing a shared vision of appropriate social order with society, and hence being justified in their exercise of power. This broadened conception of legitimacy is shown to better account for public reactions to the police than a perspective that takes an instrumental approach to policing, in which the police are evaluated by the public primarily in terms of their effectiveness in solving particular community problems or effectively controlling crime. Although such concerns are not irrelevant, they are not found to be the primary issues on the public's mind when reacting to the law and the police. Instead, the police are evaluated normatively in terms of whether they are entitled to hold power and exercise discretion about its use within the community.

The authors make their case using the results of wide-ranging British surveys that are analysed through a sophisticated and compelling approach that considers both individual-level attitudes and/or behaviours and neighbourhood context. The results first demonstrate that a broadened conception of legitimacy proposed by the authors is a central antecedent of public compliance and cooperation with the police and the law. Legitimacy is central to public deference to the police and the law, so the effectiveness of legal authorities depends simply, or even primarily, upon their ability to protect threat or use force. It depends upon the public's belief both that the police are entitled to make decisions about how and when to enforce the law, and also their sense that people should obey those decisions, as well as following the law in their everyday lives. Beyond that, policing scholars have increasingly defined success in terms of the ability of legal authorities to gain the active cooperation of the public in co-policing communities. As the authors of this volume demonstrate, such active cooperation also flows from legitimacy.

The findings reported further affirm the importance of the public's treatment with fairness and dignity in shaping their views about police legitimacy. The latter finding reinforces recent demonstrations that members of the public evaluate the actions of legal authorities primarily by evaluating the fairness of the procedures through which they exercise their authority. This procedural justice effect suggests that to maintain legitimacy, policing policies and practices need to be evaluated not only by asking whether they conform to the law and whether they are effective in combating crime, but also by considering whether the community judges them to be fair.

Taken as a whole, these findings are a powerful statement for the value of evaluating police policies and practices by reference to their impact upon police legitimacy – an approach that provides a transformative perspective with widespread implications for policing. While anyone concerned about how the police should police will value the insights in this book, they are especially timely in the context of recent efforts to understand the reasons for urban rioting in the UK and the implications of those events for the relationship between the British police and the British public, in particular the young and the members of minority communities.

Professor Tom R. Tyler,
Yale University,
January 2012

Part 1

Introduction

This book is an investigation into the psychological and sociological mechanisms driving public trust, police legitimacy and the willingness of citizens to cooperate with police officers. It was completed at a time of intense debate over the August 2011 riots, the extent of police involvement in the *News of the World* phone-hacking scandal, disproportionality in the use of stop-and-search powers, and the policing of demonstrations such as the 'Occupy' movement. All these issues and more were regularly aired in the media and other forums. Less publicly visible but arguably more fundamental, the election of the first Police and Crime Commissioners (PCCs) was only months away. The Labour Party had recently announced an 'Independent Commission' into policing; there was political wrangling over proposed cuts in the numbers of officers; and a new Commissioner had only recent taken up the reins at Scotland Yard following the rapid, and controversial, departure of his two predecessors.

Policing was at the top of the political, media and public agendas. Significant change in the structure of policing in England and Wales was afoot. Transformations were heralded by tensions in the relationship between police and public and widespread debate over the role of the police in a time of austerity. Yet we, like others, felt a strong sense of déjà vu. PCCs aside, much of the above seems eerily familiar. Scandals around the treatment of ethnic minorities, the policing of riots and other public-order events, corruption within the service, and the extent of political interference from outside it, have been issues in British policing since at least the 1970s. Politicians and senior officers have long been concerned about a decline in public trust and a crisis in police legitimacy for at least as long. Indeed, concerns about a loss of trust in, and respect for, the police were raised by the 1929 Royal Commission on the police (Weinberger 1995), as well as by its counterpart in 1962 (Royal Commission on the Police 1962).

What does the congruence in current and historical concerns tell us? First, it underlines that policing is a fundamentally controversial topic – a site of contest about the way society treats its less privileged members, about who needs protecting from whom, and about the limits of state power. Second, repeated questioning of the distribution of police activity draws attention to its impact on individuals and communities who, for whatever reason, become 'police property'. More broadly, the instrumental aims of the police – and the effects of policing on citizens – are always a key part of the social and political landscape. Third, there is an undeniable sense of nostalgia and a peculiarly British (or English) prelap-sarian vision of what policing should be (Loader and Mulcahy 2003). Fourth, and threaded through all the above, issues of fairness, probity, trust and legitimacy are placed right at the centre of a debate that has been going on for 40 years. The importance of public trust in the police is constantly restated, and its apparent decline constantly bemoaned.

The relationship between police and public stands central to all these concerns. What do people think about the police? Why do they trust it and grant it legiti-macy? Why do they cooperate with the police and criminal courts? These ques-tions seem both timely and perennial. Embedded in a wider social context, yet irreducibly personal to those involved, they play out in the context of long-term social change – such as the post-60s decline in deference and the increasing struggle of state and public institutions to maintain legitimacy in a globalised, multi-polar world (Reiner 1992; 2010) – as well as the immediate, micro-level interaction between officer and citizen (Waddington 1999). The implications of a loss of public trust, and the implications of a de-legitimation of the police, are enormous: at both ideological and mundane levels, the police rely on the consent, assistance and cooperation of the public. Policing by consent is a fine phrase, but it means little if we do not understand why people defer to officers, offer them support, or provide them with information. In this book we place people's use and experience of policing centre-stage.

Leaving aside questions concerning the police organisation, the links between police and other agencies, and the laws that govern or should govern police activity – as important as these issues are – we concentrate instead on the ways members of the public think, behave and react in relation to the police. Exploring the perceived social distance between police and the public, two points orient the discussion. First, trust in the police, while both multi-faceted and multi-sourced, rests most importantly on fairness judgements (Tyler and Huo 2002). Second, the legitimacy of the police – a complex social phenomenon involving individual, organisational and institutional elements (Bottoms and Tankebe 2012) – is none-theless constituted in a fundamental way by the beliefs, assessments and actions of the people it serves (Beetham 1991).

These ideas are explained and expanded on in the chapters that follow. Our approach is intensely empirical. Trust and legitimacy are social facts; their pres-ence or absence has important material implications for individuals, communi-ties and the police itself. Using social survey data, primarily from London, we trace a path from the roots of trust (or mistrust) through the factors that influ-ence the trust judgements people make, to the effect that trust has on legitimacy and the ways legitimacy plays out in public propensities to cooperate, or not, with police. Although these pathways find expression primarily at the individual level, the underlying causal mechanisms seem to refer to the importance of social groups in people's lives. One reason why people care so deeply about the fairness of the police is that the police represent a social group most find important and to which most feel affiliation – the nation state or community. Fairness indicates status and respect within this group (Tyler and Blader 2000). Despite its social psychological bent, this book fits well with other more sociological accounts of

British policing that have stressed the symbolic role of the police in providing a bridge between nation, community and self (Girling *et al.* 2000; Loader and Mulcahy 2003).

'The police' in London and beyond

Our data consider public understandings of a police service rooted in a city that claims modern policing as part of its own legacy. The Metropolitan Police consciously draw on this history to form part of its own 'founding myth'. So it is useful at this early juncture to address the history of policing and to define what is meant by 'police' in the context of this book.

Over the past 200 years or so, the police service in Great Britain, as elsewhere, emerged from previous modes of policing to become an organised body of people with a specific set of duties and responsibilities limited primarily to crime and the maintenance of order. Exactly when the first such 'police force' came into being is unclear – mid-eighteenth-century Paris had the *lieutenant general de police*, commanding a force of around 3,000 men (Emsley 2007: 65), and similar arrangements were in place in other European cities around the same time. But it was the establishment of the Metropolitan Police in 1829 that is still generally cited as the first instance of a police force in the modern sense (Reiner 2010).

Much of the debate about police and policing revolves around research on the institution of policing itself. Despite this, precise definitions of what the police actually is – either substantively or formally – have proved elusive (Manning 2010). The sheer variety of police organisations, and the range of policing activities in which they are involved, may mean a single definition is unachievable. Yet Bittner's (1975) much-quoted definition retains significant appeal; the police are the body responsible for dealing with situations requiring 'non-negotiably coercible' remedies. Bittner conceptualises policing through the eyes of the public, who conceive what the police are to be determined by what they do, or more precisely, how they are used. People 'locate' the police by reference to the tools it has to address the huge range of situations it is called upon to deal with. Famously, these situations can be defined as moments when 'something-that-ought-not-to-be-happening' is occurring, 'about-which-someone-had-better-do-something-now' (Bittner 1975).

Linking this public-generated definition of the police to the idea that the modern state is the monopolist of the use of legitimate force, Bittner positions the (potential) use of force as the central element of the police's role and its 'offer' to the public. In ideal-typical terms, procedures applied by police to remedy a situation cannot be opposed by the public. If they are, then force may be used to ensure that it is the will of the officers that prevails. After all, people call the police in order that it 'does something' and many of these calls concern immediate, specific conflicts where an imposed solution is desired or required. The police can be – and are – called upon in almost any situation involving disagreement, threat or the possibility of danger (that is, from lost pets to crowd control to actual crimes). Although many such situations will be only tangentially connected to the criminal law, all imply expectations that the police will provide at least proximal solutions by drawing on the authority the potential use of force provides.

But the public police are not the only policing actor, in mature democracies or anywhere else. In the UK at least it has become increasingly obvious over the past 15 to 20 years that positioning the police as the only, or even the primary, agent of policing is an outdated idea. Indeed some authors have noted that to a greater or lesser extent the public police have never held this role and that 'policing beyond the police' (Crawford 2003) or private policing has always been an important element in the maintenance of public order (Johnston 1992). Many commentators have begun to talk of 'security networks' (Newburn 2001), within which private security guards, CCTV, and other correlates of 'mass private property' (Shearing and Stenning 1981) work alongside or with the police both in the enforcement of law and order and in many of the traditional police service functions. Furthermore the New Labour government triggered a massive growth in quasi-public policing – Police Community Support Officers (PCSOs), Street Wardens, and so on – who occupy an area of middle ground, publicly employed but with few of the legal and symbolic powers available to sworn police officers. More than ever there is a need to conceptualise the police – whether as the publicly funded guardians and arbitrators of the law, or as the holders of the monopoly of the legitimate use of force, or both – separately from the activities of policing, which in modern society is conducted by many disparate institutions and bodies, as well as via those informal social controls which have always operated to impose and regulate behavioural norms. In much academic and policy discourse, police and policing are increasingly treated as two distinct areas of concern, with the latter enclosing the former as well as many other activities, organisations and social behaviours.

Yet, there is little evidence to suggest that such distinctions are made by citizens who still draw on public policing to assist them and who still believe that a visible, uniformed police presence is linked to security. Indeed, there may be much justification for the public's apparent unwillingness to let go of 'policing by the police'. Not because an array of other organisations is uninvolved in policing, but rather that the rise of diverse 'security networks' has not led to a decline in the power of the public police, nor a significant shift of its core responsibilities to other agencies (Newburn and Reiner 2004). Although the paramount position of the UK police as state organised and funded specialists in the provision of policing has been challenged by the growth of plural policing, there has been a gradual accretion of powers to the public police over the past 20 years, particularly through the passage of legislation designed to combat terrorism. This has left police officers with a set of powers that 'far exceeds' those of the ordinary citizen (ibid: 606) and, equally, earlier generations of police. The public police may have much more competition than previously, but they also have considerably more power, and arguably an ever increasing public profile, especially in the debates about security and safety.

There is surely little doubt that the majority of people, when asked who 'does' policing, would answer 'the police', meaning sworn officers with all the traditional set of responsibilities and abilities, the monopoly of the use of legitimate force, and (usually) dressed in a blue uniform. Moreover, when the public are asked about how to enhance security, they often reply they want to see 'more uniforms' visible on the street. For this reason if nothing else we use the term 'police' to refer exclusively to the public police and not to other agencies involved in modern day policing.

Our book studies people's experience of this police, their beliefs about its trustworthiness, their recognition and justification of police power, and their willingness to cooperate with legal authorities. And as we elaborate in Chapter 1, we take a distinctively interdisciplinary perspective. From a psychological perspective we show the validity of an extended version of Tyler's influential procedural justice model of policing; from a sociological perspective we highlight the social ecology of people's orientations to the police, linking informal policing processes operating in local neighbourhoods to people's inferences about the justified action of the police. So let us turn to an outline of our objectives and a catalogue of our contributions.

1   Social and moral connections

This book is about the bond between the police and the public. Why do people trust the police? Why do they grant legitimacy to officers and the institution? Why do they cooperate with the police and criminal courts? These are important questions because they speak to the vital nature of *policing by consent*. First, the public deserve and desire a police force that is legitimate, just, effective and restrained in its use of power. Second, the police depend upon trust, legitimacy and the cooperation of the public to function in an effective and fair manner. Third, contacts between police and public – for example through stop-and-search – have the potential to catastrophically damage people's trust in police, thus eroding the legitimacy of the law and the right of legal authorities to command common support.

We present in these pages the findings from a major study into the police-related experiences, attitudes and behaviours of Londoners. Our analyses highlight the vital nature of public trust and police legitimacy. From a policy perspective, our findings speak to the continued importance of the British idea of 'policing by consent'. Policing works best when the police can encourage normative commitment to legal authorities (Banton 1964; Bittner 1975; Smith 2007; Hough 2007a; Hough *et al.* 2010; Reiner 2010). Absent such commitment, a sole reliance on the threat or use of force drives a wedge between the police and those they serve, with significant economic and social implications. Adversarial police tactics risk the legitimacy of legal authorities, and the quickest way for the police to lose public consent is through mistreatment and unjust action.

We also add to a growing international literature on public trust and police legitimacy (e.g. Tyler and Huo 2002; Sunshine and Tyler 2003b; Reisig *et al.* 2007; Murphy *et al.* 2009; Tankebe 2009; Reisig and Lloyd 2009; Hough *et al.* 2010; Murphy and Cherney 2011; Cherney and Murphy 2011; Gau 2011; Elliott *et al.* 2011; Hasibi and Weisburd 2011; Stott *et al.* 2011; Jonathan-Zamir and Weisburd 2011; Ward *et al.* 2011; Kochel 2011; Bradford 2011a; Jackson *et al.* 2011, 2012a; Tyler *et al.* 2011b; van Craen 2012; Côté-Lussier in press; Huq *et al.* 2011; and Jackson *et al.* 2012a). Bridging psychological and sociological levels of analysis, we consider individual and neighbourhood factors that explain variation in trust, legitimacy and cooperation across London. Linking fair and respectful treatment to trust and legitimacy, we show that legitimacy finds practical expression in people's sense of obligation to defer to authorities, alignment with the morals that officers represent, and willingness to cooperate with the police and criminal courts. Demonstrating the important role of people's use and experience of policing, we show that contacts between police and public – for example through stop-and-search – have the potential to catastrophically damage people's trust, as well as erode the legitimacy of the law and the right of legal authorities to command common support.

The findings we present in the following pages together form four core contributions. First, we conduct the most comprehensive test of Tyler's psychological model of cooperation with the police outside the US (Tyler 2004, 2006a, 2006b, 2007, 2011a; Schulhofer *et al.* 2010; Huq *et al.* 2011). Theories of procedural justice state that if people in authority behave fairly and respectfully to those they direct, the latter will regard the authority of the former as legitimate, will defer to this authority, and will feel that the power that officials wield is justified (Sunshine and Tyler 2003a; Tyler *et al.* in press; Jackson *et al.* 2011). Taking into account the diverse neighbourhoods in which Londoners live, we find that this model works well in the capital. We conclude with the idea that the police must strive to treat those they encounter fairly and respectfully, and that failure to do so undermines people's sense that police officers are themselves worthy of respect and that the law defines acceptable behaviour. Fairness helps secure long-term commitment to the rule of law. Police unfairness makes the task of dealing with crime and disorder more difficult in the long run.

The second contribution is to extend Tyler's definition of police legitimacy (see Tyler 2006a, 2006b; Tyler *et al.* in press). Legitimacy refers to a fundamental property of legal institutions, the right to govern, and the recognition by the governed of that right (Jackson *et al.* 2011). When citizens see criminal justice institutions as legitimate, they recognise the system's authority to determine the law, to govern through the use of coercive force, to punish those who act illegally and to expect from members of the public cooperation and obedience. Crucially, we show that legitimacy is not just public recognition of power (people's duty to obey), it is also public justification of power (a sense of moral alignment with the institution).[1] This is important given ongoing debates over the form and texture of police legitimacy (Reisig *et al.* 2007; Gau 2011; Jackson *et al.* 2011; Bottoms and Tankebe in press).

Third, we uncover the social ecology of trust, legitimacy and cooperation. Is the social and structural context important to public trust and police legitimacy? Is living in a disadvantaged and residentially unstable area a factor? Is living in a disorderly area that lacks collective social resources and ties also important? We find that neighbourhood context is more important than individual-level characteristics such as age, ethnicity and work status. Highlighting the special significance of social characteristics of the neighbourhood in which people live, we argue how the legitimacy of the police is premised in part on what it is: namely, the physical embodiment of social control activities. Informal social controls are most evident when residents hold the neighbourhood in mutual regard, when they uphold the locally accepted obligations of civility, and when they outwardly disdain the flouting of those obligations. When order is maintained and informal social controls are strong, the police seem justified in their holding of power, but when a neighbourhood does not informally police its members, the police seem unjustified in their monopoly over social force and regulation.

Fourth, London is one of the most diverse cities in the world. One might therefore expect to see large-scale variation in what Londoners want from the police. But we do not find this to be the case. People from different groups and from different communities want similar things from the police; they judge the police in largely similar ways; they want to live in orderly neighbourhoods that enjoy social cohesion and fair regulation; and their attitudes toward the police are wrapped up in the health of subtle, informal processes of social control. They want fair and respectful treatment and fair and respectful decision-making from the police. And their legitimising beliefs concerning the police involve not just obligation to obey, but also a sense of moral alignment with the police's role as a regulatory agent (with the exception noted below). They cooperate with the police not just when they trust officers, but also when they believe that police authority is legitimate and justified.

Structure of the book

Our book has five parts. In Chapters 1 and 2 we summarise the findings and outline our methodology. Part 2 then takes the 'long view': building upon Bradford (2011b) and pooling data from 25 years of the British Crime Survey, we show trends and trajectories in public confidence in the police (Chapter 3) and public contact with the police (Chapter 4). Parts 3 and 4 move to a large-scale, interdisciplinary study of Londoners conducted between 2007 and 2009. In Chapters 5 to 10 we address trust in the police via the London study. We begin with a definition of trust in the police (Chapter 5). We then move to the role of newspaper reportage in public confidence (Chapter 6), the effects of neighbourhood context (Chapter 7) and police-initiated contact (Chapter 8) on public trust, a focus on trust among young males from Black and Minority Ethnic (BME) groups (Chapter 9), and an examination of the importance of victimisation and public-initiated contact in assessments of police trustworthiness (Chapter 10).

Part 4 shifts to police legitimacy. Starting with definitions (Chapter 11), we then consider neighbourhood context (Chapter 12) and police contact with the police (Chapter 13). Part 5 completes the study. Chapter 14 tests the full procedural justice model of cooperation, examining whether the model holds across key social groups. Chapter 15 turns one last time to our special population, namely, young BME males from the four most ethnically diverse boroughs in London. The book finishes with a discussion of the implications for policing policy and practice.

The rest of this chapter expands upon our four main findings which together form the contribution of this book.

Just and fair authority

The first contribution is to test Tyler's psychological model of cooperation with the police for the first time in the UK. Drawing upon data from a major survey of Londoners with a representative sample of just over 40,000 individuals living in just under 5,000 neighbourhoods (funded by the London Metropolitan Police Service), we model individuals within their neighbourhood context. Exploring the influence of individual characteristics, individual experiences and psychological attributes, we adjust for neighbourhood properties. Adding to a British literature on the social and moral connection between the police and the public (Fitzgerald *et al.* 2002; Loader and Mulcahy 2003; Jackson and Sunshine 2007; Bradford *et al.* 2009b; Hohl *et al.* 2010; Hough *et al.* 2010; Jackson *et al.* 2011; Bradford 2011a; Bradford and Jackson 2011), our data highlight the centrality of authorisation and accountability in trust, legitimacy and cooperation.

Building upon Tyler's seminal work (Tyler 2006a, 2006b; Sunshine and Tyler 2003a; Tyler and Huo 2002), we show that police authority is justified in the eyes of Londoners when the police treat citizens with fairness and dignity (and when people believe that the police treat citizens with fairness and dignity). For authority to be conferred, people need to believe that the police are fair in their procedures and just in their treatment and decision-taking. Public encounters with the police are critical in this process. Indeed, procedural justice is especially important among a special population who tend to have a more fractious, adversarial and confrontational relationship to the police. Drilling into the experiences, attitudes and behaviours of young males from a range of different ethnic minority communities, we find that people who are more willing to call the police, more likely to come forward as witnesses, and more likely to identify suspects in court, also tend to defer to the police, to feel obligated to obey the decisions and directives of officers, and to feel that the police have a right to determine appropriate behaviour.

Why is the fairness of police treatment and decision-making important in public trust, legitimacy and cooperation? For an answer to this question we must turn to theoretical and empirical work on procedural justice. A series of US-based studies has shown how the exercise of authority via the application of fair process strengthens the social bonds between individuals and authorities (Tyler and Huo 2002; Sunshine and Tyler 2003b; Tyler 2006a, 2011b). People comply and cooperate first when they believe that agents of the law are rightful holders of authority, and second when they imbue the legal system with the corresponding duty to obey (Tyler 2006a, 2006b). Feelings of identification with the police and courts – and a willingness to defer to their instructions – generate the belief that authorities have the right to dictate appropriate behaviour, thus activating self-regulatory mechanisms. People then defer to and cooperate with legitimate authorities because they feel it is the right thing to do so (Tyler 2006a, 2006b, 2008).

Fostering the idea that the individual and the police are 'on the same side', procedural justice is marked and demonstrated by neutrality and transparency, by fair, equitable and respectful treatment, and by a feeling of control ('voice' – Hirschman 1970).[2] At the root of Tyler's group-value model is shared group membership (as well as a relational conception of justice reasoning). Individuals are motivated to feel valued members of social groups; they derive self-relevant information through the quality of their interactions with group representatives

(Tyler *et al.* 1996); and strikingly for justice systems, individuals seem to value fairness, decency and transparency (in interpersonal treatment and decision-making) over instrumental concerns (Tyler and Huo 2002; Belvedere *et al.* 2005; Gau and Brunson 2010; Hinds 2009; Mastrofski *et al.* 1996; Reisig and Chandek 2001).[3]

Individuals establish connections even in groups with only tenuous bases for group identification (Lind and Tyler 1988; Tyler and Lind 1992; Tajfel and Turner 1986; Mulford *et al.* 2008). They are sensitive to signs and symbols that communicate information about their status and position within a group (de Cremer and Tyler 2005; Tyler 1999). Central to this perspective is the way in which police officers exercise their authority – particularly via fair interpersonal treatment and fair decision-making. How the police treat people communicates their status within the group that the police represent (Tyler and Blader 2003), such as the nation, state or community (Jackson and Bradford 2009; Loader and Mulcahy 2003; Reiner 2000; Waddington 1999).

Tyler and Blader's (2003) group engagement model predicts that people identify strongly with groups that provide favourable status evaluations. Feeling pride and respect via their connection to the group, they gain confidence in their identity through their association to that group. They also cooperate with organisations when those organisations serve the social function of providing individuals with a favourable identity and a positive sense of self (Blader and Tyler 2009). Pride and respect within the group are especially important here: if people feel pride in the group, and if they believe that they are accorded respect, then their motives will be transferred from the personal to the group level. Defining themselves in terms of their group membership, they will be more willing to act cooperatively on behalf of that group. The goals of the police become their own goals.

The experience of procedural justice or injustice communicates status within the group. Of particular relevance in this context is the idea that procedural injustice can communicate a stigmatisation by legal authorities that results from their application of negative stereotypes (Tyler and Wakslak 2004). If people perceive that the way police officers treat them is based not on what people are doing, but on their race, gender or age, police behaviour carries negative identity implications. It raises questions about whether those on the receiving end are accorded rights pertaining to membership of the superordinate group (or the rights accorded to group members in good standing):

> The example of racial profiling illustrates the risks a person undertakes when merging one's sense of self into a group. If people are drawing their sense of self from a superordinate group membership, then demeaning and disrespectful treatment from that superordinate group will undermine their feelings of favourable self-esteem and self-worth. It will communicate marginality and exclusion from important protections that are extended to most other group members – for example, 'freedom from arbitrary arrest and seizure.'

(Tyler and Blader 2003: 359)

Legitimacy as both recognition and justification of power

Our second contribution is more conceptual: namely, to develop and test a new theoretical definition of police legitimacy. In the US, police legitimacy may find its practical expression in public feelings of obligation. This is legitimacy as recognition of power – it is the belief that the police have authority and that individuals have a corresponding duty to obey (Tyler 2006a, 2006b).

But in England and Wales the history – or perhaps the ideology – of policing by consent may have left citizens with closer affective bonds with the police. Public connection with the police may be based not just on the feeling that one should obey the commands of officers, but also on a sense of shared moral values and an identification grounded in the social and cultural significance of the police (Loader and Mulcahy 2003; Jackson and Sunshine 2007). As Smith (2007: 280) says:

> Legitimacy depends on what Reiner (2000: 55) has called the mystical sense of an identification between the police and the British people. It depends on the myth that police and people share a single set of coherent and consistent norms and values, and that the police have a unique function in using force if necessary to impose them.

Following Hough *et al.* (2010) and Jackson *et al.* (2012a), we operate on the basis that people partly justify the power of the police when they believe that the police operate in ways that accord with the ethical and normative frameworks of members of community.

Tyler typically measures legitimacy using two sub-scales (e.g. Sunshine and Tyler 2003a). The first is felt obligation to obey the police. Would an individual do what the police told them to do even if they disagreed? Would an individual do what the police told them to do even if they did not like the way that the officer was treating them? The second is trust and confidence. Does the individual believe that the police are 'trustworthy, honest and concerned about the well-being of the people they deal with'? (Tyler 2011a: 256).[4] The resulting scale reflects the willingness of citizens to accept decisions and abide by directives and rules. Obligation to obey is a motivational (and normative) force based upon internalisation of values: people adopt the value of deference to authority (the belief that it is morally just to obey authorities); they authorise the police to dictate appropriate behaviour and they feel a corresponding duty to obey (Kelman and Hamilton 1989; Tyler 2006a, 2006b); and they cooperate because they believe that the police have a legitimate right to influence citizens and that citizens have an obligation to accept this influence (c.f. French and Raven 1959). Legitimacy is thus demonstrated by citizens when they believe – and act upon this belief – that they have a duty to obey and cooperate with the police (Tyler 2006a, 2006b). As Tyler (2011a: 256) says: ' … the police are legitimate if people defer to their decisions and follow their directives.'

In our study we show the importance of this public recognition of police power: we highlight the significance of Londoners' feelings of obligation to police authority. But we also show that legitimacy is a kind of justification of police power that is grounded in a sense that the police represent appropriate and shared moral values. In other words, we view legitimacy as not only obligation, authorisation and consent to power (Tyler 2006a, 2006b) but also alignment with the moral, ethical and normative positions of the police (Hough *et al.* 2010; Jackson *et al.* 2011, 2012a, 2012b; Tyler *et al.* in press). Conferring legitimacy on an institution is to grant them the right to exist, the right to determine authority and the right to exert power. And this, we propose, is partly a stance or act based on the police being morally justified in the eyes of the policed.

Moral alignment is a sense of shared moral values and group solidarity with the police. Based on a sense of shared moral purpose – assessments that the police are pursuing and defending right and proper values – moral alignment constitutes, in part, the conferred right of the police to possess the power to govern. People give up some of their freedoms in exchange for police regulation of social life and moral order. By indicating that this surrender will not be abused, a sense of moral alignment between citizens and the police cements the deal (c.f. Rawls 1995). Absent moral alignment, people may be less inclined to cede regulatory authority to the police. Importantly, we show that obligation to obey the police and moral alignment with the police are both significant predictors of willingness to cooperate, with moral alignment a particularly strong predictor in the general London sample.

Why might moral alignment shape cooperation? Shared moral values strengthen the connection between citizens and the institutions. When the police are seen not to share a basic moral framework, people's commitment to cooperate are expected to be relatively weak. Conversely, when people feel aligned with the moral values of an authority in a group setting they will act in ways that support the group that the authority represents, activating shared goals and shared commitment to social order and control. In particular, we assume that moral alignment is a motivational and normative force based on the social psychological processes of identification and internalisation (Kelman 2006; Jackson *et al.* 2012a). The motivational force of identification is partly based on the idea that people who feel morally aligned also identify with the police as a source of moral values. They accept a reciprocal-role relationship (the law-abiding and upstanding citizen); they feel a corresponding need to meet the expectations of that role (Kelman 2006); and the transition of self-perception from individual to group transforms goals or motives, thus placing greater weight to the outcomes of the group as a whole (Tyler 2011a; Blader and Tyler 2009; Tyler and Blader 2003; Tajfel and Turner 1986; Turner 1974; Turner *et al.* 1979).

The motivational force of internalisation is partly based on the idea that people who feel morally aligned also take on the values of the police as their own. This provides an important basis for cooperation. A large psychological literature shows that a powerful human motivation is the desire to act in accord with one's values about what is morally right and wrong. For example, Tyler and Blader (2005) found that employees in a management setting were motivated by the assessment that their work organisation acts in ways that are consistent with their own moral values (see also de Cremer *et al.* 2010). They cooperate with the police because to cooperate is to work towards shared goals – particularly the co-production of social order and control.

Our data are consistent with the idea that people identify with and internalise the goals of police and policing, in that felt obligation and moral alignment with the police are strong predictors of the willingness to cooperate with legal authorities.[5] But we also show that procedural fairness is a strong predictor of both obligation to obey and moral alignment with the police. People value fairness, decency and transparency (in interpersonal treatment and decision-making) over instrumental concerns (c.f. Tyler and Huo 2002; Belvedere *et al.* 2005; Gau and Brunson 2010; Hinds 2009; Mastrofski *et al.* 1996; Reisig and Chandek 2001); they want to feel valued members of social groups; they derive self-relevant information through the quality of their interactions with group representatives (Tyler *et al.* 1996); and fair, decent and respectful treatment fosters motive-based trust (Tyler and Blader 2003: 356) and moral alignment with the authorities of that group (Jackson *et al.* in press). Procedural justice communicates pride and status in the group, but it also seems to activate identification (we hand over our individual self-interest to group interest) and internalisation of the moral values of the police. So when the police act in procedurally just ways, they legitimise themselves in the eyes of the citizens they regulate.

The social ecology of trust and legitimacy

Our first two contributions are psychological. As just outlined, they are based on our empirical examination of individual-level associations between contact, trust, legitimacy and cooperation. We interpret observed correlations with reference to the mechanisms that underpin procedural justice, identification, authorisation and social influence. And critically, these mechanisms have been assessed and demonstrated via experimental and observational studies (for a review, see Tyler 2011a).

Our third and fourth contributions are more sociological. Addressing the different experiences and beliefs of diverse individuals across diverse social and structural contexts, we explore the social ecology of trust and legitimacy (Sampson *et al.* 1997; Sampson and Bartusch 1998; c.f. Brunton-Smith and Sturgis 2011). Examining the social and structural aspects of the neighbourhood context, our analysis shows not only significant between-neighbourhood variation in contact, trust, legitimacy and cooperation. We also shed light on why individuals who live in the neighbourhood tend to have similar outlooks on the police.

A series of Chicago studies (Sampson and Bartusch 1998; Kirk and Matsuda 2011; Kirk and Papachristos 2011) has linked structural characteristics of the neighbourhood to legal cynicism (the belief that the norms and rules enshrined in the laws of a society are not personally binding) and satisfaction with policing (instrumental and/or calculative trust in the job that the police are doing). First, concentrated disadvantage, segregation and institutional neglect are thought to breed a more general sense of cynicism and distance from society. Second, aggressive policing is thought to cluster in certain neighbourhoods, generating antagonism among some of the residents. Third, neighbourhood residents talk and interact. A sub-culture of legal cynicism and distrust in policing is thought to emerge, with legitimacy and illegitimacy shaped by sub-culture and contact that is 'augmented and solidified through communication and social interaction among neighbourhood residents' (Kirk and Papachristos 2011: 3).

We investigate whether normative orientations towards the law emerge not only from direct and indirect experiences with legal authorities (that cluster in neighbourhoods) but also from the structure of diverse London neighbourhoods. We show that neighbourhood context matters in London, but we also show that it matters for different reasons than in Chicago. First, we find that concentrated disadvantage is positively associated with police legitimacy; that is, the effect goes in the opposite direction to that which might be expected. We find that people in disadvantaged neighbourhoods tend to confer more rather than less legitimacy to the police. Perhaps they justify police power because they are more reliant on that power?[6]

Second, structural characteristics such as concentrated disadvantage are nowhere near as important in explaining variation in public trust, police legitimacy and cooperation with legal authorities as social characteristics of the neighbourhood. We find that collective efficacy and disorder are especially strong predictors of trust and legitimacy. We show that low police legitimacy clusters in disorderly neighbourhoods with weak informal social control mechanisms, that lack not only a sense of shared values but also a willingness among local residents to act upon those values for the collective good. People invest greater legitimacy in the police when they live in a neighbourhood that exerts strong normative pressures on the social value of regulation, orderliness and law-abidingness. Londoners, it seems, infer the strength and legitimacy of formal social controls from the strength of informal social controls (Reiner 2010; Jackson and Bradford 2009).

Why might the legitimacy of the police be influenced by the presence and strength of informal processes of social control? An important clue can be found in the fact that policing is not only done by 'the police' (c.f. Brodeur 2010). Other agencies, both state and private (and crucially the public) are also engaged in the activity of policing. Seen in this light, policing is a field in Bourdieu's sense (Bourdieu 1993; Emirbayer and Johnson 2008), that is, a structured space of positions or roles that is occupied by a variety of actors, and fields define specific stakes and interests, structure behaviours, and orient actors toward goals (Bourdieu 1993). The police are located and work within the field of social activity concerned with and directed toward social control. They are an 'institutionalized organization' (Scott 2001) that represents, indeed embodies, activity conducted within the field and the ends to which it is directed. More pertinently to our study, people seem to infer the success of formal policing from the success of informal policing. The legitimacy of the police is premised in part on *what it is*: namely, the physical embodiment of social control activity. When this activity is seen to be successful, the police garner legitimacy. But when social control mechanisms are seen to be failing, the police lose legitimacy. Understanding the social 'location' of the police allows insight into processes by which police legitimacy is simultaneously challenged and reinforced by urban disorder and the breakdown of shared values.[7]

We also examine whether the psychological model 'breaks down' once we adjust for neighbourhood context. Prior research shows strong associations between trust, legitimacy and cooperation at the individual level. But is this a function of shared social context? Residents of some neighbourhoods may be generally supportive of the police; they may believe that the police are fair, legitimate and worthy of cooperation; and each of these beliefs may be reflections of what is really important. A generally 'hot and positive' or 'cold and negative' view of the police may be determined by context and sub-culture. Residents of other neighbourhoods may be generally antagonistic – whether for cultural, historical, social or political reasons (or for any combination of these reasons). Finding that beliefs correlate in individuals may reflect the fact that individuals live in different neighbourhoods. Without adjusting for context we may erroneously conclude that there are important psychological processes going on here.[8]

Testing the procedural justice model within a multi-level framework, we show that the links between trust, legitimacy and cooperation are not mutually determined by social context. The individual-level associations between contact, trust, legitimacy and cooperation are not, we conclude, simply a function of neighbourhood context. The procedural justice model works well even when we adjust for social context.

Multiple pathways to cooperation, or, different things to different people?

Finally, we address the question of whether Tyler's procedural justice model generalises across different social groups and contexts. Is procedural justice portable across diverse social groups and contexts? We show that neighbourhood effects and individual-level correlations between contact, trust, legitimacy and cooperation operate side by side. But we also show that the central processes of Tyler's framework are not modulated by social context and situated action. We find that the associations between contact, trust, legitimacy and cooperation are not – in the main – different for different groups in different contexts.

Reiner (1992, 2000) provides the most influential analysis of the history of police legitimacy in Britain. The police, he argues, have moved in ideological terms from the status of the 'sacred' (in a golden age of an ordered and settled England the police had an iconic status) to the 'profane' (where the police are just another public service). Where once the police occupied an iconic and identity-bearing status of British life, public confidence is now 'tentative and brittle ... to be renegotiated case by case' (Reiner 2000: 162). A number of explanations for this have been proposed (e.g. Loader and Mulcahy 2003; Hough 2003; Reiner 2000). But two are particularly relevant here. First, there have been transformations in the political economy. The 1970s and early 1980s saw soaring inflation, rising unemployment and increasing levels of industrial and social conflict, with the police often called upon in particular moments of discord (the miners' strikes for instance, see McCabe *et al.* 1988). Tense and troubled relations developed between the police and particular communities that are often structurally excluded. Second, there have been changing values and expectations as society has become more diverse. This brings with it a greater variety of expectations from different communities (Rowe 2002). How, in an increasingly individualistic and pluralistic society, can the police hope to operate as an 'effective symbol of a unitary order' (Reiner 1992: 779)?

Strikingly, we find not only that procedural justice is important for all groups across London. The links between contact, procedural justice, legitimacy and cooperation generalise across diverse social groups and contexts. The one exception is among a group or set of groups that tend to have a more adversarial relationship with the police, for whom it is typically more a source of deterrence and conflict than service and protection. For young males from various minority ethnic groups, who live in four of the most diverse London boroughs, we find that one aspect of legitimacy (duty to obey) is far more important than the other aspect of legitimacy (moral alignment). For this special population (or groups of special populations), who tend to have a more fractious and antagonistic relationship with the police, it is a felt obligation to obey the police that is more important in explaining why people cooperate with legal authorities than moral alignment with the police. These individuals base their relationship with the police on feelings of obligation, censure and duty. For people who are more regularly policed, it is the authority of the police based on a sense of procedural justice and consent that is more important.

Perhaps, among people more likely to feel they are 'police property', the police are seen less as a body that regulates other people and more as a force of intrusion and regulation. They experience the police as a regulator of their behaviour on a personal level. Their conception of the legitimacy of the police is shaped by this connection and the internalisation of the value that one should obey authority – or that one should disobey illegitimate authority. While for the general population of London, who might tend to view the police more as a public service, and as a source of the regulation of other people's behaviour, moral alignment is a more important predictor of cooperation than obligation to obey the police. Consistent with the idea of policing by consent that still has symbolic meaning in the British context, Londoners in general thus seem to base their cooperative relationship with the police on shared moral purpose and common commitment to collective goals. The police and the public are to work together to regulate social order; people want the police to express and defend appropriate norms and values; and they withdraw consent to the police (and willingness to cooperate) when officers are believed not to be policing according to a shared moral purpose.

The social influence of legitimate institutions

Putting our four contributions together in one statement, this volume presents an integrative framework of trust, legitimacy and cooperation that spans both psychological and sociological levels of analysis. We present a new conceptualisation of public trust and police legitimacy; we highlight the importance of public encounters with the police (and especially procedural justice) in this new model of trust and legitimacy; and we explore whether the effects of procedural justice and legitimacy shift across social groups and contexts. Tyler's procedural justice model of policing works well in London. But the social ecology of trust and legitimacy across diverse London neighbourhoods is also important. The quality of informal policing in a neighbourhood is linked to people's trust and the perceived legitimacy of the police.

As outlined at the start of this chapter, the findings we present in the following chapters speak to the still influential idea of policing by consent. When police behave in a procedurally fair manner, people are encouraged to feel ready and able to cooperate with officers, to feel it is right and proper to support the police, to be more willing to engage with them to address the problems they face in their communities. And they do so not when they are incentivised by aggressive policing, nor necessarily when they see the possibility of a direct material return, but when such cooperation becomes valid in itself (because it seen as an effort to work toward a common goal). As Tyler *et al.* (in press) argue, the individual and collective propensity to cooperate with the police can itself be a form of social capital.

The social and moral connection between the police and the public lies at the heart of the co-production of social order. People who feel aligned with the moral values of the police (c.f. Sunshine and Tyler 2003b; Jackson and Sunshine 2007; Bradford and Jackson 2011) tend to report being motivated to aid the police and courts. Like a felt obligation to obey the police, moral alignment emerges as a relational rather than an instrumental drive that is based on social connections, identification and shared identities (Jackson and Sunshine 2007; Jackson *et al.* 2012a). Legitimacy is based not on material interests and personal concerns about crime and risk, but on a normative motivation that is rooted in social connections and identification. Legitimacy strengthens the motivation to cooperate because (a) the goals accord with one's moral values so they are shared goals and (b) people value the social connection they have with the police and the group the police represents.

We turn, in the next chapter, to the issue of methodology. But before doing so, a note on the recent riots in England is perhaps in order. The finishing touches to this book were made not long after the August 2011 events, when London and cities across England witnessed the biggest outbreak of urban unrest for a generation. Naturally, a detailed account of the riots, their aetiology and implications, is beyond the scope of the present volume. Suffice to say, both the proximate cause of the riots – the shooting of Mark Duggan and, in particular, the way police appeared to deal with his family in its aftermath – speak powerfully to some of the key themes of this book, as does the way unrest and looting spread among disaffected and marginalised youth across the capital and beyond. In working-class communities in London and elsewhere, some young people may have de-legitimised the police to a very significant degree. They do not feel an obligation to defer to and obey officers; they do not feel that the police represent and embody values they themselves share. A barrier to criminality may thus have been attenuated (Jackson *et al.* 2012b). And while the reasons for this state of affairs are inevitably complex – and while the legitimacy of the police will be only one component of any explanation of the rioting – the need for police to act in ways that enhance, or at least do not undermine, legitimacy was reiterated by the August 2011 events. In particular, we might point to the disproportionate impact of police stop-and-search activity within the communities involved, and the often visceral reaction people have when this kind of police activity is perceived to be unfair in its intention or application.

It would be wrong to infer from the riots that there has been a complete break-down in the relationship between police and public. Even in the most heavily affected areas, the vast majority of young people did not take part in the distur-bances. Yet, in some parts of London and other cities the consent of the public to the role of the police is plainly tenuous. This is a situation that should concern us all. Policing by consent has been and continues to be the dominant ideological underpinning of the British policing model. While there must be doubts about the extent to which they were ever whole-heartedly applied – policing has also always been about controlling the 'dangerous classes' and maintaining the social status quo (Choongh 1997) – Robert Peel's nine principles of law enforcement (Reith 1948) remain instructive as both long-term goals and, we believe, a set of criteria by which the majority of the British public still judge the police.

Peel's principles also correspond closely with some of the ideas outlined above and detailed in the chapters ahead. Ideas such as the police depending on the approval of the public, that active cooperation between police and public is a pre-requisite of successful policing, and that the excessive use of force diminishes such cooperation appear as relevant now as they did in 1948, or indeed 1848. Peel (or at least Reith's reconstruction of Peel) also stressed the need for police officers to act impartially, with courtesy, and in a spirit of self-sacrifice. Finally, and famously, the principles underlined the importance of the link between police and public: the police are the public and the public are the police, and police officers are no more than uniformed citizens paid to do something all should be doing in some way or at some time.

What is most striking – in terms of both the evidence presented below and other work examining the views of marginalised individuals and communities (Brunson and Miller 2006; Sharp and Atherton 2007) – is that the relevance of Peel's principles extends deep into communities that might appear on other criteria to be completely disengaged from policing. People in London, whatever their class or ethnic background, appear to desire a bottom-up form of policing that works with communities, that gains consent, that encourages people to police themselves. They want to feel that the police represent them and share their values. A key factor in the legitimacy of the British police is an alignment of police and public values, a sense of shared ends and agreed means. When police act in ways that damage this sense – when they transgress basic principles first mooted nearly 200 years ago – they risk undermining legitimacy and damaging the public cooperation upon which they ultimately rely.

2 Design of the study

The centrepiece of this study is a representative-sample survey of London entitled the London Metropolitan Police's Public Attitudes Survey (METPAS). We analyse data from face-to-face interviews conducted with just over 40,000 respondents who live in just under 5,000 neighbourhoods (neighbourhood is defined here according to Lower Super Output Area geography). Interviews were conducted between 1 April 2007 and 31 March 2009.

We investigate the social ecology of public trust and police legitimacy in London. Generating new measures of the social and structural characteristics of the neighbourhood in which individuals live, and applying the work of Sampson and colleagues on neighbourhood context (e.g. Sampson *et al.* 1997, and Sampson and Bartusch 1998), we calculate levels of concentrated disadvantage, residential instability and ethnic composition. Considering the structural characteristics of London neighbourhoods, we use a factorial ecology approach to generate a series of structural indices that characterise key dimensions of area differentiation (Morenoff and Sampson 1997; Brunton-Smith 2008; Brunton-Smith and Sturgis 2011). We also consider social characteristics, generating measures of collective efficacy, disorder and worry about crime at the neighbourhood level. Aggregating individual-level variables estimated from the observed sample, we estimate cluster-level means as weighted averages of the sample mean and the grand mean (Kuha *et al.* 2011). Exploiting the partial pooling inherent in multi-level modelling (Gelman and Hill 2007), we correct for the low within-cluster sample size that generates small-area estimation problems.

Our analyses in this book are driven by two core questions. First, why do some individuals in a given neighbourhood invest more trust and legitimacy in the police (and are more willing to cooperate with the police) than their neighbours? In other words, why might individual A who lives next door to individual B differ from his or her neighbour? Second, why do some neighbourhoods contain more trusting individuals (and people who invest more legitimacy in the police) than others? Put another way, why might people in neighbourhood C be more ready to cooperate than people in neighbourhood D? Answers to these questions are provided by testing Tyler's procedural justice model of legitimacy and cooperation, as well as extending Sampson's work on the social ecology of normative orientations to the law. We highlight the pattern of individual and neighbourhood predictors in trust and legitimacy across London, estimating individual-level and neighbourhood-level variation using multilevel modelling, but we also report the findings from a booster sample that explores the lived experience of 1,000 young males from Black and Minority Ethnic (BME) groups living in four London boroughs with high concentrations of ethnic minorities. This allows us to drill into the experiences of a group who tend to have a more adversarial and tense relationship with the police.

To strengthen our analysis, we draw upon two other data sources. In Part 2 we present pooled data from eleven sweeps of the British Crime Survey (BCS). This provides a historical perspective on trends and trajectories in public confidence and police contact in England and Wales. In Part 3 we draw upon another dataset, alongside the METPAS and our special population sample. Analysing newspaper coverage of policing during the period of the survey fieldwork, we link Londoners' views (captured in the METPAS) to media intensity, content and themes from newspaper coverage of policing and the police.

In the pages that follow we outline the various methodologies. We take the various datasets in the order that they arise. So we begin with the data analysed in Part 2 of our book. After describing the BCS, we then turn to the METPAS, which is the main focus of Parts 3, 4 and 5.

Setting the scene: 25 years of the British Crime Survey

In Chapters 3 and 4 we track trends and trajectories in confidence in the police and contact with the police over the past 25 years or so. In order to contextualise the findings of the rest of the book, we show how predictors of confidence and contact have shifted over the years. Pooling data from the 1984 to 2006 sweeps of the BCS,[1] our dataset presents rich opportunities and important insights. We show a convergence – not divergence – of levels of confidence in the police across key sociological variables (c.f. Bradford 2011b). If differences in confidence across age, gender, class and ethnicity have weakened over the past 25 years, then key explanations of variation seem to lie elsewhere.

The lack of strong variation in socio-demographic variables then motivates much of the rest of the book, which focuses on public contact, neighbourhood context and so forth. Our analysis of the BCS data allows us to replicate Skogan's (2006) finding of asymmetry in the effect of contact with the police in the mid-1990s in England and Wales. We show that asymmetry in the effect of 'good' and 'bad' contact has become less pronounced over the years (Bradford *et al.* 2009b), with the effect of 'good' contact becoming increasingly positive. We conclude that contact remains key – and that the police are able to exert a positive influence when they interact with citizens and treat people with dignity and respect.

On a methodological note, our pooled BCS dataset presents a number of difficulties. Beyond a few core items, questions have varied significantly over the years. Not only did pertinent questions enter the survey at different points in time, some were subsequently dropped – sometimes permanently, sometimes only for a period of time. On other occasions, the question format has changed. This means that data from later years are not comparable with those from earlier periods. In some sweeps (such as 1992, 1994 and 2003/04) an expansive set of questions on personal contact with the police were fielded that were comparable. But in alternative years (1996, 1998, 2004/05) the survey contained many fewer questions on this topic.

METPAS: the Metropolitan Police Service Public Attitudes Survey

In Parts 3 and 4 we report findings from the METPAS. This is a random-proba-bility, face-to-face survey that is based on a three-stage sample selection process (households, dwelling units and individuals). First, a random probability sample of household addresses was drawn. Second, a random selection of a dwelling units was made in cases where a single address included more than one unit. Third, a randomly selected adult was picked for interview (in cases where a household contained more than one adult). We consider data from the 2007/08 and 2008/09 sweeps (adding 2009/10 in Chapter 6). The achieved response rate was 60 per cent.

Individuals in neighbourhoods

The utility of disentangling and investigating individual and neighbourhood level effects in public attitudes towards the police has been demonstrated in a good deal of US criminology (Sampson and Bartusch 1998; Reisig and Parks 2000; Wu *et al.* 2009; and Schuck *et al.* 2008). Reisig and Parks (2000) found, for example, that 5 per cent of the variation in satisfaction with the police was between neighbourhoods in Indianapolis, Indiana and St Petersburg, Florida. Concentrated disadvantage and homicide rates at the neighbourhood level explained around three-quarters of this variation. Wu *et al.* (2009) also found variation in satisfaction with the police between neighbourhoods. Explaining this variation were racial and class composition of the neighbourhood, as well as concentrated disadvantage, residential mobility and levels of violent crime.

What does 'neighbourhood' mean in such work? Guided by the availability of relevant area-based data, definitions of neighbourhoods in studies such as these have applied generally defined spatial units to all residents within them (Sampson *et al.* 2002). Studies differentiate neighbourhoods on the basis of a range of geographic boundaries, with neighbourhood effects often assessed in relation to differences between administrative units such as cities, census tracts and city blocks in the American context, and electoral wards, postcode sectors and regions in the UK context.[3]

Studies that locate individuals within their geographical context are based upon the idea not only that neighbourhoods exist, but also that neighbourhoods are meaningful to people. An important tension exists between objective and subjective definitions of neighbourhood. Qualitative community studies stress the subjective meanings that physical and social spaces have for individuals (Weiss 2007), where the neighbourhood is a place for activities to occur, a set of social relationships, a place defined by its relationships with institutions, or a symbolic unit with a recognised identity (Chaskin 1998). Crucially, neighbourhoods are defined and experienced differently by different people, depending on the relative importance of material and social characteristics, such as physical barriers, landmarks and roads, as well as demographic structure, political factors and the extent of friendship networks. In addition to viewing neighbourhood boundaries as dependent on the experiences and perceptions of the individual, qualitative community studies also allow for multiple overlapping neighbourhood definitions to be important for each person. Neighbourhoods can refer to different spatial zones depending on the type of social interactions that are being examined.

Constructing neighbourhoods specifically for each individual captures the fact that people often rely on different neighbourhood definitions to others around them. But it also makes them unsuitable for multilevel analyses. If it is no longer possible to identify discrete geographic boundaries that individuals are clustered within (with different boundaries applied to each person), then the definition fails to incorporate the dependency among bespoke neighbourhoods that share some of the same geographic space. And because each person belongs to a unique bespoke neighbourhood, this type of approach requires contextual data that is specific to the individual, restricting the breadth of available data.

'Electoral wards' are commonly used to classify quantitative neighbourhood boundaries in the UK. Varying considerably in size and scale, from less than 1,000 to more than 30,000 residents, comparability is however difficult (Gibbons *et al.* 2005; MacAllister *et al.* 2001). Electoral wards also represent political boundaries rather than clear geographic markings, making them somewhat arbitrary as measures of a local area. They are frequently subject to shifts in location, making them problematic when analyses are conducted over a number of years.[4] More recent neighbourhood studies use more carefully defined area classifications, going some way to dealing with the limitations identified in much quantitative area effects research (see for example Johnston *et al.* 2005a). Based around the construction of 'bespoke neighbourhoods' that are specific to each individual in a sample, they are typically formed by clustering enumeration districts (the smallest geographic unit defined for the collection of census data) that are in the closest spatial proximity to each respondent (Johnston *et al.* 2005b; Macallister *et al.* 2001). This results in local areas – specific to each sampled individual – with each local neighbourhood smaller and more statistically stable than other available geographic units. 'Bespoke neighbourhoods' have been defined at a number of spatial scales from the nearest 500 individuals to the respondent up to the nearest 10,000, allowing more detailed analyses of area-level influences at different levels of aggregation.

In this book we adopt census Super Output Area (SOA) geography boundaries, constructed using a methodology similar to the creation of 'bespoke neighbourhoods'. They were introduced as a stable geography for disseminating local area statistics from 2001 onwards. Rather than defining areas that are specific to each respondent, the constructed boundaries are common to all households within a local area, making SOAs suitable for multilevel analyses. The increased internal stability – when compared with other potential area geographies – makes them particularly suitable for our analysis, where the principal focus is on the shared influence of local areas on individuals.

SOAs also cover a significantly smaller local area than the neighbourhood boundaries that have typically been used in area studies. Enabling a more detailed assessment of small area influences on individuals' levels of trust, legitimacy and cooperation, we can examine more clearly how characteristics of the area immediately surrounding the individual influence their levels of confidence. Like all other empirical assessments of neighbourhood effects, however, the selection of these spatial units has primarily been influenced by data availability. This means that, while they offer many benefits over other spatial units that have previously been used, they cannot directly incorporate many of the elements that have been identified as important in theoretical treatments of the neighbourhoods.

The lower level of the Super Output Area hierarchy (LSOA) was selected with an average cluster size of eight respondents in the METPAS – this is a sufficient number of respondents to construct more complex models of area variation in trust, legitimacy and cooperation. Importantly, LSOAs are small enough to act as a reasonable approximation for the locality of the respondent: they are more consistent in size than the alternative geographies that have previously been used to measure context effects.

Analysing the METPAS

In Chapter 5 we show that trust can be decomposed into (a) trust in police effectiveness and (b) trust in police fairness and intentions and/or interests. We use latent variable modelling, specifically standard linear factor analysis in its confirmatory form (see Bollen 1989, for an overview), to examine both how the survey items measure the latent constructs and whether the latent variables relate to each other. First, we use factor analysis to derive new variables that summarise the survey items in a single measure for each dimension of trust; these will then be used in proceeding analysis. Second, we examine the dimensionality of the data; we identify whether there are one, two or three underlying factors that best summarise the data.

In Chapter 6 we analyse newspaper coverage of the police and policing via the manual coding of 9,000 articles. Our media analysis considers different aspects of police coverage in five major London newspapers over a three-year period. Survey respondents were asked which newspaper(s) they read regularly (if any). Together with the interview date, this allows us to link the intensity and tone of coverage to public trust in the police.

In Chapter 7 we then consider variation of trust at the level of the individual and neighbourhood. We examine basic socio-demographic predictors and we bring into the equation key social and structural characteristics of the neighbourhood. In Chapters 8 and 9 we estimate the effects of contact with the police and victimisation, showing not only the importance of people's experience of crime and the police, but also of neighbourhood structural characteristics as well as collective social properties. Our findings underline the deeply relational nature of the link between the police and their public(s), not just in the encounters people have with officers, but also in the links between trust in the police, neighbourhood disorder and collective efficacy.

Part 4 then turns to police legitimacy. As with trust, we begin with an analysis of the meaning and measurement of legitimacy, finding that it is reflected by both obligation to obey and moral alignment. We then move to explain significant variation in obligation and alignment. We consider socio-demographic predictors; we partition the variance into individual and neighbourhood components (Chapter 12); and we assess contact with the police (Chapter 13). The pattern continues in Part 5, which considers cooperation.

Naturally the data places limits on the conclusions that we can reach. Causality is a function of research design characteristics. Experiments (or the exploitation of naturally occurring variation that approximates random assignment) provide the leverage and identification to infer causal mechanisms (Morgan and Winship 2007), and statistics applied to observable data are a poor substitute for manipulation and random assignment. So we make no causal claims based on the patterns of associations we identify.

But the survey is a good methodology for the current study. This is because of the very simple idea that what we are really interested in is the lived experience of individuals across London and how this relates to their social context. Londoners live in certain neighbourhoods; they have (or don't have) trust in the police; and they invest (or don't invest) legitimacy in the police. The patterns of associations between these clusters of beliefs, attitudes and preferences at the individual and neighbourhood levels are the result of their experiences and dispositions, and it is these experiences and dispositions that will shape public support for particular criminal justice policies (and get the attention from policy-makers and the mass media).

The BME booster: young males from Black and Minority Ethnic groups

In order to drill into the experiences, attitudes and beliefs of a population made up of people who typically have a somewhat more tense and confrontational relationship to the police, we also consider data from a booster sample of 1,000 Black and Minority Ethnic (BME) males aged 16–30. In each of Hounslow, Newham, Southwark and Tower Hamlets – the four London Boroughs with some of the highest concentration of BME populations – 250 interviews were carried out by the market research company that fielded the METPAS. The first stage of the sample design was the selection of wards within each selected borough, where the chance of selection was in proportion to the number of BMEs in the ward. Within each selected ward, the selection of census output areas was then weighted in proportion to the number of BMEs in the census output area (OA). The approach taken in this booster survey was as follows:

- (within each selected borough) random probability selection of five census wards weighted according to number of BMEs in each ward;
- (within each selected ward) random probability selection of five OAs weighted according to number of BMEs in each OA;

- for each selected OA, identify all OAs adjoining or near to it, and randomly select four others. This gives a total of five sampling points – each comprising five 'clustered' OAs; and,
- provide the interviewer team with all the addresses in the selected sample point (from Postcode Address File, PAF) and instruct interviewers to free-find ten young male BMEs.

Twenty-five sampling points (ten interviews in each) were issued for each borough, giving 100 sample points in all. A disadvantage of a quota-based approach is the likelihood of bias related to interviewee characteristics. For example, people who are likely to be out and about during the day or evening, and people afraid of answering the door to strangers, may tend to be under-represented. This sort of bias is difficult to handle by explicit weighting factors. However, this stricture also applies to an extent to the random address method, unless repeated attempts are made to re-contact non-replying addresses. Table 1.1 shows the ethnic diversity of the sample.

In Part 2, we look at trends and trajectories in public attitudes towards the police over the past decades. We examine shifts in the importance of class socio-demographic variables in explaining public trust in the police, and the shifting influence of context.

Table 1.1 Ethnic minority groups in the BME booster sample

	N	%
Bangladeshi	263	26
Indian	225	22
African	196	19
Pakistan	84	8
Caribbean	83	8
Any other Asian background	48	5
Any other ethnic group	27	3
White and Black Caribbean	21	2
Any other mixed background	18	2
Chinese	17	2
White and Black African	11	1
Any other Black background	10	1
White and Asian	9	1

Source: London Metropolitan Police BME booster survey, n=1,000

Part 2

Trends and trajectories

We begin with two scene-setting empirical chapters. What follows is not intended to be an exhaustive review of the recent history of police–public relations. Such a review would naturally require a book all of its own. Instead, our intention is to provide an impressionistic but evidenced overview of the 20-plus years from 1984 to 2005/06. This therefore provides an important springboard for the rest of the book.

Looking at confidence in the police and contacts with officers, we revisit and expand on analysis already presented elsewhere (Bradford 2011b) to consider how trends have played out not only in general but among specific sections of the population. Examining what has happened to public opinions of the police since the early 1980s, we show a homogenisation of experience and opinion over time across important socio-demographic and experiential categories. Pooling data from 11 sweeps of the British Crime Survey (BCS), we show a growing similarity in experiences of the police – and confidence in the police – over social categories such as age, gender and ethnicity. Classic sociological variables thus appear relatively unimportant now compared to 20 years ago. We also show that the impact of public contact with the police has become more symmetrical over time. 'Good' contact has become more strongly associated with higher levels of confidence over time, opening up the possibility that the police can improve trust and confidence through the exercise of procedural justice (Tyler and Fagan 2008; Bradford *et al.* 2009a; Myhill and Bradford 2011).

However, a number of provisos are required at the outset. First, the content of the BCS has changed over time, with questions being introduced in a particular year, later dropped, and sometimes reappearing. Very often, consistent time series over the entire period are not available. Rather than discuss the availability of questions at every stage, the analysis that follows is usually presented such that it covers the longest possible time period possible given the subject at hand (ideally 1984 to 2005/06, but very often less than this). As ever, data availability limits the types of analysis that is possible.

Second, while one aspect of this book is an implicit critique of simplistic ideas concerning the definition of trust and confidence in the police, such ideas are unfortunately all that are available in the early years of the BCS. Questions about the trustworthiness of the police (rather than some overall confidence in the job that the police are doing) do not appear consistently in the survey even in later years. When we talk in these two chapters about 'confidence in the police' we are referring to responses the following question: 'taking everything into account, how good a job do you think the police in this area are doing?' (For a discussion of confidence and trust, see Jackson and Bradford 2010.) This question appeared in identical format in every BCS from 1984 to 2003/04 (before changing format slightly: see Chapter 3).

The two chapters that follow provide a very broad overview of public opinion; they do not cover the more nuanced forms of trust and legitimacy we cover later on in the book (see Chapter 5). Finally, the formats of socio-demographic variables available across the entire period often do not match what would be considered current best practice. When considering police–public relations between 1984 and 2005/06 we concentrate below on four such variables: age, gender, economic activity status and ethnicity. Of these the first three are unproblematic. But the recording of ethnicity in the BCS changed over time from a very simple White/Black/Asian/Other categorisation in 1984 to a much larger 16-group classification in the late 1990s (to match that used in the 2001 census). This is far from ideal because we are limited to the classification used in the earliest period when comparing across time.

3 Twenty-five years of public confidence in the police

Tracking the responses given by respondents to the 1984 to 2005/06 sweeps of the British Crime Survey (BCS) to the general job-rating question – 'how good a job do you think the police are doing?' – we first sketch out the broad (and well-known in UK criminology) picture of change in public confidence in the police since the 1980s. We then examine whether aspects like age, gender, ethnicity and economic status have become more or less important in public confidence over the 20-plus years.[1]

Trends and trajectories

As described by Bradford (2011b), there are two main accounts of the historical trajectory of trust and confidence in the British police. According to the first account, public confidence has been declining since the 'golden age' of the 1950s (Reiner 2000: 48), when the police stood almost unchallenged as protectors of law and order and moral representatives of community and nation. In the 60 years since – so this account goes – this position has been seriously undermined by a process of 'desacralisation' and disenchantment, driven by a wide variety of economic and social developments that have combined to knock the police off the pedestal which they once occupied (Reiner 2000; Newburn 2003). Problematic relationships between the police and the socially marginal or excluded are central to this account, particularly in relation to youth and ethnic minority groups (Hall *et al*. 1978; Gilroy 1987; Keith 1993; Loader 1996; Reiner 2000). Police maltreatment of people from these groups has become common knowledge, and publicity has been given to any number of policing scandals – such as the death of Blair Peach, the Brixton riots, the Stephen Lawrence investigation, and the 2011 shooting of Mark Duggan that triggered the English riots of August 2011.

Consumerist attitudes toward the police (Morgan and Newburn 1997; Loader 1999; Jones and Newburn 2002) and the organisation's attempts to demystify itself into another mundane institution of government (Loader 1999; Reiner 2000) form a second key component of this account. New Public Management (NPM) ideas about policing in the mid-1990s (Martin 2003; Hough 2007a) are also important. Operating at both the public and organisational level, these processes seem bound up with the 'desacralisation' described by Reiner, concerned as they are with the positioning and management of the police as 'just another' public service – a service, moreover, that is subject to market forces and the power of the sovereign consumer.

The second account, stresses greater continuity in public confidence over time. Emphasis is placed on feelings of affect toward and ownership of the police, at least among certain sections of the population (Loader and Mulcahy 2003). The last half-century may have created challenges to the police arising from social diversification, the decline of deference and changes in the political economy of the United Kingdom. But there remains a sustained sense of identification with the police, particularly among those who turn to it as a symbol of stability in an increasingly disorientating and apparently threatening world. This account finds resonance with studies that have highlighted the extent to which support for the police is as much bound up with concerns about disorder and social cohesion as it is with crime per se (e.g. Girling *et al*. 2000; Jackson and Sunshine 2007; Jackson and Bradford 2009; although see Sindall *et al*. 2012). It questions the extent of any overall decline in trust and confidence: consider, for example, the relatively high levels of support for the police found in the BCS and elsewhere, especially compared to that for other public services.

Late modernity and the homogenisation of experience

The impact of 'late modernity' on public opinions of the police looms large in accounts of the trajectory of public trust and confidence over time. Phenomena such as consumerism, neo-liberal economics and globalisation seem relevant, with social theorists such as Anthony Giddens, Ulrich Beck and Zygmunt Bauman arguing that growing social atomisation and individuation are key elements of the late modern condition (Bauman 2005, 2007; Beck 1992; Beck and Beck-Gernsheim 2002; Giddens 1991). On these accounts, people's life experiences have been homogenised by the pressures of living in 'over-developed' countries such as the UK. Just as the high streets of British towns have become increasingly similar to each other – due in large part to globalisation and the hegemony of global brands – so too have the choices, lives and indeed world-views of those who use them. Old patterns of difference and demarcation, along lines of age, gender, ethnicity, sexuality, class or locality, have also been undermined. Critically, they have not been replaced by new patterns that lend equally diverse yet strong structures to people's lives. Rather, a web of fleeting, multiple and contradictory social identities and roles characterise the existence of many, the number and ephemerality of which, ironically, make individuals more and not less similar to each other than was hitherto the case.

A tension exists in these accounts: experience and identity seem to have become both more homogenised and more diverse (and indeed more contingent). Exploring this tension is a key theme in the work of the theorists listed above (see, for example, Bauman 2002). But for present purposes, our point is rather more mundane. Put simply, it seems unlikely that the conditions described by Beck, Bauman *et al*. will provide individuals with firm grounds for differentiated understandings of the police, or regularised experiences with officers, in a way that more fixed roles and identities may have done 60 or more years ago. Then and previously, who you were and what you did were strongly linked. Interlinked identities and behaviours may have predicted differential experiences of the police. Consider the different relationships with the police suggested by being an Edwardian 'street urchin', a worker in London's docks, a suburban housewife, or a gentleman farmer. At the present time, however, the behaviours associated with particular social roles or positions may have spilled over, blurred and disengaged from association with particular social groups or identities.

Similarly, the space of policing seems to have changed. The way the social and physical environment is constructed and used has altered significantly and along many different dimensions, leading some to talk of a 'flattening' of space very similar to the social homogenisation described above (Harvey 1990). To give just one example, the identikit shopping and entertainment 'strips' of many British towns may have exerted a centripetal effect on the night-time economy (Hadfield 2007), and may have generated experiences of policing that are more similar across population groups than those generated by more variegated patterns of socialising.

When considering the relationship between police and public, these processes have been in many ways positive, both in their origins and in their current outcomes. Individuals from previously oppressed social groups can now at least hope for, and indeed expect, a different experience of the police than their fore-bears. To be an out gay man in the late 1960s will usually have meant a very definite (and negative) 'knowledge' of the police. To be an out gay man now some-times still means the same, yet some gay men now serve in the police, while others exert control over the police when sitting on local councils and other bodies.

At the same time, such 'levelling up' processes have been matched by equiva-lent processes 'levelling off' the spread and focus of policing, as security has become more pervasive and police activity has widened in scope (Loader 2006). Policing was classically directed against the urban poor and other 'dangerous classes', and its most important arena was the city's public space. This, again, is often still the case. But a culture of control (Garland 2001) places many more people in situations where they might encounter the police than was hitherto the case. A familiar example is middle-class experiences with traffic police (Wells 2008). Widespread use of the car over the last half-century may have meant that people who in the past were very rarely exposed to 'negative' confrontations with police have been increasingly exposed to the way officers are able to intrude forcefully into citizens' lives.

The list of examples could be lengthened. But the point here is that when thinking about public opinions surrounding the police, perhaps the old sociolog-ical certainties of gender, age and ethnicity are less relevant now than they may have been in the past. We need new ways to think about how people come to form their opinions of the police and what the implications of these opinions might be.

We should, of course, note the continued importance of identity (Spalek 2008) and social, cultural and economic status for individuals' experiences of the police. Total homogeneity is impossible, and significant variations in the relationship between the police and its various publics remain. Most notably, people from some ethnic minority groups continue to encounter specific styles of policing as a result of their minority status (Bowling and Philips 2007), and young working-class people continue to be the objects of styles of policing quite different to those used in other situations (Loader 1996; McAra and McVie 2005). However, there is little evidence that those on the receiving end of such treatment hold the radically different views of police that are sometime imagined. Indeed, studies examining the relationship between excluded groups and the police often conclude that the marginalised do not necessarily want the police to 'just go away' – they simply want the same sorts of policing that they see others receiving (see, for example, Carr *et al.* 2007). Their expectations and ideas about policing are similar to those not excluded on grounds of ethnicity, age or class, for all that their actual experiences of policing are very different.

In sum, some important trends in recent social theory point to an increasing, although not overwhelming, process of homogenisation in experience and opinion, from which the police are unlikely to have been excluded. We now turn to using this notion as heuristic, we now turn to examine the story told by successive sweeps of the BCS and the wider literature on the history of policing.

Public confidence in policing over the past 20 years

Studies show considerable variation in levels of confidence in the different branches of the British criminal justice system (CJS), with the police habitually coming top. The police are the object of considerably higher levels of confidence (Roberts and Hough 2005) or ratings of performance (Fitzgerald *et al.* 2002; Jansson *et al.* 2007) than other agencies. Public trust in the police is also higher than trust in parliament or local councils (e.g. DCLG 2010). But the police fare less well compared with other public services. For example, Fitzgerald *et al.* (2002) reported that while just 18 per cent of Londoners in 2000 thought the police (local or national) did a very good job, 37 per cent gave this opinion for doctors, 39 per cent for teachers, 64 per cent for nurses and 73 per cent for firemen. In comparison, 20 per cent rated social workers as very good, with just 11 per cent giving judges this score. Time will tell whether the *News of the World* phone hacking scandal and the 2011 riots and looting will have a lasting effect on trust and confidence in the police.

The relatively poor performance of the police in this regard continues to trigger concern around public feelings toward the police and the CJS more widely. How, then, have things changed and developed over time? On all the available evidence, trust and confidence appear to have been declining since the 1960s (Hough 2007b). Early assessments of public opinions about the police suggested extremely high levels of support. Consider the 1962 Royal Commission on the Police, which reported findings from a random sample survey assessing public views of the police. The authors noted that: 'No less than 83 per cent of those interviewed professed great respect for the police, 16 per cent said they had mixed feelings, and only 1 per cent said they had little or no respect' (Royal Commission on the Police 1962: 103).

A decade later, Belson (1975) reported on a survey of Londoners that found that 73 per cent of adults had 'a lot' of respect for the police, 25 per cent had 'some' respect and just 2 per cent had 'not much' respect. Similarly, 61 per cent said they were 'very satisfied' with the police, with a further 35 per cent 'fairly' satisfied. Only 4 per cent were dissatisfied in some way (ibid: 7).

Despite the generally extremely positive picture painted by both these early studies, differences between younger and older people were already an area of concern. The Royal Commission noted 'a measure of antipathy towards the police' (Royal Commission on the Police 1962: 103–4) among the youngest respondents aged 18–25. Belson (1975: 7) reported that only 44 per cent of young people (aged 12–20) had 'a lot' of respect for the police (compared with the figure of 73 per cent for all adults noted above). These early reports therefore contain hints of a divergence in the views of the youngest age groups, something which proved to be a theme in the later BCS reports.

Qualitative work further cautions against too rosy a picture of public opinion in the immediate post-war years. Using oral history accounts of ex-officers who served from the 1920s through to the 1960s, Weinberger (1995) describes a well-respected and generally well-liked police force operating within a situation which was not, however, free from tension. The policing of everyday public order caused friction between police and those who relied on street-life, both legal and semi-legal, for their living; traffic policing was also mentioned as a site of dissent and difficulty. Most tellingly, in a passage that resonates with Williams' (1964) account of a perennial nostalgia for a golden age just passed, Weinberger notes that:

> Disquiet over police behaviour in the 1920s, especially in the Metropolis …
> (culminated) in the 1929 Royal Commission on the police. These inquiries
> revealed a degree of illegal behaviour that led the Home Secretary to admit
> that the police had lost public trust and needed to regain the 'full support and
> sympathy – as they used to have 20 or even 10 years ago – and the affection
> of the public as a whole'.
>
> (Weinberger 1995: 167)

The story that emerges is one in which, within a paradigm of what by modern standards was a very popular police force, public disquiet and growing distrust after the war years through to the 1960s was specifically related to (a) growing concerns about police scandals, corruption and abuse of power, (b) growing public awareness of both its own rights and of the fact that a police officer's word was not necessarily law and (c) these trends inculcating a growing fear of, and declining trust in, the police.

These trends reached a crisis point in the early 1980s, marked by, among other things, urban riots in London, Bristol and Liverpool, which were in many ways directed at the police, and the use, at the behest of the then Conservative government, of heavy-handed policing tactics against striking miners and other workers. It was in this atmosphere that the first Policing for London study was carried out (Smith 1983; Smith and Gray 1985). Based on an extensive programme of research, this study set out to create the conditions for 'reasoned public debate' about the role of policing in a modern Britain. Survey evidence reported from the study found high levels of public disquiet about the honesty and integrity of the police (25 per cent thought that the police 'often' used threats during questioning, for example), that people were sometimes stopped without good reason (over two-thirds of 'West Indian' respondents felt this way) and, among ethnic minority respondents in particular, that some groups in society are treated unfairly by the police. Overall, the report found that:

> There need to be mechanisms that try to achieve a measure of harmony between how the police behave … and how people wish and expect them to … . Whatever the mechanism is, it will tend to be seen within the police force as a means of obtaining public support for the policies and practices they believe are right; and outside the police force as a means of ensuring that policing policy is adapted to meet public expectations.
>
> (Smith and Gray 1985: 15–16)

The first British Crime Survey (BCS) was also conducted at precisely this juncture, 1982, and further waves followed with increasing regularity. A key finding presented by successive waves of the BCS was indeed an apparent decline in confidence in the local police over time (Jackson *et al.* 2009; Bradford 2011b; Jansson 2008).

However, findings from the BCS suggest a more nuanced picture than that of a monotonic decline, suggesting a middle way in the debate between Reiner and Loader and Mulcahy outlined above. A central issue in this debate is the meaning of 'fairly good' responses to the relevant BCS question: do they mean 'pretty good', 'OK', 'not great' or 'don't know' (Hough 2007b)? Some favour taking the words at face value (Loader and Mulcahy 2003), while others stress that in collo-quial English 'fairly good' can mean almost anything – probably being function-ally equivalent to a collective 'don't know'. If people really thought the police were doing a good job, they would use the 'very good' response category (Hough 2007b). If we look only at the 'very good' responses, then support certainly did crumble during the 1980s and 1990s: this is, in essence, Reiner's position. If we look at 'very' and 'fairly good' combined, then public support for the police looks much more stable: this is Loader and Mulcahy's position.

Fortunately the core question referring to the local police changed format in 2003/04, allowing comparison of the old format with a less ambiguous 'excellent/ good/fair' formulation. The implications of the change are shown clearly in Figure 3.1, which underlines the importance of the apparently esoteric debate over the meaning of 'very' and 'fairly' good. If 'fairly good' really does mean 'don't know', as Hough suggests, then support for the police was indeed at an all-time low in the early 2000s. However, if it can be taken at face value then support was very much higher. In fact the change to the question format in 2003/04, the results of which are also shown, suggests that Hough was perhaps half correct. For example, while only 7 per cent of people rated their local police as 'excellent' in 2005/06, a further 44 per cent gave an unequivocal 'good' response. For all that levels of confidence in the police are lower than in the past, at the very least Figure 3.1 suggests a bedrock of support which has remained constant over recent years, and which even seems to be increasing slightly (see Flatley *et al.* 2010).

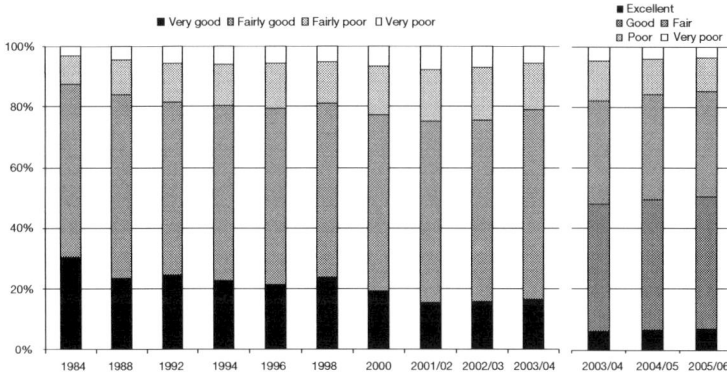

Figure 3.1 Ratings of the local police, 1984 to 2005/06.

Source: British Crime Survey 1984 to 2005/06

Notes: Responses to question 'How good a job are the police in this area doing'. Response categories changed in 2003/04, which is shown on both old and new basis for comparison.

Reports of the death of public confidence in the police appear, then, to be premature. But the BCS trend shown in Figure 3.1 and the earlier data outlined above together do suggest something quite significant occurred over the 40 years from 1960 to 2000. Trust and confidence in the British police was undermined during this period, for all that it did not disappear. To examine this issue in more depth we now shift to looking at changes in confidence within specific population groups. Given the timespan involved – 20 years, in most analyses – we concentrate primarily on confidence as indicated by 'very good' responses to the BCS question, since the meaning of this question is likely to have remained relatively invariant over time. We are therefore considering what might be seen as strong indications of support for the police.

Age

It is generally well documented (for example Allen *et al*., 2006) that older people have on average more favourable views of the police. If a process of 'desacralisation' or disenchantment has occurred since the late 1950s, then older people, brought up at a time when views of the police were very much more favourable, may have been somewhat insulated from it. Younger people, brought up in less deferent times and lacking any residue of feeling and affect, may in contrast have experienced far greater declines. The reservoirs of support for the police which Girling *et al*. (2000) describe might be expected to be stronger among older people.

Yet there is another possibility. Older people, alive at a time when 80 per cent of people thought the English police where the 'best in the world' (Home Office

1962, quoted in Loader and Mulcahy 2003: 4) may feel more 'let down' or otherwise disenchanted by more recent events, resulting in a greater comparative fall in trust and confidence. Younger people, especially the youngest of those brought up in the 1970s and 1980s, may in turn be immune from such disenchantment since they have primarily experienced what Reiner (2000: 47) has called 'post-legitimacy'. This is characterised as the most recent historical period in which the police, despite having survived the legitimation crises of the 1970s and 1980s, and retaining significant public support, are now just one among a number of public services and may be treated in analogous ways. Among younger people the decline in trust and confidence may have bottomed out and active questioning of legitimacy set aside (ibid.). Older people, because they grew up in a different social climate, may still be in the process of arriving at the same position.

Examining in more detail the consistent series of questions used from 1984 to 2003/04, Figure 3.2 demonstrates that the decline in strong support for the police was not uniform across different age groups. It was greatest in the most elderly, 75 plus age group (falling from over 45 per cent in 1984 to less than 20 per cent in 2003/04) and smallest among the youngest, 16–24, age group (20 per cent to 15 per cent). Indeed by this measure trust and confidence in the police increased slightly in the 16–24 age group between 1994 and 2003/04. The outcome of these changes was that while in 1984 there was a strong gradation by age levels of strong support for the police, with older people much more supportive than younger, by 2003/04 this had almost disappeared, such that there was relatively little variation by age in the later period. One other pattern of note from Figure 3.2 is the timing of the greatest part of the decline. For those aged 25–44, and arguably 45–54, it was between 1984 and 1994: for older people, and especially the eldest, 75 plus, age group, it was between 1994 and 2003/04.

Of course, Figure 3.2 needs to be treated with caution; there are many alternative interpretations to that given above. Those who were aged 55–64 in 1984 (for example) were not the same as those who were aged 55–64 in 1994 (who were then aged 65–74). So the apparent reduction in trust and confidence within age groups may be confounded by change across age groups. If people in a young age group start with a low opinion at time A which they carry forward to time B, when they are in an older age group, this would appear as a reduction in confidence when it had in fact remained stable.

One way to deal with the problem outlined above is the technique of pseudo-cohort analysis. Results from such an analysis are shown in Table 3.1. This technique assumes that if two samples are drawn from the same population ten years apart, 20-year-olds in the first sample are 'the same' people as 30-year-olds in the second. This idea can be better understood with reference to the table (where age groups are used because of small sample sizes). Consider the cohort born in 1963–69, who were aged 16–21 in 1984. In that year 21 per cent of this cohort thought their local police were doing a very good job, compared with 16 per cent in 1994 (when they were aged 26–31) and 15 per cent in 2003/04 (when they were aged 36–41). This group already had a relatively low opinion of the police in 1984; this declined further by 1994, after which it appeared to remain relatively stable.

■1984 ▨1994 ▫2003/04

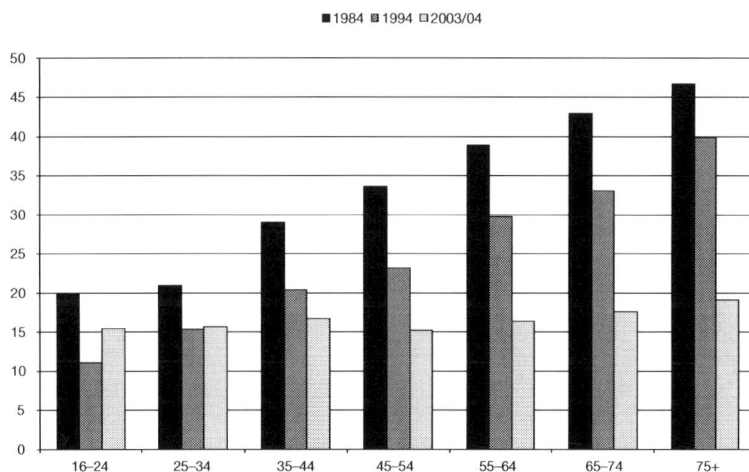

Figure 3.2 Proportion rating the local police 'very good': by age.
Source: British Crime Survey 1984; 1994; 2003/04

Table 3.1 Proportion rating local police as 'very good': by age

	Percentages					
	16–21	*26–31*	*36–41*	*46–51*	*56–61*	*66–71*
1984	21	19	29	33	38	43
1994	11	16	21	24	30	32
2003/04	15	16	15	16	16	17

Source: British Crime Survey 1984; 1994; 2003/04

The general message of Table 3.1 is clear; the fall in trust and confidence was greater among older people. Some 29 per cent of those aged 36–41 in 1984 indicated strong support for their local police, but by 2003/04 only 16 per cent of the same cohort, now aged 56–61, did so. For those aged 46–51 in 1984 and 66–71 in 2003/04 the same proportions were 33 per cent and 17 per cent, respectively. The contrast with the youngest cohorts shown is strong. By 2003/04 there was almost no variation by birth cohort in levels of strong support for the police, in marked contrast to the picture just 20 years before.

While there was certainly a strong levelling down in opinions according to the old four-category question, variation in confidence by age has not entirely disappeared. According to the 2008/09 BCS, for example, 50 per cent of 16–24-year-olds rated their local police as excellent or good, compared with 54 per cent of 35–44-year-olds, 50 per cent of the 55–64 group, and 60 per cent of the over-75s (Flatley *et al.* 2010: 124). Yet, as these figures suggest, any linear association between age and confidence does seem to have been lost, suggesting perhaps that it is factors associated with different age groups (for example higher levels of street stops in the youngest, greater levels of car use among the middle-aged) that are behind the small variations in confidence observed. We explore these issues in greater depth in Chapter 7.

Gender

In contrast to variation in confidence by age, as recorded by the old four-category confidence question, there was relatively little difference between men and women in levels of support for the police in 1984: and what little variation there was had entirely disappeared by 2003/04. In the earlier year, 33 per cent of women rated the police as very good, compared with 29 per cent of men (11 per cent of women gave a 'fairly' or 'very poor' response, compared with 14 per cent of men). By the latter year, 17 per cent of women gave a 'very good' rating, while 16 per cent of men did the same (compared with 20 per cent and 22 per cent, respectively, who gave 'fairly' or 'very poor' responses). However, in 2008/09, using the new five-category question, 56 per cent women rated their local police as excellent or good, compared with 51 per cent of men. Marked similarity between the genders is the key message, however, and it is often hard to distinguish between the opinions of men and women once relevant factors are controlled for.

Ethnic group

The last three decades has been a period in which severe tensions have been played out between the police and members of many ethnic minority communities. From the use of 'sus' laws in the 1970s and early 1980s to target young Black men, through to the disastrous handling of the Stephen Lawrence murder enquiry, relationships between police and many sections of the Black community have been particularly difficult. More recently, the terrorist attacks in New York in 2001 and London in 2005 have presaged changes in the relationship between police and British Asians in general and of course British Muslims in particular.

But it would be a mistake to assume that change will only ever be in a negative direction. Fully aware of the difficulties in relationships with ethnic minority groups, the police have been attempting through a variety of programmes and policies to improve the situation (Miller *et al.* 2000; Dalgliesh and Myhill 2004; Innes 2007). The success of these remains in question, and more recent policies based on the 'Prevent' counter-terrorism agenda have been highly controversial, but efforts to improve relations between police and ethnic minority communities may well have had some effect.

Equally, relationships between the police and the majority White British population are unlikely to have remained static. There are a number of possible trajectories but underlying causes are likely to centre on those structures of feeling (Williams 1964; c.f. Loader and Mulcahy 2003) which position the police as key representatives of state, nation and community. These associations are likely to be particularly prevalent among the White British population, significant sections of which hark back to the 1950s and a police force of the imagination that represents a high point in national and social cohesion (Girling *et al.* 2000). Change since then may have been particularly strongly felt among sections of the White British population as old certainties have been swept away by the kinds of social processes described by Bauman, Beck and others. Many of those from the White 'group' may therefore be particularly prone to placing the police on a pedestal, holding them up as representatives of the way things were and should be. With some caveats, this is roughly the position of many of the White, middle-class respondents in Girling *et al.*'s (2000) study. Trust and confidence in the police in the White group may have declined less, relative to other ethnic groups, as these structures of feeling have provided some insulation from the overall decline.

On the other hand, opinions of the police, archetypal representatives of the nation/state, may have been particularly affected by the perceived failure of the state to provide security and stability. Declines in trust and confidence have been greater among those that in the past held the police in the highest regard as they blame the police for apparent breakdowns in order, civility and in community cohesion (Jackson and Sunshine 2007; Jackson and Bradford 2009). Feelings of disappointment and disenchantment may also have a role here, the highest edifices (of affect) having the furthest to fall (Girling *et al.* 2000).

Ethnic categorisations in the BCS

As we noted above, the ethnic group questions used in the BCS developed over time from a simple White/Black/Asian/Other classification in 1984 through to adoption of the full 16-group census classification in 2001 (Office for National Statistics 2003). This means that comparisons of ethnic group over time are limited to the simplest classification used in the earliest period available. This is not entirely satisfactory since socio-economic variation and differences in cultural background within broad ethnic (or racial) categories such as 'Black' are often greater than variation between that category and other similarly broad groupings ('White' or 'Asian') (Dobbs *et al.* 2006). On the other hand, people's contact with the police may be affected more by their 'race' – for example, police reactions to visible markers of ethnic difference such as skin colour – than their own self-assessed ethnicity.

In terms of ethnic categorisations, we move in this chapter from viewing the long-term historical picture in the most general terms to looking at the most recent situation through a much finer-grained lens. This allows us to view developments over the longest timespan possible while also taking into account the idea that cultural variation within, for example, the 'Black' group, may be very considerable, and act to obscure the picture.

Ethnic variation in trust and confidence

If patterns of opinion among different age groups look like they have become more similar over time, what is the situation for different ethnic groups? In fact the picture here is more complex. Support for the police appeared to decline steadily among the White group, with 'very good' ratings falling from 31 per cent to 15 per cent over the 20 years. In contrast, support in the Black and Asian groups fell sharply between 1984 and 1988 and then fluctuated after that, notably ending in both cases at slightly higher levels in 2003/04 than was the case among Whites.[2] Yet, overall the message is similar to that described above in relation to age. The biggest change in opinions over the whole 20 year period occurred in the group with the greatest confidence in the police in 1984, the Whites, and opinions appeared to be more homogeneous in 2003/04 than they had been in 1984.

Moving to a more recent timeframe allows the very general Asian-Black-White classification to be unpacked somewhat. Figure 3.3 uses only BCS data from 1994 onwards, when the ethnic group classification became more detailed.

The decline in the White group remains. However, it seems that over this ten-year period 'strong' confidence among Pakistanis and Bangladeshis fell by more than was the case for the Indian group, although by 2003/04 there was little difference between the two groups (note also how the 'Indian' and 'Pakistani/Bangladeshi' groups behave slightly differently to the 'Asian' group shown in Figure 3.3 – this is presumably due to the inclusion in the Asian category of

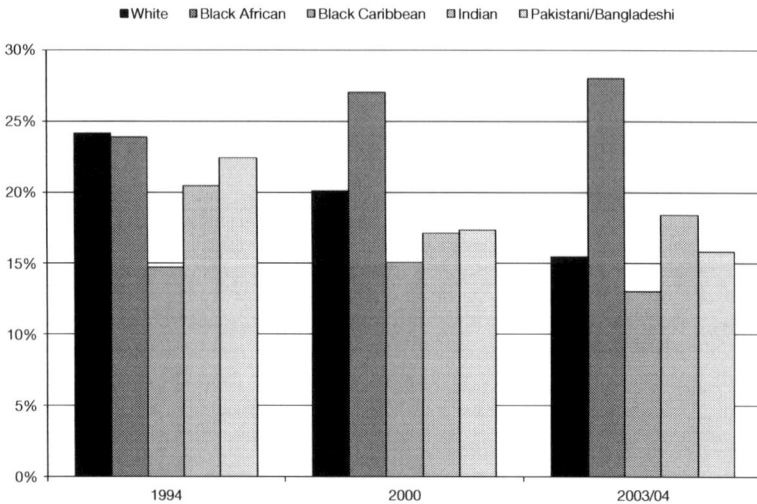

Figure 3.3 Proportion rating the local police 'very good': by broad ethnic category.

Source: British Crime Survey 1984; 1988; 1994; 2000; 2003/04

other ethnic or national groups). More striking is the difference between Black Africans and Black Caribbeans. While confidence was low among the latter group in 1994 and remained that way through to 2003/04, levels of strong support among Black Africans rose over the decade, in complete contrast to the other groups shown, and indeed almost all the other data presented in this chapter. The Black African group experienced considerable population growth over the period shown, much of which will have been from immigration – it may be that those born overseas have a higher opinion of the British police than those born in the country itself. With the exception of the Black African group, however, the general picture of more similar views in later period remains – and this, to repeat, was largely due to declines in confidence among those groups who previously held the most favourable views.

More recent data from the BCS confirm that opinion in the White British group remains lower than in most other ethnic groups. In 2008/09, for example, 52 per cent of White British people rated their local police as excellent or good; average ratings were higher in the British Asian ethnic groups (Indian 58 per cent, Pakistani 61 per cent, and Bangladeshi 60 per cent) and markedly higher in the Black African (68 per cent). By contrast, average ratings were lower in the Black Caribbean group (43 per cent) and, notably, the Mixed White and Black Caribbean (34 per cent). It is worth noting, however, that many – although certainly not all – of these differences disappear in multivariate analyses, likely as they are to be confounded by variation in contact experiences and other factors relevant to trust and confidence.

Economic activity status

Just as young people and those from ethnic minority groups may be 'over-policed and under-protected', with significant potential implications for their confidence in the police, economic activity status might also be a key predictor. Whether someone is employed full-time or part-time, is unemployed, or is a student or retired can affect their use of public space, for example, and hence their exposure to both crime and police (Waddington *et al.* 2004). Furthermore, unemployment in particular may have implications for individuals' sense of integration with the community and society more widely. In as much as the police represent these structures, trust and confidence may be affected by such alienation.

Significant variation in opinions of the police by economic activity status might therefore be expected – and in the earlier sweeps of the BCS this is indeed what is found. Instead of the bivariate associations displayed elsewhere in this chapter, Figure 3.4 shows fitted probabilities generated from a multinomial logistic regression model that reveal the effect of economic activity on confidence net of the effect of age, gender and ethnicity. Unlike age and gender, economic activity status is not an 'innate' characteristic of an individual, nor is it usually as closely tied to identity as is ethnicity. As a variable it is also extremely unevenly distributed across the population. It was, therefore, important to take account of at least some potential confounders in order to home in on the relationship at issue.

Figure 3.4 shows that retired people in the earlier years of the BCS were much more likely to give 'very good' ratings than others – and as predicted above, unemployed people were less likely than those in employment to do the same. But as the 1990s progressed to the turn of the new millennium, the difference in levels of strong confidence between people of different employment statuses shrunk, and had essentially disappeared by 2003/04. The one exception was students, who in the earlier years were much less likely to confess strong support for the police than others; by 2003/04, they were more likely to do so.

Bringing it all together

So far in this chapter we have discussed various socio-demographic factors in isolation from other factors. Yet, Hough (2003) discusses the way in which the views of "white, middle-class, middle-aged" Londoners converged with those of more socially and economically excluded groups between the two 'Policing for London' surveys conducted in 1983 and 2000/01. The BCS data support this view, and Figure 3.5 below demonstrates graphically the extent of this convergence. Generated from a multinomial logistic regression model it shows the predicted probabilities of rating the local police as 'very good' for two 'average' individuals, one 50-year-old White man, in employment living outside the inner city and the other a 20-year-old unemployed man from an ethnic minority living in the inner city, who have otherwise similar characteristics (in terms of the

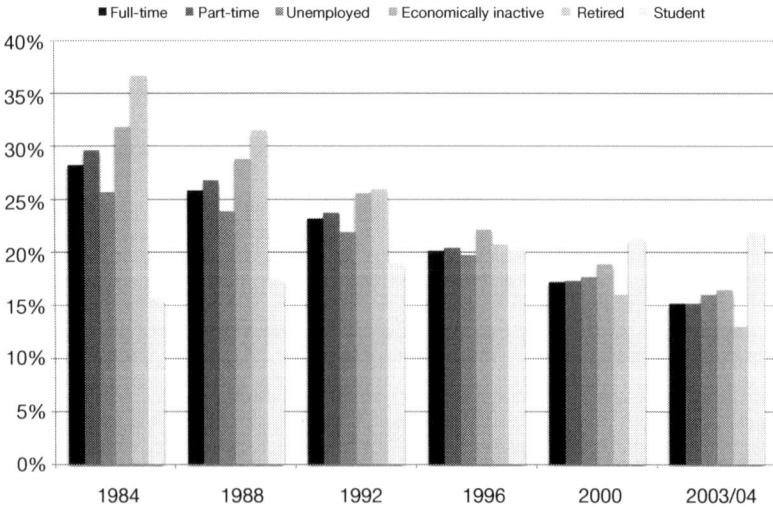

Figure 3.4 Predicted probability of giving the local police a 'very good' rating by employment status, 1984 to 2003/04.

Source: British Crime Survey

—— 50-year-old White man living outside inner city

▬ ▬ 20-year-old man from ethnic minority, living in inner city

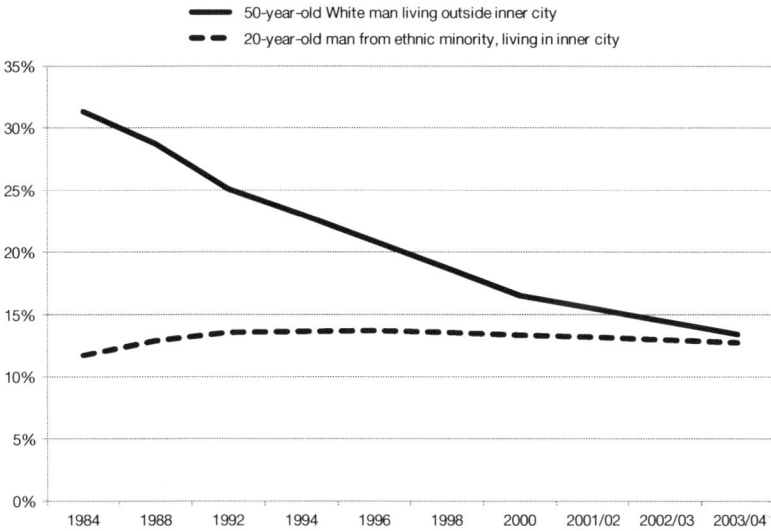

Figure 3.5 Probability of rating local police as very good: 'average' individuals.

Source: British Crime Survey 1984 to 2003/04

Notes: Estimated probabilities calculated holding constant: household size; car access; education (degree or not); housing tenure (social renter or not); employment status, victim status.

variables included in the model, at least). The extent of the convergence between the two is striking, and clearly demonstrates that levels of 'strong' support for the police declined markedly over the period among people who previously maintained relatively high levels of confidence, making them much more similar to those who, throughout the two decades shown, had low levels of confidence.

Summary

In this chapter we have examined how the relationship between age, gender, ethnicity and employment status, and opinions of the police, varied between the mid-1980s and the mid-2000s. Predictably, confidence in the police varies across these important social categories, but more surprisingly perhaps, this variation appears to have shrunk over time. By 2003/04, older people were not more likely to think the local police did a 'very good' job than younger people; women were not more likely than men; White people were not more likely than those from ethnic minority groups; and students are more likely to indicate strong support for the police than people with other economic activity statuses.

Opinions of the police appear, according to these measures at least, to have become rather more homogeneous over time. Obviously this idea needs to be carefully delimited. For example, it is rather unlikely that the truly marginalised and excluded are represented in any significant way in sample surveys such as the BCS. And it is probable that there are pockets of England and Wales where radically different views of the police hold sway – places where confidence is virtually absent, where local cultures inculcate antagonistic postures toward authorities such as police and, indeed, which experience a very different style of policing to the majority of the population. In addition, more recent waves of the BCS, and other sources, suggest that while variations in confidence across the categories used here are relatively small, they do still exist. Most notably White British people, on all available evidence, now appear to have significantly lower levels of confidence than those from many other ethnic groups, with the notable exception of the Black Caribbean group.

Perhaps the key point, however, is that public confidence in the police is in no way determined by age, gender, ethnicity or employment status – four of the key variables that are often thought to represent who people are and, often, the things that they do. In fact, these characteristics have only rather weak associations with opinions of the police.

What does influence public confidence in the police? Recall that, according to Beck, Bauman and others, changes to the structure and importance of established social categories (and the formation of new, more ephemeral categories) is intimately linked to forces that predict a growing similarity in individuals' experiences. Perhaps it is exactly these experiences that influence people's opinions? We turn next to personal contact with officers. What change has occurred in the number and types of contact that people have with the police?

4   Twenty-five years of public contact with the police

In Chapter 3 we examined change over time in the socio-demographic corre-lates of confidence in the police. We showed an increasing similarity of views across different population groups. While important variations remain, opinions of the police now vary relatively little over classic sociological variables such as age and ethnicity. If these characteristics are only weakly correlated with opin-ions of the police, we should look elsewhere for sources of variation in public trust (and perhaps, by extension, in police legitimacy and cooperation with legal authorities).

Much of the rest of this book is concerned with just this question. What accounts for individual and neighbourhood variation in trust, legitimacy and cooperation? Personal contact is well known to predict confidence (Skogan 2006; Tyler and Fagan 2008; Bradford *et al.* 2009a). People's experiences of the police may be powerful predictors of trust, legitimacy and cooperation. This chapter outlines the recent history of personal contacts with the police and judgements about the quality of these encounters. We examine how rates of personal contact with police have changed over time; we ask whether the way such encounters are judged by the public has also changed; and we investigate developments in the relationship between contact and confidence over the past 25 years or so.

Encounters between police and public

While personal contact with officers is an important element in the formation of opinions about the police, there is no reason to suspect that the intensity of such interactions is constant. Could it be that the changes in trust and confi-dence discussed in Chapter 3 mirror, at least in part, changes in rates of contact or how such contacts are judged? Can homogenisation of opinion be related to homogenisation of experience? Many recent developments in policing policy, for example the implementation of the National Reassurance Policing Programme (NRPP), are predicated on increasing the levels of contact with the public. There also appears to be an assumption that citizen contacts with the police will increase over time as the provision of security becomes ever more pervasive (Loader 2006; Loader and Walker 2007).

They are many reasons why a uniform upward trend in rates of contact is, however, unlikely. Crime levels have fluctuated dramatically over the last 30 years (Jansson 2008), influencing numbers and patterns of contact between police and public in relation to both calls for service and, possibly, stop-and-search and other police-initiated contacts. Equally, the use of public space has changed, for reasons ranging from the continued increase in the use of the car to changing patterns of socialisation, with implications for the availability of the public to the police (and vice versa). Finally, incentives and disincentives to report victimisation to the police have also changed, as for example the growth of household insurances acted as an increasing incentive to report certain types of victimisation.

Change in the way marginalised and minority groups are policed may also have altered rates of contact. Attempts to address the case of how socially excluded groups (particularly ethnic minorities) are treated by police (Reiner 2000) have involved policies by police and government to deal with the flagrant inequities in policing that were revealed over the course of the 1980s and 1990s (Scarman 1982; Macpherson 1999; Miller *et al.* 2000). While the effectiveness of these efforts is a moot point (Bowling and Philips 2002), it seems hard to imagine that they will have had no effect on public experiences of the police. That said, the continued disproportionality in experiences of stop-and-search activity (Bowling and Philips 2007; Miller *et al.* 2000) suggests that improvements, if they exist at all, must have been in the way contacts are handled by officers, rather than in successful attempts to address imbalances in the proportion of people from ethnic minorities who come into contact with police in this way.

Contact with the police 1988 to 2005/06

Overall rates of contact with the police fell significantly between 1988 and 2005/06. Figure 4.1 shows that the proportion of people who had initiated a contact with the police in the last year in 2005/06 was around half that in 1988. If security has become more pervasive in the last 25 years (Loader 2006), this does not seem to be reflected in greater levels of personal contact between officers and public. In part this mirrors a decline in victimisation (as recorded by the BCS) over the same period. But it is interesting to note that, while the decline in self-initiated contacts was essentially uni-directional, victimisation rates actually rose from 1988 to 1994/96 before falling back. Although the overall decrease in self-initiated contacts from 1988 to 2005/06 can probably be explained in part by falling crime rates, this seems not to be the only factor involved.

Rates of police-initiated contact – and police stops in particular – were also lower in 2005/06 than in 1988, although the difference was much smaller. Police-initiated contacts mirrored victimisation rates more closely, increasing to 1996 before falling from then on. It is important to note that it is the experience of the public which is at issue here (the figures are based on survey data), and for a wide variety of reasons change in the level of BCS stops may differ from change as indicated by police-recorded stops (see Bradford 2011b).

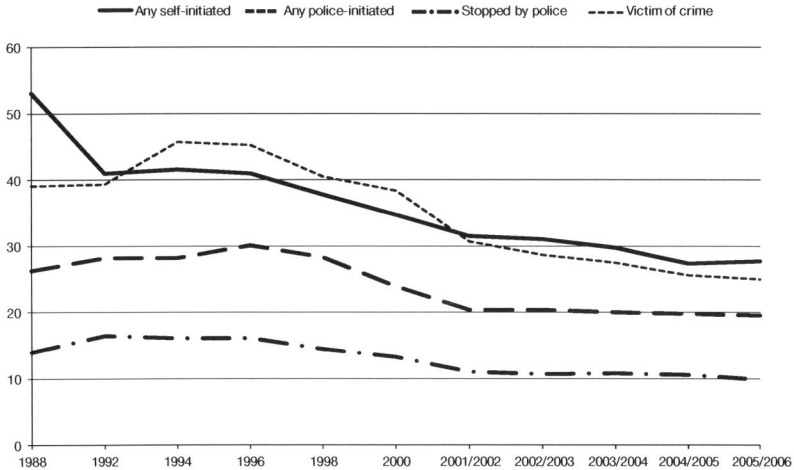

Figure 4.1 Contact with the police and victimisation rate: 1988 to 2005/06.

Source: British Crime Survey

Notes: 2001/02 contains data from entire calendar year of 2001.

Self-initiated contacts and sub-group analysis

We now turn to specific forms of contact as these were experienced across the four socio-demographic categories covered in Chapter 3: age, gender, ethnicity and employment status. Before looking at the impact of police-stop activity, we first consider self-initiated contacts.

Age

The overall decline in rates of self-initiated contact was repeated for all age groups, and the biggest changes occurred among those age groups most likely to initiate contact in 1988 and the smallest among those least likely. Although homogenisation across the age range was not as strong here as it was for public confidence in the police, overall decline in use of the police does seem to have occurred alongside a relative homogenisation across different age groups. Since the most common reason for contacting the police is to report a crime, either as witness or victim (Allen *et al.* 2006; Bradford *et al.* 2009a), at least part of the reason for this relative homogenisation must lie in changes in the level of crime. It may be that, since crime has a disproportionate impact on the young (Walker *et al.* 2006), falling crime rates will have a greater effect in the younger age groups, and make the experience of the young more similar to that of older people.

Gender

Over the period from 1988 to 2005/06 there was a dramatic convergence in the rates of self-initiated contact among men and women. In the earlier years, 46 per cent of women reported contacting the police in the past 12 months, compared with 61 per cent of men. By 2000, these figures were 30 per cent compared with 37 per cent, respectively – and by 2005/06, 28 per cent of both men and women reported such contact.

This is a striking change over such a short time period. In part, it might be explained by the change in the rate of victimisation – in 1988, 37 per cent of women reported having been a victim of crime in the previous 12 months, compared with 41 per cent of men. By 2005/06, the victimisation rate was 24 per cent for women and 25 per cent for men. Yet there may be many other reasons behind the convergence in experience between men and women. We might speculate that changes in work patterns might be a factor as more women entered the workforce over the course of the 1980s and 1990s; changes in household structures might have had an effect as more women lived on their own or headed households on their own; and changes in gender roles. Such speculation is beyond the scope of the present work, leaving us merely to note, again, a growing similarity in experience over time across a key socio-demographic category.

Ethnic group

A similar pattern is found across the very broad 'ethnic' categories that are available from the earliest years of the BCS. In 1988, 45 per cent of Asians reported self-initiated contact with the police, compared with 54 per cent of Whites and 56 per cent of Blacks. By 2005/06 these figures were 23 per cent, 28 per cent and 29 per cent respectively. Taking into account the sampling variation reflected in the 95 per cent confidence intervals round these numbers, it becomes impossible to distinguish between the rates of contact for each group in the latter year. Some caution is needed here, since the social variation within each of these categories is likely to be as wide as the variations between them (compare, for example, the different histories and experiences of British Indians, Pakistanis and Bangladeshis). However, we found very similar results using the more detailed ethnic group classification available in the later years of the survey. In 2005/06, only Indians reported a significantly lower rate of self-initiated contact than the White group.

Economic activity status

Levels of self-initiated contact among people of different employment statuses also generally converged between 1988 and 2005/06. In 1988, those who were retired or who were economically inactive were notably less likely to initiate a contact with police than their economically active counterparts; by 2005/2006 the gap between the groups had shrunk significantly.

Police-initiated contacts

We now turn from self-initiated to police-initiated contacts. As noted earlier, the proportion of people experiencing a police stop rose between 1988 and the mid-1990s before falling back; the changes mirror those of police-recorded crime rates. By 2005/06, the number of police-initiated contacts was slightly below 1988 levels.

Age

This overall trend occurred almost uniformly in all age groups, with the biggest fluctuations occurring in the 16–34 age range. The variation in stop rates between age groups was higher in the 'high-crime' early 1990s than in the 'low-crime' period a decade later. For example, 45 per cent of 16–24-year-olds reported a recent police stop (either on foot or in a car) in 1994, as did 51 per cent of 25–34-year-olds. By contrast, 34 per cent of 55–64-year-olds, and 26 per cent of 65–74-year-olds reported a stop in the same year. By 2005/06, 30 per cent of 16–24-year-olds, 35 per cent of 25–34-year-olds, 27 per cent of 55–64-year-olds, and 18 per cent of 65–74-year-olds reported a police stop in the past year.

There are two readings of these numbers. On the one hand, there appears to be a flattening out of experience in the latter years, especially around 2001/02. On the other hand, there is consistency over time in that stop rates and differences in experience between age groups are broadly similar across the period, notably in 2005/06 compared with earlier years when the victimisation rate was substantially higher. Finally, despite a 15-point reduction in the rate of victimisation, people of all ages were only slightly less likely to be stopped than people of an equivalent age in 1988.

Ethnic group

Differences in stop rates by broad ethnic category were also largely maintained across the period, in spite of the fluctuation in the overall stop rate. People from Black ethnic groups were more likely than those from White or Asian groups to be stopped in 1988, and this remained the case right through to 2005/06. However, variations between ethnic groups narrowed in the period up to 2001/02, after which they began to increase again. One possible reason for this might be events around the time of the Stephen Lawrence enquiry and its aftermath, leading to a decline in police-stop activity as the service grappled with charges of institutional racism. Over time – perhaps alongside the effects of 9/11 – such prerogatives faded and old patterns seem to have reasserted themselves.

Economic activity status

Whether a person is employed, unemployed or retired can in itself have very little bearing on the stop decisions made by police officers. Rather, it is personal characteristics and especially behaviours which are correlated with employment status which must be the relevant factors. Any change in the rate of stops across groups of individuals with different employment statuses might therefore be down to changes in the composition of the group and entirely unrelated to simply being, for example, unemployed. Once these 'compositional' factors have been taken into account, any remaining variation between economic activity status and the chances of being stopped by the police can be more firmly attributed to characteristics associated with the different statuses. So, for example, if after controlling for age, gender and ethnic group, unemployed people were still more likely to be stopped, this would more firmly suggest that it is factors associated with being unemployed – such as being 'out and about' during the day and available for the police to stop – which are important.

We used binary logistic regression models that controlled for age, gender and ethnic group to predict probabilities of having experienced a police stop in the last year across various economic activity statuses. There was a marked convergence over the period shown, with the partial exception of the unemployed, whose chance of being stopped rose relative to the other groups over time, and who were significantly more likely to be stopped in 2005/06 than those either in employment or economically inactive. Overall, with the exception of the unemployed, the salience of a person's employment or economic activity status for their risk of being-stopped by the police shrunk over time.

Modelling the experience of police stops

Table 4.1 presents results from two logistic regression models predicting the odds of experiencing a car or foot-stop, or any police-initiated contact, over the period 1988–2005/06. The survey year is entered as an independent variable, as was its square (the statistical significance of which demonstrates that there was a curvilinear relationship between time period and the chances of experiencing police-initiated contact), and interactions between (a) time and age, and (b) time and broad ethnic category.

Table 4.1 Binary logistic regression models predicting odds of having experienced police-initiated contact in previous years (1=experienced police-initiated contact).

	Stopped in car/on foot			Any police initiative contact		
	Odds ratio	95% Confidence interval		Odds ratio	95% Confidence interval	
Age	0.95***	0.95	0.96	0.97***	0.97	0.98
Sex (ref: male) Female	0.48***	0.46	0.50	0.67***	0.65	0.70
Broad ethnic category (ref: White) Black	1.42***	1.16	1.74	1.04	0.88	1.24
Asian	0.68***	0.55	0.83	0.59***	0.50	0.69
Other	1.20	0.72	1.98	1.51**	1.00	2.28

	Odds ratio	Stopped in car/on foot 95% Confidence interval		Odds ratio	Any police initiative contact 95% Confidence interval	
Car access (ref: no) Yes	2.09***	1.96	2.22	1.51***	1.44	1.58
Place of residence (ref: not inner city)	1.00	0.95	1.05	0.96**	0.91	1.00
Inner city	0.97**	0.95	1.00	0.98*	0.96	1.00
Household size Number of children in household	0.88***	0.84	0.92	0.99	0.96	1.03
Eudcation (ref: below university degree) Batchelor's degree and above	0.91***	0.86	0.96	1.00	0.96	1.05
Tenancy (ref: all others) Council renter	1.16***	1.10	1.23	1.11***	1.07	1.16
Household income (ref: middle bands) Lowest	0.93	0.83	1.04	0.90**	0.82	0.99
Highest	1.21***	1.13	1.29	1.19***	1.13	1.25
Employment status (ref: employed/other econ. Inactive) Part-time	1.03	0.96	1.09	1.04	0.99	1.09
Unemployed	1.25***	1.16	1.34	1.19***	1.12	1.26
Retired	0.89***	0.82	0.97	0.91***	0.86	0.96
Student	0.92*	0.83	1.02	0.94	0.86	1.03
Marital status (ref: other) Single	1.26***	1.19	1.33	1.10***	1.06	1.15
Victim of crime in previous 12 months (ref: no) Yes	1.36***	1.30	1.41	1.39***	1.34	1.43
Self-initiated contact in previous 12 months (ref: no) Any self-initiated contact	1.69***	1.63	1.77	2.02***	1.95	2.08
Survey year	1.05***	1.03	1.08	1.05***	1.03	1.07
Square of survey year	1.00***	1.00	1.00	1.00***	1.00	1.00
Interactions Survey year*age	1.00***	1.00	1.00	1.00***	1.00	1.00
Survey year*Black	1.00	0.98	1.01	1.00	0.99	1.01
Survey year*asian	1.02**	1.00	1.03	1.02***	1.01	1.03
Survey year+other	0.99	0.96	1.02	0.98**	0.95	1.00

Source: British Crime Survey 1988–2005/06.

Note
Unweighted n=102,624 for the first fitted model (stopped in car/on foot); 102,611 for the second fitted model (any police initiated contact)
* significant at the 5% level, ** significant at the 1% level, *** significant at the 0.1% level.

The coefficients for time period and its square, presented in Table 4.1, confirm that from 1988 to 2005/06 the odds of a person being stopped by the police, independent of their personal characteristics, first increased and then fell back to the 1988 level. The pattern for all police-initiated contacts was almost identical. In terms of the model this can perhaps be thought of as a 'pure' police activity effect (although obviously occurring in the light of the changes in the crime rate and the political and social climate), since it represents the chances of being stopped net of an individual's characteristics or circumstances. Controlling for this temporal effect, and the other characteristics included in the model, over the whole period the odds of being stopped fell with age; while compared with the White groups those from Black ethnic groups had greater, and those from the Asian groups lower, odds of being stopped. Again these patterns were generally (and unsurprisingly) repeated for all police-initiated contacts, although based on these results, it appears that people from the Black groups had no greater odds of any police-initiated contact than those from the White groups.

However, the effect of the interaction terms between age and time, ethnic group and time period mean things are a little more complicated. The positive value for the age–time interaction in the police-stop model suggests that as time went on, the odds of contact among older people increased relative to those of younger people: across the period, the odds of experiencing a police stop among older people grew more similar to those of younger people, although it should be noted that younger people still had considerably greater chances of being stopped in 2005/06. Similarly, the odds of people from the Asian groups experiencing a stop increased over time relative to those of people from the White groups; but, in contrast, the time period had no significant effect on odds of experiencing a stop among those from the Black groups. In concrete terms, these findings suggest that, net of other factors, in 1988 Asians were the least likely to experience a stop, followed by Whites, with those from the Black groups the most likely. By 2005/06 there was almost no difference between Whites and Asians, but those from the Black groups still had significantly higher odds of being stopped.

The experience of police stops has, net of other factors, therefore become more similar among people of different ages and broad ethnic categories; but, despite this, and despite changes in policing policy and practice, younger people and those from Black ethnic groups are still more likely than others to experience such encounters with the police. With regard to the former, this is perhaps understandable; but as Bowling and Philips (2007) discuss, disproportionality in the experience of stop-and-search activity among Black people continues to be a major problem, possibly even calling into question the use of the technique as it is currently employed.

Turning to the Asian groups, it has been suggested that both police and wider social stereotyping may in the past have protected Asian people from this type of police activity, because, among a number of unfavourable stereotypes, Asians were seen as broadly law-abiding (Jefferson 1992). While the extent to which this was ever true is doubtful, the advent of Islamist terrorism as well as other factors means it almost certainly is not the case now (Webster 2004). It is within these broader patterns that the relative increase in the experience of stops among Asians can perhaps be understood, as cultural and political change and new security concerns have combined to even out the experience of police stops in the White and Asian ethnic groups. It will be interesting to see whether in future years Asians, on this measure, come to experience more police attention than Whites.

In sum it appears that, regarding contact with the police among people of different ages or from different ethnic backgrounds, the story over the period 1988 to 2005/06 was one of a gradual homogenisation of experience within an overall framework of a decline in the proportion of people experiencing contact with the police. This was, of course, an incomplete and sometimes contradictory process. Any homogenisation of experience which did occur appeared to be of a lesser magnitude than that found in opinions of the police reported in Chapter 3. However, such change as there was over the period, from fluctuations in the crime rate through to terrorist attacks, combined to produce patterns of personal experience that were more similar across different population groups in 2005/06 than they had been in 1988.

Change in public judgements of contacts with police

Just as changes in policing policies, practices and in society more widely will have affected rates of personal contact with the police, they may also have altered the ways in which contacts are experienced and judged, and also the processes through which such encounters affect overall opinions. It is well known that many of those who have had recent contact with the police, and in particular those who have had unsatisfactory contact, have lower levels of trust and confidence (Allen *et al.* 2006; Bradford *et al.* 2009a; Skogan 2006). More contested, but seemingly still present, is a positive impact on trust, confidence and legitimacy from personal contacts which are judged satisfactory by the public (Bradford *et al.* 2009a; Tyler and Fagan 2008).

But there is no reason to suspect such effects are constant over time. Factors associated with the late-modern condition, described above, that may have levelled down experiences of contact with the police may also have affected how those experiences are judged. A growing consumerist orientation would in particular predict that assessments of contacts, especially self-initiated or service contacts, would become more critical over time as individuals grew to expect more from the police. This would impact trust and confidence in a direct way if dissatisfaction with contact grew. A consumerist orientation might also imply a growing threat to the policing 'brand' as more critical orientations broaden the extent to which individual (bad) experiences are generalised to the entire organisation.

On the other hand, growing consumerism need not inevitably imply more negative effects from personal contacts. Might police 'customers' develop brand loyalty if they receive good service? On the face of it such an outcome appears unlikely: police customers will expect a good service, and a positively assessed encounter under such circumstances might not lead through into an improved assessment of the police overall, since a positive outcome was expected at the outset (Skogan 2006). But the possibility remains open and, indeed, one of the key tenets of recent government policing policy has been that trust and confidence can be enhanced by making policing more citizen (or consumer) oriented.

Public assessments of the quality of contacts with the police

Experiences of police contact, in as much as they changed between 1988 and 2005/06, appear to have become more homogeneous over time. What, then, of judgements about those contacts? If personal contact with the police largely affects trust and confidence through assessments of the way in which police handled the encounter, changes in these assessments over time may have been a factor in the decline in trust and confidence.

People's views about their contacts with the police did indeed change over time. Dissatisfaction with self-initiated and 'other' police-initiated contacts (that is, not vehicle or foot stops) grew markedly between 1992 and 2005/06: dissatisfaction with self-initiated contacts, for example, grew from less than 20 per cent in 1992 to more than 30 per cent in 2005/06. By contrast, dissatisfaction with police car stops was almost unchanged over the same period. At this very broad level it might be suggested that the changes for self-initiated contacts reflect a more consumer-oriented approach to these contacts among the public (Loader 1999), which seems would almost inevitably lead to greater dissatisfaction. Such an orientation may also have affected opinions about cars stops; however, police have made concerted efforts to improve the way they deal with people during such encounters (Miller *et al.* 2000; Shiner 2006) that might have offset any negative outcomes from such a change. These ideas are examined in more detail below, where discussion will be constrained to the period 1994 to 2003/04 due to limited availability of data.

Why should people grow more dissatisfied with police contact? It seems doubtful that the ten years from 1994 to 2003/4, over which time dissatisfaction with self-initiated contacts changed significantly, witnessed major variation in the outcomes police were able to offer the public. Tyler's studies on procedural justice and other work in this area suggests in any case that material outcomes are not uppermost in people's minds when they make judgements about their contacts with the police (Bradford *et al.* 2009[a or b?]; Tyler 1990; Tyler and Huo 2002; Tyler and Fagan 2008). Reasons for the growth in dissatisfaction must therefore lie elsewhere. Two plausible suggestions are, first, that a growing consumer orientation among the public toward policing means that 'services' found to be adequate in earlier periods were at later dates more critically assessed (Newburn 2003); second, a growth in negative orientations toward the police may have translated into more negative assessments of personal contacts. In many ways both ideas have similar aetiology, namely the idea that processes of desubordination (Reiner 1992; c.f. Miliband 1978) have stripped the police of much of the protection they once received from public deference toward them.

If there has been a process of desurbordination, dissatisfaction with self-initiated contact might be expected to vary with age: for example, because older people retain deference toward police lost by their younger counterparts; the extent of these variations may have changed over time. Figure 4.2 examines this idea, comparing changes in dissatisfaction with self-initiated contacts and vehicle stops. It demonstrates that there were marked differences between age groups within and across years. Most strikingly, there was considerably less variation by age in dissatisfaction with self-initiated contacts in 2003/04 than there was in 1994. If the relatively small number people aged 65–74 are excluded, the same is true for car stops. For self-initiated contacts this reduction in variation again occurred because older people 'caught up' with younger ones. For example, 26 per cent of 16–24-year-olds were dissatisfied with such contacts in 1994, compared with 32 per cent in 2003/04 – for 55–64-year-olds these proportions were 16 per cent and 34 per cent respectively. For car stops the picture was subtly different, and here dissatisfaction fell over the ten years among those aged under 45 but increased among 45–64-year-olds.

That changes of the magnitude shown in Figure 4.2 occurred over only a ten-year period is remarkable. The social and political context in which these encounters occurred is likely to have been an important influence: it is interesting that for the youngest people dissatisfaction with these types of contact was highest in 2000, a time when the police were receiving a considerable amount of 'bad press'. Overall, however, the sense is once again that opinions of the police, or here police actions, were 'levelled down' over the decade to become considerably more homogeneous by the end of it. Perhaps there really was a residue of deference retained by older people in the 1990s that was substantially weakened by the mid-2000s.

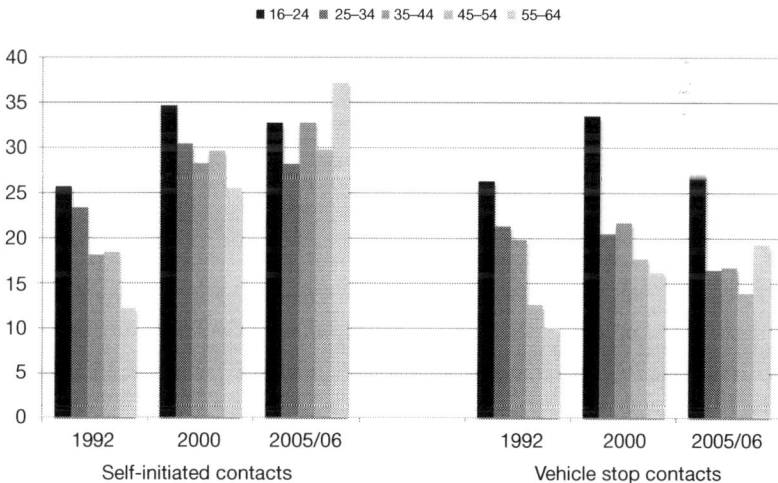

Figure 4.2 Proportion dissatisfied with police contact: by year, age and type of contact.
Source: British Crime Survey

Opinion formation during self-initiated contacts

It appears, then, that there has been something of a convergence of views regarding assessments of contacts with the police. But can causes for this be identified? The BCS allows some investigation of what drives satisfaction (or dissatisfaction) with police–public encounters by asking those who experienced them a number of questions about the events and their reactions. Multinomial logistic regression models were estimated to investigate if and how the factors affecting satisfaction with self-initiated contacts changed over the period from 1994 to 2005/06. As well as socio-demographic variables, a number of explanatory variables representing respondents' feelings about the contact were included: whether the respondent felt they had been kept informed about what was happening to a sufficient extent, whether they thought the officers involved appeared interested and made enough effort, and also whether they had had to wait for police to arrive. Overall the findings suggested that there was little change in the relative importance of these different aspects of experience over the decade. There was one exception, however: the importance of police providing information grew over time. There is evidence elsewhere to suggest that the provision of information to people is of particular importance in affecting public opinion (Bradford *et al.* 2009a; Hohl *et al.* 2010), and it seems this may be an increasingly salient aspect of people's assessments of the police. The regression modelling also confirmed the change in the effect of age described above. Even when conditioning on the other variables in the model, young people were considerably more likely to be dissatisfied with this type of contact than older people in 1994, but a decade later the probability of dissatisfaction was more or less equal across all age groups. This suggests, again, a levelling down (to less favourable assessments) over the period examined.

Bringing it all together: change in the impact of contact on confidence

In our review of the historical picture thus far, we have considered confidence in and contact with the police as separate issues. However, the two are deeply intertwined. Personal contact with officers is a driver of trust in the police, with the association between contact and confidence well known (Skogan 2006; Bradford *et al.* 2009).. On average, people who have had recent contact with the police have lower levels of confidence than those who have not, a situation unlike that pertaining for many other public services (Stanko *et al.* 2009). To bring this section of the book to a close, we examine how the effect of contact on confidence changed over time.

Skogan (2006) demonstrates that there is a marked asymmetry in the impact of personal contact on confidence in the police. Using data from the 1992 BCS, as well as other sources, he shows that while negative contacts are strongly associated with lower levels of confidence, positive contacts have only a very weak association with higher levels of confidence. This finding has been replicated on numerous occasions, although there is considerable debate about the extent of this asymmetry (Bradford *et al.* 2009a; Gau 2010; Myhill and Bradford 2011;

Rosenbaum *et al.* 2005; Tyler and Fagan 2008), with some studies finding considerably more symmetry than Skogan suggests.

To illustrate how the effect of contact on confidence changed over the 1990s and into the new millennium, Figure 4.3 shows the variation in ratings of the local police among those who had contact with the police in 1992, 2000 and 2003/04. Each bar represents the difference in the proportion of respondents rating their local police as very or fairly good, compared with those who had no contact (the zero line). As Skogan suggested, there was almost complete asymmetry in 1992. People who had unsatisfactory contact were much less likely than those who with no recent contact to give the local police a good rating. There was almost no difference, however, in the ratings given by the no contact and satisfactory contact groups. However, over time there was a small but significant increase in the difference between the satisfactory and no contact groups, such that by 2003/04 people who had positive self- or police-initiated contacts were more likely to give the local police a good rating.

These results were replicated in a multivariate analysis that controlled for a wide range of potentially confounding factors. Even after age, gender, ethnicity, employment status, victimisation and a range of other factors were taken into account, there was a growing symmetry in the effect of contact on confidence

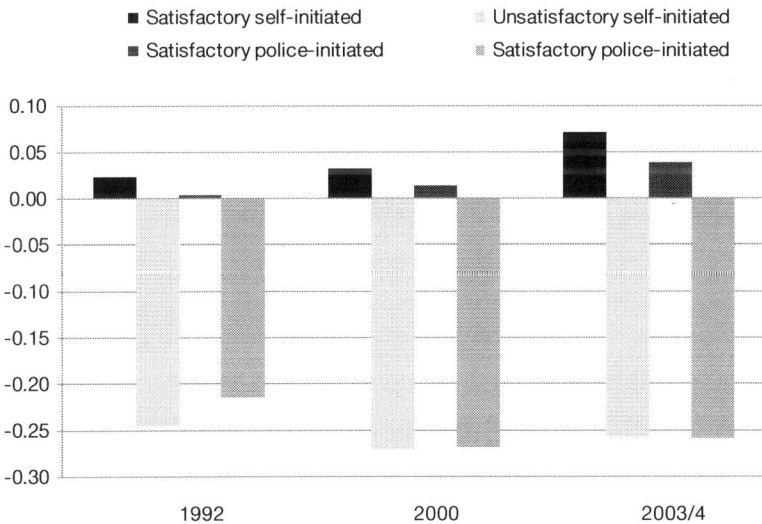

Figure 4.3 Variation in 'good' ratings of police: differences from 'no contact' group by contact experience.

Source: British Crime Survey

over the period 1992–2003/04, albeit that the statistical effect of negative contact remained far stronger than that of positive contact (see Bradford 2011b).

There may be many reasons for the apparent increase in the effect of positive contact over time. One might be increasingly consumerist attitudes toward the police: perhaps people are willing to give the police a small 'reward' for good service. However, in common with many commentators we believe there is marked resistance among the public to seeing the police in this way. The symbolic and relational aspects of policing are likely to remain far more important to most people, most of the time, for all that some influence from the growing consumerisation of society is probably inevitable (Girling *et al.* 2000; Loader and Mulcahy 2003; Reiner 2000; Tyler and Huo 2002). Tyler's work on procedural justice has demonstrated that people do not often judge interactions with police in cost-benefit terms, nor are they most interested in what the police can provide to them in a material sense. They do, however, pay close attention to how they are treated by officers, and they will enter into encounters with a whole range of expectations about what might transpire and how the police should behave.

The nature of these expectations will have changed over time. Growth in symmetry is therefore probably linked to the more general processes of social change described above, of which consumerisation is just one facet. Trust in the police will always have been tested against experience. But there may have been more factors that previously intervened in, influenced or mediated the effect of contact on confidence. Smith (2007) suggests that many people with little personal experience of officers' behaviour – middle-class groups, older people – may place the police on a pedestal, even seeing the institution as above reproach and criticism. Direct encounters with officers are likely to be unsettling and potentially undermining of trust for such people, leaving little room for positive encounters to enhance trust. More generally, people with high opinions of the police may enter into interactions with high expectations of officers. Theories of expectancy disconfirmation (Reisig and Chandek 2001) suggest that meeting high expectations is unlikely to result in improved opinions, while failing to meet them is very likely to undermine them. Under both conditions – placing the police on a pedestal, high expectations generated by high trust – we might well expect a strong asymmetry in the effect of contact on confidence. Both seem to have been more prevalent in the past than is the case today.

Summary

Whatever the precise trajectory and modality of change, there seems little doubt that the police have been emphatically knocked off any pedestal they once occupied (Reiner 2010). Many factors that might once have intervened between police and public have been stripped away by the processes of late modernity sketched out in Chapter 3. The dominant image of the development in policing styles over the last half century – a change from Dixon to Robocop (ibid.) – is plainly a caricature. Many people experienced extremely repressive policing in the past; conversely, recent developments in, or rediscoveries of (Innes 2004), community policing have stressed the necessity of strong, friendly links between police and public. The Dixon to Robocop story does, however, resonate at both symbolic and experiential levels. While repressive forms of policing may in the past have been largely hidden from view they are now highly visible (Greer and McLaughlin 2010). Most people are now aware that officers can and sometimes do act with excessive force and in other ways that run counter to the idea that the police are a fair and neutral arbiter in public affairs. Equally, the actual experience of police behaviour perceived to be heavy-handed seems likely to have spread far beyond groups and individuals considered to be 'police-property'. We might again point to the policing of traffic offences, often felt to be deeply unfair and oppressive to those on the receiving end (Girling *et al.* 2000).

Of course, such perceptions may often be misplaced. The point is simply that they exist and appear to be widely held. Personal experience of officers' behaviour – good and bad – is now more evenly distributed across the population, and knowledge of police malpractice is widespread, thanks to modern media conditions, meaning it is far less likely that people see the police as 'sacred and taboo' (Smith 2007). Equally, the levelling down in confidence suggests many more people will enter into encounters with officers with lower (or more realistic) expectations. One result of these interwoven processes may have been that when individuals have contact with officers they carry rather less 'baggage', in terms of excessively high expectations, a sense of awe of the police, or other factors associated with their social background or position. This may have opened up small space for positive experiences to enhance trust and confidence.

Paradoxically, then, the very processes which contributed to the decline in public confidence in the police may also have resulted in a change in the way individuals judge their encounters with officers, leading to a gradual decline in asymmetry in the effect of contact on confidence. Equally, the decline in confidence has been accompanied by and interacted with a growing similarity in experiences of the police. If we are to understand the vectors of public trust, we need to look further than socio-demographic variables and leave behind the expectation that 'who someone is' will drive their opinion of the police. Rather, it seems to be precisely their experience of police – the contact they have with officers – that has become an ever more important factor. It will not be the only one, however, and we discuss in Part 4 some of the other potential influences on public opinion. Analysis of the development of confidence and the experience of contact over the past two decades shows a clear trend towards convergence and homogenisation in the experience of contact with and confidence in the police across the socio-demographic categories of age, gender and ethnicity. With basic personal characteristics such as gender, age and ethnicity increasingly losing explanatory power, it becomes all the more important to develop a more nuanced understanding of trust in the police. In Part 3 we turn to a more detailed discussion of the concept and measurement of trust and examine key influences on public trust in the police.

Part 3

Why do people trust the police?

Part 3 moves away from tracking trajectories of confidence and contact over the past 25 years or so. In the following pages we turn to trust in the police. Drawing upon data from our London survey conducted between 2007 and 2009, we highlight the importance of the encounters that people have with officers, and we highlight the importance of neighbourhood effects on individuals' trust judgements. In Chapter 5 we examine the meaning and measurement of trust in the police. Moving beyond simplistic indicators of confidence, we differentiate between (a) trust in police effectiveness, (b) trust in police fairness and (c) trust in police intentions and shared motives.

Then, in Chapter 6 we show surprisingly weak correlations between public opinion and newspaper coverage of policing. Criminal justice practitioners and policy-makers often assume that the mass media exerts a strong causal influence on public opinion. Trust is thought to be influenced most keenly by the striking events that generate extensive media coverage, like violence between citizens, the 2011 riots and looting across major English towns and cities, and violence between the police and citizens at large-scale situations of public order. Treating newspaper coverage of police and policing as an important indicator of the tone, tenor and intensity of mass media coverage, we examine the correlation between individual-level trust and the media coverage around the time of the particular survey interview. Strikingly, our data offer little support for the idea that media coverage is an important predictor of public trust in the police.

In combination with the evidence from Part 2– that contact is important and that classic sociological variables like gender, age and ethnicity are relatively unimportant – we conclude that other sources of variation are at play. We turn to Tyler's work on procedural justice (which focuses on the encounters that people have with legal authorities) as well as Sampson's work on the social ecology of neighbourhoods. In Chapter 7 we decompose the variation into individual and neighbourhood levels, allowing for two levels of influence on the outcome variable. Using a multilevel approach that incorporates multiple levels of influence, we account for the higher-than-average similarity between residents of the same local area. Ensuring that neighbourhood level measures are incorporated as ecological effects, we treat the similarities between interviewees from the same neighbourhood as a theoretically interesting source of variation in the data to be explained. Examining whether neighbourhood characteristics explain or absorb some of the variation between neighbourhoods, our findings shed light on the social ecology of trust in the police. They confirm the relative unimportance of variables such as age, gender, class and ethnicity, apart from their indirect effect via the encounters that individuals from particular social groups have with the police.

In Chapters 8, 9 and 10 we move to police contact. We begin by examining who experiences police-initiated contact, and consistent with prior research, we find that the police tend to stop and search certain social groups more than others. We then estimate the association between being stopped by the police (for example) and trust in the police, conditioning on the neighbourhood in which an individual lives. Finally, we consider victimisation experience and public-initiated contact with police. Does crime experience predict trust? What impact has the contact that individuals have with police as a consequence of their direct and indirect experience of crime? The findings provide further support for the validity of Tyler's procedural justice framework. But first, let us consider an important question: namely, what is trust in the police?

5   What is trust in the police?

As elsewhere in our work, the current study defined trust in the police as the belief among members of the public that the police have the right intentions and are competent in the tasks assigned to them (Jackson and Bradford 2010; Hough *et al.*, 2010; Jackson *et al.* 2011; European Social Survey 2011; c.f. Hardin 2002). Spanning intentions (relational trust) and abilities (calculative trust), we assume that trust extends beyond assessments that police perform their duties effectively, to include a sense that they understand the needs of the community, that they treat members of the community fairly and with dignity, and that they give them information and also the opportunity to voice the issues they are facing in their neighbourhood.

In this chapter we present topline findings from the London survey (the Metropolitan Police Public Attitudes Survey, or the METPAS) on the nature and distribution of trust in the police. Are police officers effective and fair? Do they demonstrate the best intentions towards those they protect and police? We also consider data from our BME booster (a connected survey based on a sample of 1,000 additional individuals from Black and Minority Ethnic (BME) groups), which fields more precise measures of trust in police procedural justice. Testing the scaling properties of the separate measures of trust in police fairness and trust in police effectiveness, we examine the dimensionality of trust in the police. What does it mean to trust the police? What attributes of police trustworthiness do people evaluate most keenly, and how do the underlying dimensions relate to our specific measures?

A variety of approaches to defining trust in the police

In their discussion of public opinion concerning criminal justice systems across the world, Roberts and Hough (2005: 32) summarise a variety of different measures that researchers have assumed to measure the perceived fairness, integrity, competence and effectiveness of justice institutions. These include global questions about confidence in and satisfaction with the justice system as a whole; questions about confidence in specific branches of the system; questions about the perceived performance of the system as a whole, or specific agencies, for example in 'fighting' or dealing with crime; and levels of satisfaction with personal experiences. Roberts and Hough go on to underline that no single question will ever be enough to assess the concepts of trust and confidence; a range of indicators will always be needed to capture adequately the complexity of public opinions in this area.

In the US literature there are three general approaches to the meaning and measurement of trust, confidence and legitimacy. The first – often concerned with policy questions about racial variation in levels of support for the police and courts – treats public confidence as unproblematically related to (and measured by) simple concepts such as satisfaction with service, general support and statements of confidence. This has been the case with regard to statistics collated by the central government (Bureau of Justice Statistics 2007), as well as in academic papers that have drawn on a wealth of national and locally based surveys (Brandl *et al.* 1994; Brandl *et al.* 1997; Cao 2001; Weitzer 2002; MacDonald and Stokes 2006; for the courts, see Benesh and Howell 2001; Brooks and Jeon-Slaughter 2001). This approach assumes that attitudes toward the police can be summed up under the banner of a single question, broadly analogous to the 'how good a job' question used in the British Crime Survey and elsewhere in the UK. The assumption has been defended by Brandl *et al.* (1997: 479), who argue that: 'regardless of question forms or referent, substantively and statistically similar levels of support are produced ... perhaps respondents have more of an ideology toward the police than dynamic, peculiaristic attitudes that vary with question focus or referent.'

The second approach shares similar aims to the first, but it uses a more complex set of measures. People hold varying opinions about different aspects of policing, it is assumed, and have different 'levels' of trust in the police (e.g. national or local). Researchers use multiple measures and combine opinions across a range of different areas to create some kind of overall index. For example, Sampson and Bartusch (1998) construct a satisfaction with police scale from five items, covering police engagement with the local neighbourhood, effectiveness in dealing with crime and disorder, and responses to crime victims. Similar approaches can be seen in work by Reisig and Parks (2000), Schafer *et al.* (2003), Silver and Miller (2004), Rosenbaum *et al.* (2005) and Skogan (2006). Occasionally composite measures of one aspect of police behaviour – such as fairness – are used as proxies for general opinions of the police (Shuck and Rosenbaum 2005).

The third approach is a more comprehensive and theoretically informed exploration of what trust, confidence and legitimacy variously mean. This approach is most strongly associated with the work of Tyler and colleagues (Tyler 1990, 2001, 2004; Sunshine and Tyler 2003a, 2003b; Tyler and Huo 2002; Tyler and Wakslak 2004; Tyler and Fagan 2006; see also Reisig *et al.* 2007; Murphy *et al.* 2009; Jackson and Bradford 2010; Hough *et al.* 2010; Jackson *et al.* 2011; Gau 2011; Kochel 2011; Jackson *et al.*, in press). Here, opinions of the police and courts are assumed to be composed of different elements or sets of concerns that (although obviously related) are distinct, even potentially in conflict with each other. Crucially, the legitimacy of such authorities is separate from opinions such as satisfaction with services received or assessments of operational effectiveness.

What is trust?

Building upon Tyler's approach to the nature of trust and legitimacy, we move beyond simple measures of satisfaction with the police, or confidence in the police. In the next few pages we spell out the theoretical implications of such an approach to trust in the police.

To trust a person or an institution is to make a set of assumptions about the way they (or it) will behave in the future. Seen in these terms, trust creates a world that seems stable and coherent. A key element of any understanding of the nature of trust is therefore the link between trust and risk. Giddens (1991: 3) sees trust as a way of 'bracketing out' potential occurrences which, if all were to be considered, would induce 'paralysis of the will', or a feeling of engulf-ment at the sheer range of possible future events and potential actions. Enabling anticipation and prediction of the future, trust allows us to assume that those we trust will act in predictable ways and will behave in keeping with the person-ality they have presented to us – and of course that they may not do these things. Tolerance of uncertainty is increased by the sense that some things are certain (Luhmann 1979).

To be analytically useful, however, trust needs to be more precisely located. Barber (1983) finds trust in the expectations that actors have of each other within specific relationships (as Luhmann would also argue). Because these expectations are based on assessments of competence, predictability and motives (Luhman 1979; Hardin 2002), trust implies a social connection between the parties involved. The trustor must be able to imagine that those in whom they place their trust can understand what their interests are, and that both parties share an understanding of what it is right and wrong to do in a given circumstance. Trust is thus not only an orientation of the individual; it is also the product of a socially embedded relationship. It is inherent in and formative of many social situations, including face-to-face encounters and the complex relationships between indi-viduals and organisations, institutions and the state (Misztal 1996). When an individual places trust in another person or in an institution, they must believe that the other party is aware of the nature of the relationship between the two. This knowledge is required if the trustee is to fulfil their fiduciary responsibili-ties and understand what the trustor has risked by the act of trust.

Importantly for our study, trust involves specific expectations: that the trustee will be technically competent in the roles assigned to them; and that the trustee will carry out their fiduciary obligations, that is, in certain situations place the interests of others above their own (see also Hardin 2002). The concept of motive-based trust, developed by Tyler and colleagues (Lind and Tyler 1988; Tyler 1990; Tyler and Huo 2002), is relevant here. According to this account, trust stems less from perceptions of predictability and perceived willingness or ability to keep promises (as Luhmann and Giddens might stress), and more from estimates of character and affect. Thus viewed, trust involves the belief that others have our best interests at heart: one can assume that the police will act in predictable ways and will behave in keeping with the role that they have in society. Motive-based trust is closely linked to fiduciary trust; it is primarily social and relational rather than instrumental, and is premised on the idea that the parties involved have shared social bonds which make it possible for the one to imagine, apprehend and influence the interests of the other. Tyler and colleagues stress that fairness is the most important factor in the formation of motive-based trust. If people feel they have been treated fairly and respectfully by an authority, that they were given a voice in the interaction, they will perceive that authority to be procedurally just and a valid repository of motive-based trust (see below).

Earle and Cvetkovich (1995) go further. They claim that social trust is based primarily on salient value similarity. This is a 'groundless' trust needing no justification. Individuals require rather a lot of information about actors and institutions in order to decide whether or not to grant trust. So while the function of trust may be a reduction of cognitive complexity, the basis on which it is granted could itself require considerable cognitive effort. Rather than deducing trustworthiness from direct evidence, people infer it from 'value-bearing narratives'. Salient values consist of 'the individual's sense of the important goals (ends) and/ or processes (means) that should be followed in a particular situation' (Siegrist *et al.* 2000: 355). Trust is thus conferred not on the basis of a detailed appraisal of the likely competence and fiduciary responsibility of the actor, but on the perception of shared salient values – the evaluation of narratives regarding the roles, intentions, goals and behaviours of the police force as an organisation and as the carrier of the institution of policing.

The value-bearing narratives that people draw upon, when they make their trust judgements, could be information shortcuts, available images, social schema and the like. People trust institutions that tell stories expressing salient values that are similar to their own, whether the telling of those stories is direct, via interactions with representatives of the institutions, or indirect, via media accounts or cultural tropes. They also infer information about institutions from other aspects of their experience. Most obviously, the experience of procedural justice communicates shared group status and thus shared values. But there is also evidence that people's perceptions of the area in which they live are associated with their ideas about the police (Jackson and Sunshine 2007; Jackson and Bradford 2009; Bradford and Jackson 2010; van Craen 2012). Perhaps assessments of local crime and disorder, for example, act as cues to the formation of opinions about the police (an organisation, after all, heavily associated with these areas of life)?

Trust in the police

So what does all this mean for our understanding of the nature of trust? For us, trust in the police ranges from one's expectations about others (both intimates and strangers) to one's beliefs about social and political institutions and processes. Consider the point of contact between officer and citizen. At such moments individuals may trust officers to take the right course of action, fulfil their duty, behave fairly and to place the citizen's interests first. Or, of course, they may not. The extent to which people trust the police involves, in the first instance, judgements about effectiveness as an assessment of technical competence. But drawing on the more relational accounts outlined above, trust also involves judgements about police commitment to shared interests and priorities – this is a measure of the extent to which the police care about those it serves, its ability to understand the needs of the community, and its willingness to address these needs.

This implicates both fiduciary obligation and motive-based trust. Individuals also make assessments of the fairness with which officers treat people, a measure which, given the unique position of the police, may also imply both effectiveness and fiduciary obligation. Fairness is something police officers should 'do' as a matter of their basic remit, but it is also linked to motive-based trust.

All existing evidence suggests that in the UK trust in police fairness, caught up heavily with trust in its commitment to community values, is the most fundamental aspect of trust. As Earle (2010a: 542) notes: 'Knowing whether the intentions of the other are good or bad (relative to oneself) is more important than knowing what the other can do.' Believing officers are motivated to take into account our interests – that we and they are 'on the same side' – strengthens the belief that they are competent to do so, possibly because fairness, in particular, generates value-bearing narratives that inform other aspects of trust (Bradford 2011a; Gau 2010).

This stress on fairness and shared values over effectiveness stands in contrast to 'traditional' police performance management precepts that have held crime, arrest and conviction rates – as well as more service-related concerns such as response times – to be the core measures of police performance and, implicitly, the most important 'drivers' of public trust. Clearly such arrests and convictions, an ability to return stolen property, and timeliness in answering calls for service are – and should be – important influences on the trust people place in the police. Indeed, a basic notion that the police are at least nominally competent and in some sense worth having may be a pre-requisite for the other components of trust and legitimacy we discuss in this book. In England and Wales this baseline trust seems to be so widespread as to be almost axiomatic. By contrast, this is unlikely to be the case in many developing countries, where the police may have much to prove in terms of fundamental usefulness (see, for example, Tankebe 2009). Yet, above and beyond assessments of the fundamental utility of the police, all current evidence suggests that, in Great Britain at least, commitment to community values and fairness are more important than effectiveness. Furthermore, it is apparent that concerns about the level of crime (even fear of crime itself) have only a small association with opinions of the police (Jackson *et al.* 2009) – although this could simply mean that crime is not seen as the 'fault' of the police, and that police effectiveness remains important but is assessed in other ways.

A decision to trust?

The discussion of trust above implies some kind of active choice on the part of individuals. People assess the behaviour of the police and make judgements about its potential future behaviour. But do people really have, or make, a choice to trust the police? To all intents and purposes the police are a social given that precedes any one individual's experience of the world. Perhaps people simply proceed 'as if' they trust the police – even when police do not show themselves to be particularly trustworthy – because the functional equivalent, distrust, is enormously costly and difficult at a cognitive and a practical level. That is, acting on distrust of the police (e.g. not calling them if victimised but attempting to deal with the issue in some other way) may come not only at a significant financial and social cost to the individual; it may be difficult to even imagine, given the deeply ingrained role of the police in British social life.

It seems to us that such a situation is not only just a possibility; it also represents an important aspect of the reality of people's relationship with the police. As individuals we do have little control over the behaviour of the police and over what is expected of us in relation to it. But this is not to say that trust, either as an active process of evaluation or a more passive orientation, is not also an important aspect of this relationship. As Barber (1983) notes, the law perishes or becomes corrupt when there is no trust, and policing in a no- or low-trust environment would be very different to the type of policing most people in Britain experience. Relatedly, we would note that it is a simple empirical fact that some people and communities have lost trust in the police and do, indeed, distrust them. Not everyone thinks the police are inevitable, and not everyone would contact the police automatically if victimised at a serious level. If nothing else, we need a concept of trust in the police to help explain how such situations arise.

Measuring trust using the METPAS

Led by prior UK studies (Fitzgerald *et al.* 2002; Jackson and Sunshine 2007; Jackson and Bradford 2009; Bradford *et al.* 2009a; Jackson and Bradford 2010; Hohl *et al.* 2010), we differentiate between the trustworthiness of the police to act effectively, the trustworthiness of the police to act fairly, and the trustworthiness of the police to apprehend and share the interests, needs and priorities of the local community. So let us next consider these measures in the light of levels of trust across London. In all the following analyses, we weight the data so that the estimates refer to the general London population.

Topline findings

The first aspect of trust we investigate is trust in police effectiveness (Stoutland 2001) would call this competence). How effective do Londoners believe the police are in providing a visible patrolling presence, tackling drug dealing and gun crime, supporting victims and witnesses, responding to emergency policing, preventing terrorism, policing major events, and so on? Topline findings are found in Figure 5.1. The police are seen to be most effective at preventing terrorism, policing major events, responding to emergencies promptly and supporting victims and witnesses. They are seen to be least effective at tackling drug dealing and drug use, providing a visible patrolling presence, and tackling gun crime.

The second aspect is trust in police fairness. To what extent do Londoners believe the police would treat them with respect if they came into contact for any reason, would treat everyone fairly regardless of who they are, and would be friendly, helpful and approachable? Topline findings are found in Figure 5.1. Londoners believe that the police are relatively trustworthy with respect to treating the respondent with respect if they had contact with them, and less trustworthy with respect to treating everyone fairly regardless of who they are.

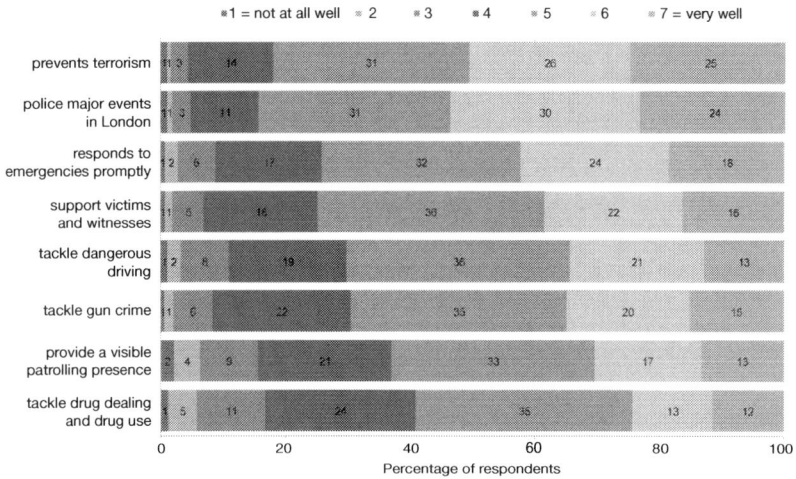

Figure 5.1 Trust in police effectiveness in London.

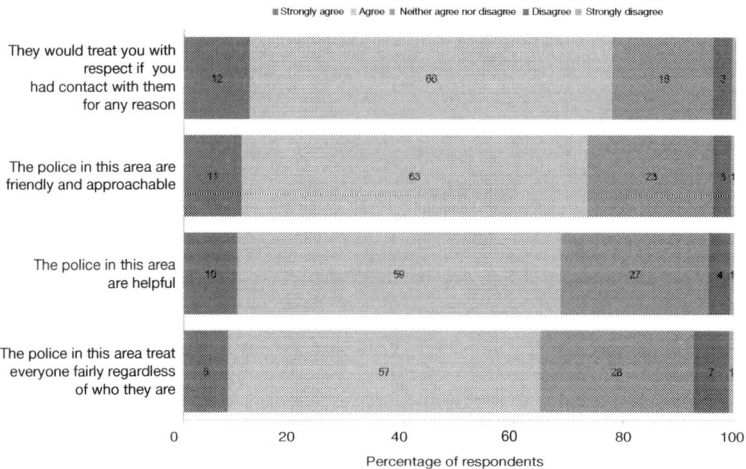

Figure 5.2 Trust in police fairness in London.

The third aspect is trust in intentions and shared interests. To what extent do Londoners believe the police can be relied on to be there when you need them, can be relied on to deal with minor crimes, deal with the things that matter to people in this community, are easy to contact, listen to the concerns of local people, and understand the issues that affect this community? A sense of trust in shared priorities and shared interests places a special emphasis on sharing low-level community interests, listening to people's concerns, and being dependable in dealing with those concerns. Topline findings are found in Figure 5.3. The police are seen to be most trustworthy to be there if one needed them to be easy to contact, and least trustworthy in dealing with minor crimes and to listen to the concerns of local people.

Scaling trust

Do these three scales measure three underlying dimensions of trust? To answer this question, latent variable modelling is our primary method of analysis. The different dimensions of trust are treated as 'latent' variables measured by a set of observed indicators, that is, survey questions. We assess the level of trust that people hold in police effectiveness (for example) by using their answers to 'build up' a picture of their underlying assessment of its efficacy. Using confirmatory factor analysis (CFA), we test three statistical models to investigate the dimensionality of confidence and trust. These three models specify 'trust and confidence' in one of three different ways:

- Model 1: one single underlying construct which spans trust in police effectiveness, fairness and shared priorities and/or shared interests;
- Model 2: two underlying constructs: (calculative) trust in effectiveness; and (relational) trust in fairness and intentions and/or shared interests;
- Model 3: three underlying constructs: (calculative) trust in police effectiveness; (justice-based) trust in fairness; and (intention-based) trust in intentions and/or shared interests.

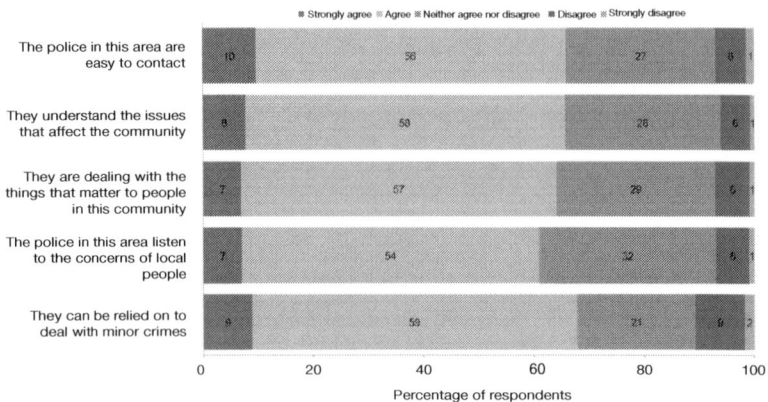

Figure 5.3 Trust in police intentions and shared interests in London.

Before turning to the findings, however, it is worth saying a few things about the methodological approach being adopted here. Measurement can be thought to constitute both a theory about observations and a proposition about the ways in which people's answers to questions reflect the substance of the phenomenon in question (Borsboom *et al.* 2003). Importantly, approaches based on latent variable modelling reflect a formal model. By testing our three models we test three theories of how particular properties captured by the particular indicators employed combine to form some underlying latent property. The response set on the questionnaire items is thought to vary as a function of the latent variable or latent variables. While the findings do not prove a causal role for the latent variable(s), in that the latent variable(s) cause people to give certain answers to particular questions, they do formulate this as a hypothesis. The fit of the model is then assessed in accordance with this hypothesis. In the case of trust in the police, between-subject covariation on trust measures is explained by invoking a latent variable (or multiple latent variables) on which individuals differ. Inter-individual differences are assessed by relating covariation in the indicators to some underlying latent variable(s).

Results from the three models are shown in Table 5.1, with the exact and approximate fit statistics indicating that model 1 fits the data poorly. Trust in the police in London thus seems not to be one homogeneous 'syndrome': people do distinguish between different aspects of police performance and behaviour when making judgements about the trustworthiness of the police. By contrast, models 2 and 3, which specify trust in police effectiveness to be separate from trust in police fairness and intentions and/or shared interests, both fitted well according to the approximate fit statistics.

At the bare minimum, then, we need to distinguish between (a) trust in police effectiveness and (b) trust in police fairness and intentions/shared interests. At first glance it may seem arbitrary to proceed with model 2 or model 3 in subsequent analysis. On the one hand, model 3 fits the data slightly better. On the other hand, model 2 fits the data, but it also has the advantage of parsimony. Crucially in favour of model 2, trust in police fairness and intentions and/or shared interests are strongly associated in model 3. There thus seems to be little discriminate validity: these do not seem to be two different constructs. Furthermore, later in the book we use trust indicators as predictors of legitimacy, and avoiding problems of multicollinearity is a powerful reason to prefer model 2.

Table 5.1 Fit statistics for one-, two- and three-factor confirmatory factor analysis solutions in London.

Model	χ^2	df	p	RMSEA	RMSEA 90% CI	CFI	TLI	SRMR
M1 One-factor	133,823	135	<.0005	0.127	0.127–0.128	0.72	0.68	0.13
M2 Two-factors	37,240	134	<.0005	0.067	0.067–0.068	0.92	0.91	0.04
M3 Three-factors	32,272	132	<.0005	0.063	0.063–0.064	0.93	0.92	0.04

Source: London METPAS survey

For most analyses in this book we therefore combine trust in police fairness and intentions and/or shared interests into one latent construct. This gives us a differentiation between a calculative trust based on effectiveness and a relational trust based on intentions and procedural justice (Tyler and Huo 2002). Figure 5.4 shows the factor loadings for model 2. Because no structural paths are constrained (i.e. because the two latent variables are allowed to covary), the fit statistics (c.f. Table 5.1) relate to the test of the measurement models, indicating

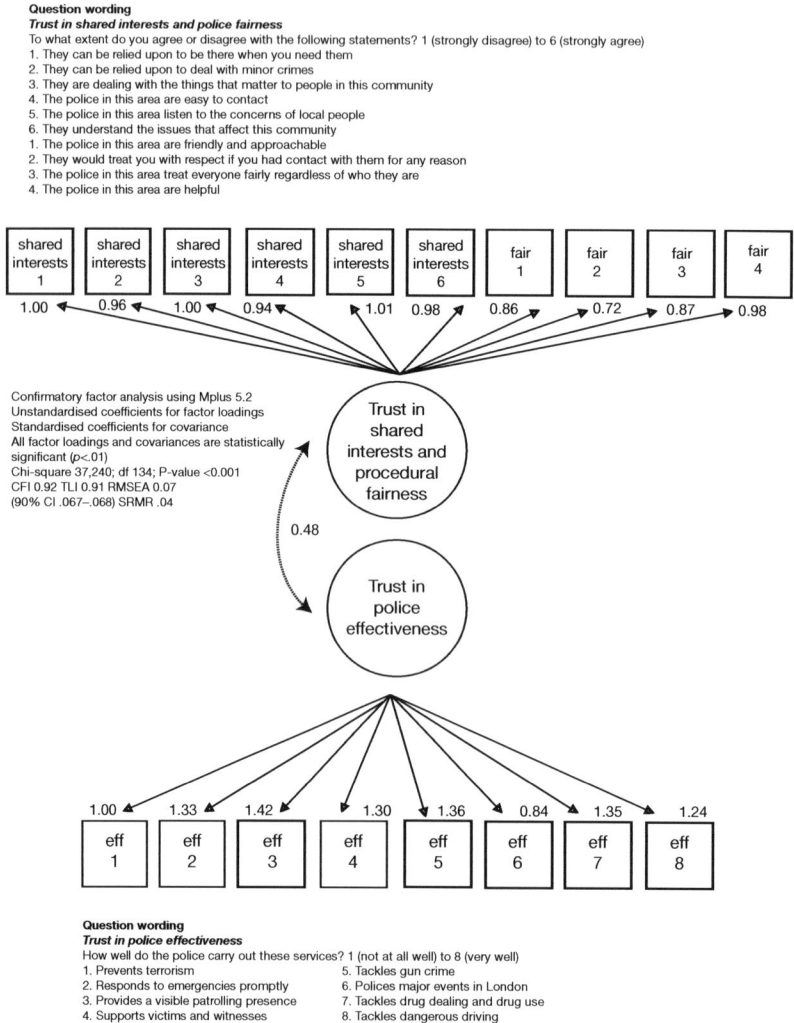

Figure 5.4 Measuring trust in the police: confirmatory factor analysis, model 2 from the METPAS sample.

that the scales have adequate reliability and the structure of the measurement model had some validity. This conclusion is strengthened by the fact that the factor loadings (validity coefficients) of the trust in effectiveness indicators were all statistically significant and of considerable magnitude (standardised coefficients: Prevents terrorism, λ=0.59; Responds to emergencies promptly, λ=0.73; Provides a visible patrolling presence, λ=0.70; Supports victims and witnesses, λ=0.75; Tackles gun crime, λ=0.71; Polices major events in London, λ=0.54; Tackles drug dealing and drug use, λ=0.70; Tackles dangerous driving, λ=0.68), as were the factor loadings of the trust in fairness and shared priority indicators (standardised coefficients: Be there when you need them, λ=0.73; Deal with minor crimes, λ=0.62; Dealing with the things that matter, λ=0.79; Easy to contact, λ=0.71; Listen to the concerns of local people, λ=0.80; Understand the issues that affect this community, λ=0.78; Friendly and approachable, λ=0.76; Would treat you with respect if you had contact, λ=0.66; Treat everyone fairly, λ=0.71; Are helpful, λ=0.82).

Measuring trust in the BME survey

The BME sample is our special population - this is a bespoke survey of young males from certain ethnic minority communities in London. The survey uses the same measures of trust as the METPAS, with one important addition: namely, the BME survey also includes four individual measures of trust in police procedural justice designed to combine to measure a fourth latent variable.

Figure 5.5 presents the findings from the new scale. To what extent do these young males believe that the police clearly explain the reasons for their actions, make decisions based on facts not opinions, use rules and procedures that are fair to everyone, and provide the opportunity for unfair decisions to be corrected? Research links the legitimacy of the police to the fairness of the procedures through which authorities exercise their authority (Tyler and Huo 2002), including allowing people a voice to present their side of the story when dealing with authorities; applying rules neutrally and consistently; treating people with dignity and respect; and appearing sincerely concerned about their well being (Tyler 2006a, 2006b, 2011a). When authority is exercised in these ways, people feel that they are receiving procedural fairness. The four key issues affecting the generation of procedural justice are: voice, neutrality, treatment with respect and dignity, and trust in authorities.

Voice means providing opportunities for individuals to participate in decision-making processes, and we find that just under 70 per cent of the sample agreed that the police 'provide the opportunity for unfair decisions to be corrected'. Neutrality refers to making decisions based on the consistent application of rules based on proper procedure rather than on personal opinions or prejudices. We find that around 65 per cent of the sample agree that the police 'make decisions based on facts not opinions'.

Treatment with respect and dignity – which includes the fairness of interpersonal treatment as well as the fairness of decision-making – is consistently one of

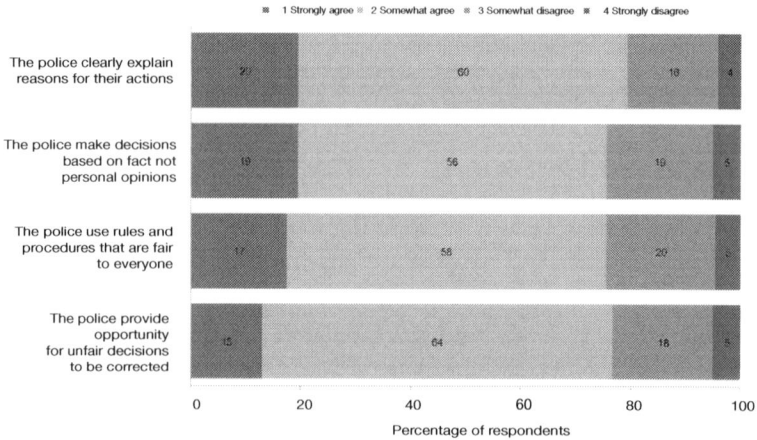

Figure 5.5 Trust in police procedural fairness in the booster sample.

the most important issues that concern people when they are dealing with author-ities. When people feel demeaned or subjected to negative stereotypes, they view themselves diminished as people and disrespected beyond what is appropriate when dealing with the law. Conversely, acknowledging people's rights and acting with courtesy leads them to feel fairly treated. We find that around two-thirds of the sample agree that the police 'use rules and procedures that are fair to everyone'. Similarly, 80 per cent of the sample agreed that the police 'clearly explain the reasons for their actions'.[1]

Topline findings on trust in police effectiveness among our young male BMEs are found in Figure 5.6. The police are seen to be most effective at preventing terrorism, policing major events and responding to emergencies promptly. They are seen to be least effective at tackling drug dealing and drug use, and tackling gun crime. This mirrors the findings from the repre-sentative sample of Londoners. Levels of trust also come close to those from the general sample.

Topline findings on trust in police fairness are found in Figure 5.7. As with the London-wide sample, the police are seen to be most trustworthy in treating the respondent with respect if they had contact with them, and less trustworthy in treating everyone fairly regardless of who they are. Again, levels of trust are similar – even a little higher.

Topline findings on trust in shared priorities and shared interests are found in Figure 5.8. Again closely mirroring the London picture, the police are seen to be most trustworthy in being there if one needed them and being easy to contact, and least trustworthy in dealing with minor crimes and listening to the concerns of local people.

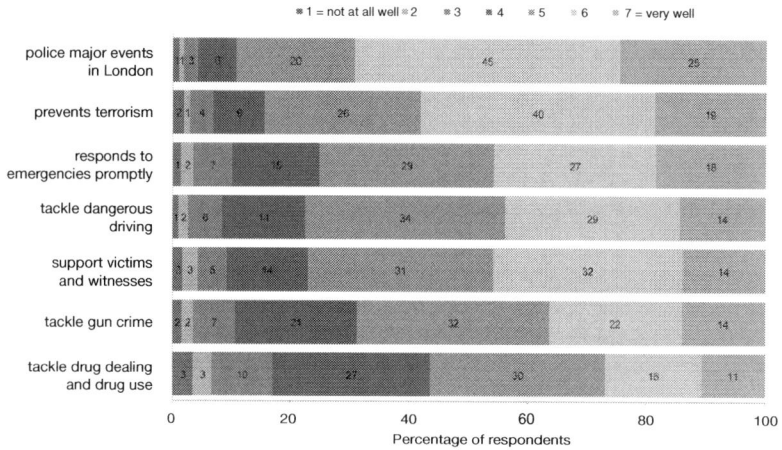

Figure 5.6 Trust in police effectiveness in the booster sample.

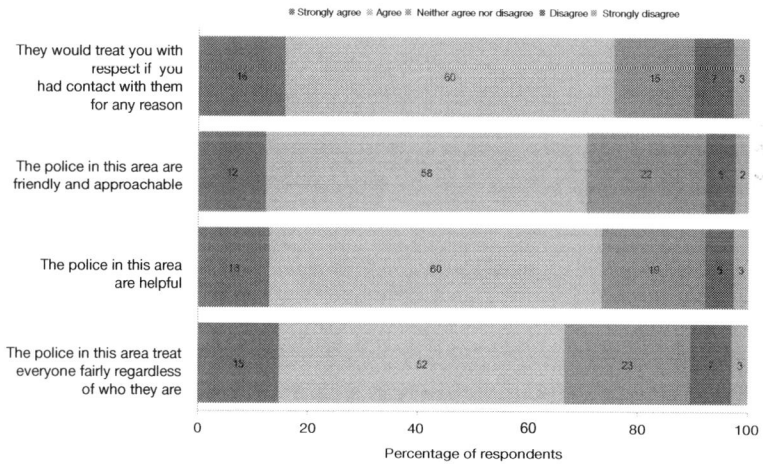

Figure 5.7 Trust in police fairness in the booster sample.

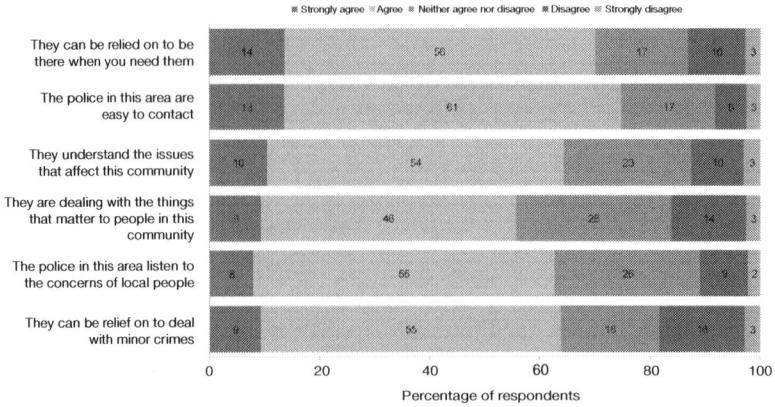

Figure 5.8 Trust in police intentions and shared interests in the booster sample.

Scaling trust

As in the METPAS, we use confirmatory factor analysis (CFA) to investigate the dimensionality of trust. This time we test a series of models that specify trust in one of six different ways:

- Model 1: one single underlying 'construct', spanning trust in police effectiveness, fairness, procedural justice and shared priorities and/or shared interests;
- Model 2a: two underlying 'constructs': trust in effectiveness; and trust in fairness, procedural justice and shared priorities and/or shared interests;
- Model 2b: two underlying 'constructs': trust in effectiveness and shared priorities and/or shared interests; and trust in fairness, procedural justice;
- Model 3a: three underlying 'constructs': trust in police effectiveness; trust in fairness and procedural justice; and trust in shared priorities and/or shared interests;
- Model 3b: three underlying 'constructs': trust in police effectiveness; trust in fairness and shared priorities and/or shared interests; and trust in procedural justice;
- Model 4: four underlying 'constructs': trust in police effectiveness; fairness; procedural justice; and shared priorities/shared interests.

Results from the six models are shown in Table 5.2. Both exact and approximate fit statistics suggest that models 1, 2a and 2b fit the data poorly. Models 3a and 3b are close to fitting. But they fall short of the accepted criteria for approximate fit statistics (CFI<.95; TLI<.951 RMSEA>.06). The only model that fits the data well is model 4. It seems, therefore, that adding more precise measures of trust in police procedural justice works to tease apart a little bit the four dimensions of trust. Equally, young, male BMEs may discriminate more acutely between different aspects of policing, perhaps because they have more experience of dealing with the police.

Table 5.2 Fit statistics for one-, two-, three- and four-factor confirmatory factor analysis solutions in the booster sample.

Model		$\chi2$	df	p	RMSEA	RMSEA 90% CI	CFI	TLI	SRMR
M1	One-factor	3,213	189	<.0005	0.125	0.122–0.129	0.74	0.71	0.09
M2a	Two-factors (effectiveness vs rest)	2,053	188	<.0005	0.099	0.095–0.103	0.84	0.82	0.06
M2b	Two-factors (effectiveness and shared interests vs rest)	2,202	188	<.0005	0.103	0.099–0.106	0.83	0.80	0.07
M3a	Three-factors (fairness combined with procedural justice)	1,347	186	<.0005	0.078	0.074–0.082	0.90	0.89	0.05
M3b	Three-factors (fairness combined with shared interests)	1,510	186	<.0005	0.084	0.080–0.088	0.89	0.87	0.05
M4	Four-factors	793	183	<.0005	0.057	0.053–0.061	0.95	0.94	0.04

Source: London METPAS BME booster survey

Figure 5.9 shows the factor loadings for model 4. The fit statistics indicate that the scales have adequate reliability, and that the structure of the measurement model had some validity. This conclusion is strengthened by the fact that the factor loadings (validity coefficients) of the trust in effectiveness indicators are (a) all statistically significant and (b) of considerable magnitude.

Summary

In this chapter we have defined trust in the police as the belief that the police are competent to do what they are tasked to do (to be effective and fair), and that they have our interests at heart (understanding and responding to the needs of the community). Our survey data suggest that there are two important aspects of trust among the general population of London. The first is trust in police effectiveness, the second is trust in police fairness and shared motives.

These findings can be compared to Stoutland's (2001) exploration of public expectations of policing in Boston. Analysing data generated from a number of qualitative interviews, she differentiated between four dimensions of trust:

1 priorities (do they care about the concerns of the community and are they meeting the specific needs of the neighbourhood?);

2   competence (are they effective at enforcing the law, securing safety and controlling crime?);
3   shared interests (if they have the best motives, do they have the resources to follow through on their promises?);
4   respectfulness (are they courteous and fair when in interactions with the public?).

Our data suggest that priorities, shared interests and respectfulness can be combined (perhaps because fairness communicates shared values and motives). But in our special population of young males from various ethnic minority groups (which fielded specific measures of procedural justice) trust seems to have four dimensions: effectiveness, fairness, procedural justice and shared interests. This may reflect the more confrontational relationship that such individuals may have with the police, compared to the general population of London (this is an important issue that we will return to later in the book).

Comparing London and our special population, we found surprisingly similar levels of trust in the police. Having explored the nature and distribution of trust across London, our next step is to try to explain variation.

We begin with the mass media (Chapter 6). Does newspaper reporting of the police and policing explain patterns of trust and confidence? We then move to neighbourhood context (Chapter 7) and people's encounters with the police (Chapters 8, 9 and 10).

Trust in shared interests

To what extent do you agree or disagree with the following statements? 1 (strongly disagree) to 6 (strongly agree)
1. They can be relied upon to be there when you need them
2. They can be relied upon to deal with minor crimes
3. They are dealing with the things that matter to people in this community
4. The police in this area are easy to contact
5. The police in this area listen to the concerns of local people
6. They understand the issues that affect this community

Trust in shared police fairness
1. The police in this area are friendly and approachable
2. They would treat you with respect if you had contact with them for any reason
3. The police in this area treat everyone fairly regardless of who they are
4. The police in this area are helpful

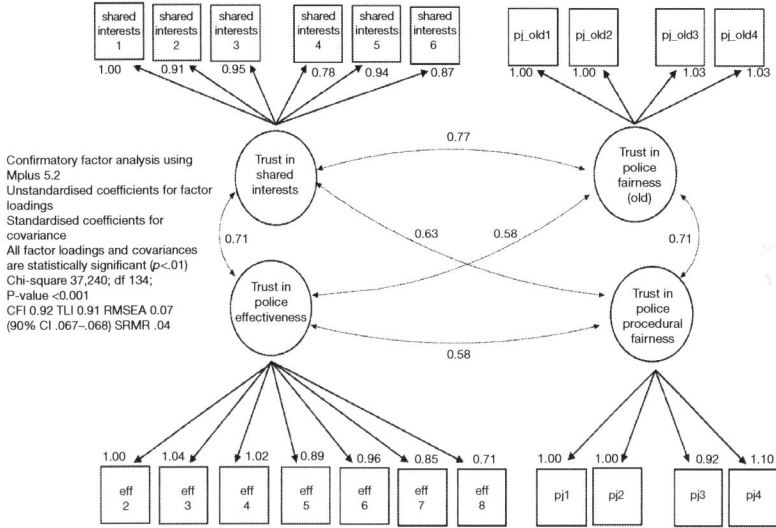

Confirmatory factor analysis using
Mplus 5.2
Unstandardised coefficients for factor loadings
Standardised coefficients for covariance
All factor loadings and covariances are statistically significant ($p<.01$)
Chi-square 37,240; df 134;
P-value <0.001
CFI 0.92 TLI 0.91 RMSEA 0.07
(90% CI .067–.068) SRMR .04

Question wording
Trust in police effectiveness
How well do the police carry out these services?
1 (not at all well) to 7 (very well)

2. Tackles drug dealing and drug use
3. Tackles gun crime
4. Supports victims and witnesses
5. Tackles dangerous driving
0. Responds to emergencies promptly
7. Prevents terrorism
8. Police major events in Londom

Question wording
Trust in police procedural justice
To what extent do you agree or disagree with the following statements?
1 (strongly disagree) to 6 (strongly agree)

1. The police use rules and procedures that are fair to everyone
2. The police clearly explain reaons for their actions
3. The police provde opportunity for unfair decisions to be corrected
4. The police make decisions based on fact not personal opinions

Figure 5.9 Measuring trust in the police: confirmatory factor analysis, model 4 from the booster sample.

6 Mass media

This chapter examines whether trust in the police is shaped – at least in part – by the mass media. Multiple media sources frame, reinforce and undermine how the public sees the police. The media may weaken public confidence through the constant scrutiny of police activities (Manning 2003), but they may also bolster the myth of an effective police service (Sparks 1992). Fictional and reality-TV formats seem to elevate police to a super-hero status (Reiner *et al.* 2000), but the media also expose police brutality, racism, corruption and blunders in crime investigations, seemingly undermining public confidence in the police (Garland 2001; Manning 2003). The media are certainly the main source of information about the police for the vast majority of the population (85 per cent according to the British Crime Survey 2009/10).[1] And according to Garland (2001) the media have not only created fear and interest in crime, they have also cultivated, nurtured and 'institutionalised' the experience of crime.

The police certainly do believe that the media are important, engaging in 'image work' in an attempt to manage 'police images' (to use the terminology of Mawby 2002). Over the past 30 years the police have created organisational structures to 'manage' the media and public relations professionally (see McGovern and Lee 2012). Media images also have political importance. For example, 'trial by media', as Greer and McLaughlin (2011) phrase it, is a palpable influence on recent police politics and crime policy (Garland 2001; Cavender 2004; Reiner 2010).

In this chapter we investigate the impact of the mass media, specifically newspaper coverage, on public trust in the police. A fair amount of academic literature has explored the police–media relationship (Chibnall 1977; Mawby 2002, 2010; Leishman and Mason 2003) and media portrayals of the police (Beckett 1997; Reiner 1997; Reiner *et al.* 2000, 2001). Our examination of variation in trust across London considers national newspaper reportage, which we treat as an important indicator of national media coverage. We link a large-scale media analysis of police coverage in five agenda-setting newspapers to the METPAS data. In this chapter we draw upon data from a three-year period between 2007 and 2010. For simplicity's sake we focus on overall confidence in the police.

Media effects studies: findings and limitations

Early media research assumed a direct causal effect of mass media on mass behaviour. The public were thought to be a vulnerable and uncritical 'sponge' that absorbs (both positive and negative) media messages. A particularly influential theory is Gerbner's cultivation theory (Gerbner and Gross (1976), with the television supposedly having a 'levelling effect' that results in more homogeneous and convergent opinions and world-views, in particular among heavy television viewers. The media are thought to have encouraged a 'mean world' view, where the world is believed to be more crime-ridden, hostile and dangerous than it actually is.

But decades of research have found little evidence of a strong direct impact of the media on public opinion. Individuals actively and consciously consume media. Looking for gratification or reinforcement, pleasure and identity construction, people respond to multiple media messages individually and actively (see, for example, Blumler and Katz 1974). Different audiences interpret and respond differently to the same media message (Livingstone 1996; Davis 2006). Some researchers in the communication field argue that studies have failed to provide any convincing evidence for a link between media consumption and behaviour across contexts and audiences, concluding that other (social) factors are far stronger than the media (Barker and Petley 1996; Gauntlett 1998).

While media effects studies on policing and crime are few and far between, some work has isolated correlations between watching crime and violence on television and aggressive and violent behaviour (Gauntlett 2001). The small number of studies that address whether media representation correlates with public opinion largely rely on survey data (Surette 1998; Callanan and Rosenberger 2011; see Reiner *et al.* 2000, for an important exception). Four studies illustrate the main survey data-based approaches and the types of conclusions they allow. First, a correlational study of US survey data (Dowler and Zawilski 2007) found a small association between the frequency of watching particular types of crime shows on television and respondents' perceptions of police misconduct. Second, Eschholz *et al.* (2002) and Dowler (2002) find a similar correlation between watching television and attitudes towards the police. Third, Weitzer (2002) studied the impact of two high-profile cases of police misconduct on public perceptions of how the police treat people, and overall confidence (see also Lasley 1994). Comparing survey data from a few years before and after these incidents, Weitzer found a quite large initial impact, particularly among ethnic minorities. After a few years, public confidence returned to its initial level prior to the high-profile incident. Fourth, Miller *et al.* (2004) combined a media analysis with data from a police-user satisfaction survey and a general public opinion survey over a nine-month timespan. Over this relatively short time period, which was free of high-profile incidents, the authors did not find evidence of a media impact on attitudes. While media coverage fluctuated, public opinions of the police remained stable. The authors concluded with the idea of a 'buffering' zone of public confidence: a certain range in which media reporting can oscillate without translating into changes in public opinion.

These studies exemplify the picture that emerges from the literature: most find small effects. But at the same time research designs are weak, and the evidence is often mixed and inconclusive (Cohen 1987; Reiner 1992; Beckett 1997; Howitt 1998; Reiner *et al.* 2000; Garland 2001; Jewkes 2004). Only Miller *et al.* (2004) collected data on media reporting that supposedly had an effect on public confidence in the police. Given the relatively stable nature of public confidence, however, the timespan of the study might have been too small to observe a media effect in the absence of high-profile events. Dowler and Zawilski (2007) relied on self-reported stated TV viewing habits, relating habits to respondents' views of the police in a cross-sectional study. Weitzer (2002) focused on the impact of high-profile events, with public opinion data measured in 3–5-year intervals. But they did not take into account actual media reporting.

In this chapter we consider the sort of representations of the police that the media may need to convey in order to influence public trust and confidence in the police. Jackson and Bradford (2010) found that overall confidence in the police was far more strongly associated with trust in police fairness and intentions than trust in police effectiveness. We might therefore expect media reporting to have the biggest impact on confidence when stories give clues about the extent to which the police share the priorities and interests of communities (for example, mention of acts that show the police listen to the local community, know and act upon local needs, or are divorced and remote from people's experiences) and act in ways that demonstrate procedural justice and fairness (or act in unfair and discourteous ways). Reporting on fairness and shared interests might include explicit mention of the police being helpful, treating people fairly and respectfully – giving due consideration to public views, as well as reporting on the absence of such shows of procedural fairness, for example police brutality, racism and abuse of police powers. By contrast, reporting on police competence and effectiveness in handling crime cases might have less impact on public confidence in the police.

While the procedural justice model has mostly been applied to – and thought about in the context of – direct encounters with police, it has not been addressed in the context of media effects. It thus remains to be seen whether mediated cues about the procedural fairness of the police are important in shaping trust and confidence in the police.

Hypotheses and data

We test the following set of hypotheses:

- Reporting on police activities that demonstrate community engagement has a positive impact on confidence in the police;
- Reporting on fair and respectful police treatment has a positive effect on confidence in the police and reporting on the absence of procedural fairness, especially the extreme case of police misconduct, has a negative impact on public confidence in the police;
- Reporting on how effective the police are in dealing with crime has a negative impact if the reporting is critical, and has a positive impact if the evaluation is positive; and,

- The effect of press reporting on community engagement and procedural fairness is larger than the effect of reporting on police effectiveness, because the latter is the 'weakest' driver of confidence.

We combine our large-scale population representative survey of Londoners (interviewed between April 2007 and March 2010) with a media analysis that measures, through manual coding of 9,000 articles, various aspects of police coverage in five major London newspapers over the same three-year period. Survey respondents were asked which newspaper(s), if any, they read regularly, and combined with the interview date, we can assign the media measures for the newspaper and time point to every observation in the survey dataset.

The content analysis of newspaper reporting covers articles published during the fieldwork of the METPAS between April 2007 and March 2010. Monthly measurement intervals were chosen, since this is the smallest time interval that allows the METPAS sample size to remain large enough for separate analyses of different newspaper readerships. The five agenda-setting newspapers – the *Guardian*, *The Times*, the *Daily Mail*, the *Mirror* and the *Sun* – include quality broadsheets, mid-market papers as well as tabloids, selected so as to cover a range of political leanings and world-views. The articles were retrieved from Lexis-Nexis searching for articles with the terms 'police', 'cops', 'Yard' or the 'Met' in the headline and 'London' anywhere in the text. Within any given newspaper and month, all articles were coded if there were fewer than 50 articles. If a newspaper published more than 50 articles with any of the keywords in it within a month, a random sampling procedure was used to select 50 articles for coding, with replacement of 'false-positives.' False-positives are articles that are duplicates, fictional, historical or otherwise outside the scope of the study. For example, the reporting on the Madeleine McCann case (of a missing British girl in the summer of 2007) has been excluded, unless British police was explicitly mentioned in the article, because it was Portuguese police investigating the case. A total of 9,290 articles were selected and coded: 40.8 per cent of those were false-positives. So the media measures are estimated based on 5,495 articles.

A survey question on newspaper readership included in the METPAS is used to match respondents to the media 'treatment' they were most likely to have received. The total sample size of the survey is 61,436 respondents. Of these, 25,439 respondents read one of the five newspapers and were included in the study. A further 4,218 respondents read two or more of these five papers. They are excluded because one would have to make specific assumptions about how reading more than one newspaper plays out to be able to decide whether one can assign them to a 'primary' newspaper or alternatively average, multiply or otherwise aggregate the 'media treatments' the respondents received from the two or more newspapers. Such assumptions might be hard to justify, and in any case are arguably not necessary to answer the research questions at hand. Excluding these cases should not introduce any bias as the purpose of this study is to generalise on the effect that exposure to the five newspapers has on public opinion: for this purpose it is more sensible to focus on those respondents who received 'undiluted' treatment rather than a mix of treatments when it is not clear how multi-readership changes the effect.

Measurement of concepts

Public confidence in the police was measured using the standard single item question 'How good a job are the police doing in this local area?' Respondents were asked to answer this question on rating scale from 1='very poor' to 5='excellent.' A latent trait score is used to measure trust in the fairness and shared interests of the police.[2]

In the content analysis, the intensity of media reporting was measured by the number of Lexis-Nexis returned articles minus the false-positives. For a month in which there were more than 50 articles and thus only a randomly selected sample of them was coded, the total number of valid articles was estimated by multiplying the total number of retrieved articles by the proportion of valid articles (non-false-positive) articles in the coded sample. The measurement of specific characteristics of media reporting was done through manual coding. Five coders coded the 9,290 articles using a coding frame that, together with detailed explanations and instructions, defines the measures as follows:

- False-positives (no=0, yes=1)
- Acts of police community engagement (mentioned=1 or not=0)
- Police treatment: misconduct (mentioned=1 or not=0) and treatment in direct encounters (not mentioned=0, poor treatment=1, explicitly fair/respectful treatment=2)
- Police effectiveness: in a specific crime case and separately, organisation as a whole (not mentioned=0, negative=1, neutral=2, positive=3, ambiguous=4)
- Crime statistics (no=0, yes=1)
- Overall tone (negative=1, neutral=2, positive=3 and ambiguous=4)

The coding frame was pre-tested by two coders on 50 articles. To ensure reliability between all coders, coders were trained thoroughly, the coding frame had precise and comprehensive descriptions for each measure, and ambiguous articles were discussed with the primary researcher throughout the coding processes. To minimise potential bias introduced through the assignment of newspapers to coders (and months to coders), a randomisation procedure was used to allocate newspaper articles to coders. Inter-coder reliability was tested by double coding 200 articles. Inter-coder agreement was good for all variables; the lowest kappa was 0.50 and the percentage of inconsistently coded articles less than 10 per cent for each of the variables.

Data from the content analysis were then aggregated into proportions of articles (out of the total number of articles within month and newspaper) mentioning, for example, police community engagement, within a given newspaper and month. Because the media measures are monthly rather than daily, survey respondents could not be assigned an accurate measure of their media exposure over the past month. Instead, media measures had to be weighted to a moving 30.5-days window depending on the day of the month a respondent had been interviewed. For example, a respondent interviewed on 27 May would be given the average exposure of 27/31 of the May measure and 4/30 of the April measure while a respondent interviewed on 3 May would get 3/31 of the May measure and 27/30 of the April measure.

Results

Descriptive analysis of police portrayals

Before testing the set of hypotheses, we first describe how reporting on the police developed over the three-year period and how police portrayals differ between newspapers. Figure 6.1 shows the observed and the smoothed trajectory of the intensity of police coverage across the five agenda-setting newspapers.

Police coverage increased from 2007 to 2008, and then declined from 2009 onwards. On average there are 33 articles per month and newspaper – with a standard deviation of 19.25 articles, a minimum of 7 articles and a maximum of about 100 articles per newspaper and month. There is, however, much variation within this three-year period. The overall trend is dented with blips and spikes, with the spikes coinciding with notable crime and policing events. Table 6.1 gives a chronological overview.

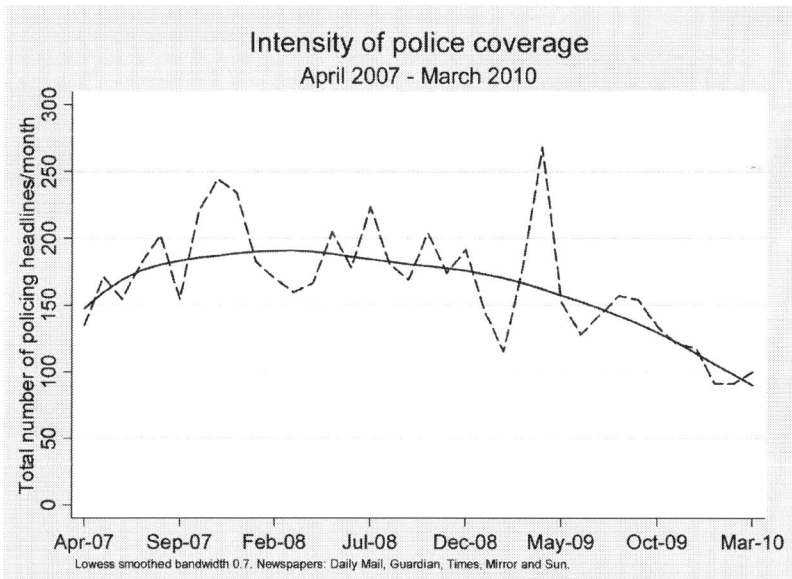

Figure 6.1 Total number of articles referring to police in the headline.

Table 6.1 Notable crime and policing events between April 2007 and March 2010.

Date	Event
July 2007	Crown Prosecution Service drops 'cash for honours' investigation without charges. 'Cash for honours' refers to the practice of awarding life peerages in return for political donations. 'Cash for honours' caused a major political scandal followed by extensive police investigation in 2006 and 2007.
October 2007	Met questioned over cost of futile 'cash for honours' investigation. Sir Ian Blair criticised over his bonus pay.
November 2007	Met criticised for large unaccounted credit card expenses.
December 2007	Pay dispute between the police and the Home Secretary Jacqui Smith.
January 2008	Ipswich murder trail opens after the arrest of the serial killer Steve Wright.
May 2008	Police foil terror attack in Exeter.
June 2008	Met internal racism allegations against Sir Ian Blair.
July 2008	Nepotism allegations against Sir Ian Blair.
October 2008	Opening of trial for police misconduct in the shooting of Jean Charles de Menezes (2005). Sir Ian Blair resigns as the commissioner of the Metropolitan Police London.
December 2008	Jury returns open verdict in de Menezes trial. Critique of police blunders in the arrest of MP Damian Green and earlier investigations such as the murder of Rachel Nickell (1992).
January 2009	Sir Paul Stephenson announced as the new commissioner of the Metropolitan Police London.
April 2009	G20 protest policing, death of Ian Tomlinson after beating by police officers.
July 2009	Beginning of allegations against *News of the World* of hacking the phones of major public figures.
October 2009	Inquest of police failures in the case of Fiona Pilkington who killed her disabled daughter and herself in 2007 after years of abuse and anti-social behaviour by youths of which police knew.
February 2010	Further revelations in the *News of the World* phone hacking scandal.

The biggest spike in newspaper coverage is found in the reporting of questionable policing tactics at the G20 protests that appeared brutal, humiliating and inappropriate (April 2009, 268 articles). Particularly intense coverage showed how Ian Tomlinson, a physically weak newspaper vendor bypassing the protests, collapsed and died after being assaulted by a police officer. Autumn 2007 saw a second period of intensive coverage (220 articles in October, 244 articles in November and 234 articles in December). In October 2007 the press gave intense coverage to the questioning of the police by MPs over the cost of the large-scale 'cash for honours' investigation of political donations made in exchange for peerages. The investigation had proven futile two months earlier when the Crown Prosecution Service decided to press no charges. In October 2007 assistant commissioner John Yates accused Sir Ian Blair of obstructing the 'cash for honours' investigation followed by public and police internal disapproval of Ian Blair's bonus pay. In the following month, November 2007, criticism continued over large credit card expenses the Metropolitan Police could not account for. In December 2007, policing headlines were dominated by the pay dispute between the police and the home secretary Jacqui Smith.

The third biggest spike in police coverage was in July 2008 (223 articles). Sir Ian Blair was accused of nepotism in helping a friend to obtain a major IT contract with the Met. This came shortly after he faced accusations of Met internal racism against Asian officers the previous month. The next biggest spike, October 2008 (204 articles), marks the opening of the trial for police misconduct in the killing of Jean Charles de Menezes on 1 October 2008 which received intense coverage and was followed by renewed calls for Sir Ian Blair to resign, which he did within the same month. Jean Charles de Menezes was a Brazilian man shot in the head seven times by police officers at a London underground station in July 2005 after he had been misidentified as one of the terrorist suspects in the London bombings. The de Menezes case, the policing of the G20 protests, the scandals around Sir Ian Blair, and the expensive yet futile 'cash for honours' inquest account for seven of the eight highest spikes in media coverage.

Turning next to the tone of newspaper reporting, Figure 6.2 shows that the majority of the newspaper articles remain neutral or ambiguous (40.1 per cent, and 20.3 per cent, respectively).

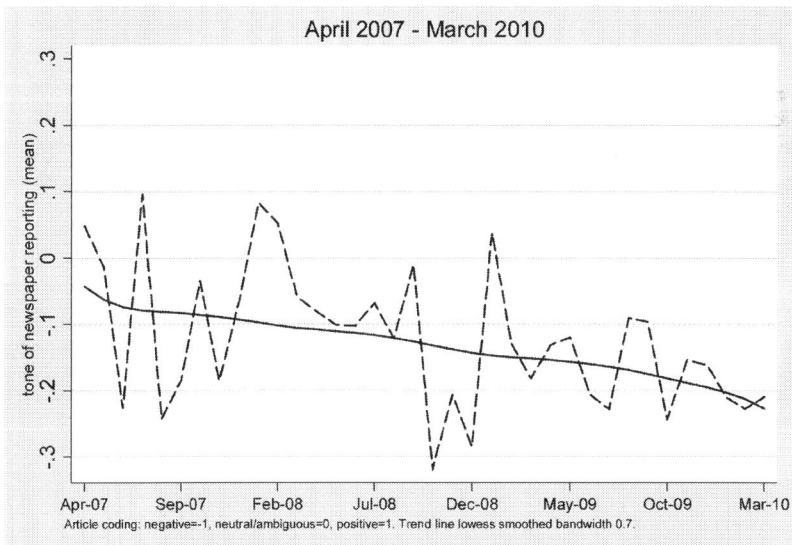

Figure 6.2 Tone of press reporting over time.

Negative articles tend to outweigh positive articles (25.5 per cent negative articles compared to 3.3 per cent positive articles). This finding could be explained by what newspapers deem newsworthy, as newspapers are the most critical media outlet, as opposed to movies and television which paint a much more positive picture, especially fictional and semi-fictional formats (Reiner 2010). We see a slight shift toward a more negative reporting, although the three-year period might not be enough to establish a long-term trend. The tone of police reporting is volatile and depends on current events. Unsurprisingly, we observe the most negative reporting in the months of intense coverage of major police scandals: October 2008 (de Menezes trial, Blair resignation), December 2008 (police blunders), October 2009 (Fiona Pilkington case) and in August 2007 (Heathrow climate protests, police blunders in various ongoing investigations). The months in which positive reporting outweighed negative police reporting are few: July 2007 (the police hand the 'cash for honours' case to the Crown Prosecution Service, confident the evidence would lead to charges), January and February 2008 (Ipswich murder trial). Positive reporting also outweighed negative reporting in the comparatively eventless and scandal-free months when policing coverage was largely confined to the police investigating crime cases (April 2007 and January 2009).

Figure 6.3 shows trends in the contents of the newspaper articles. Across time the composition of newspaper reporting remained largely stable, with no significant trends emerging. There are, however, a few spikes that coincide with the aforementioned key events. Most articles are about police investigations in a specific crime case (57 per cent). Less than 40 per cent comment

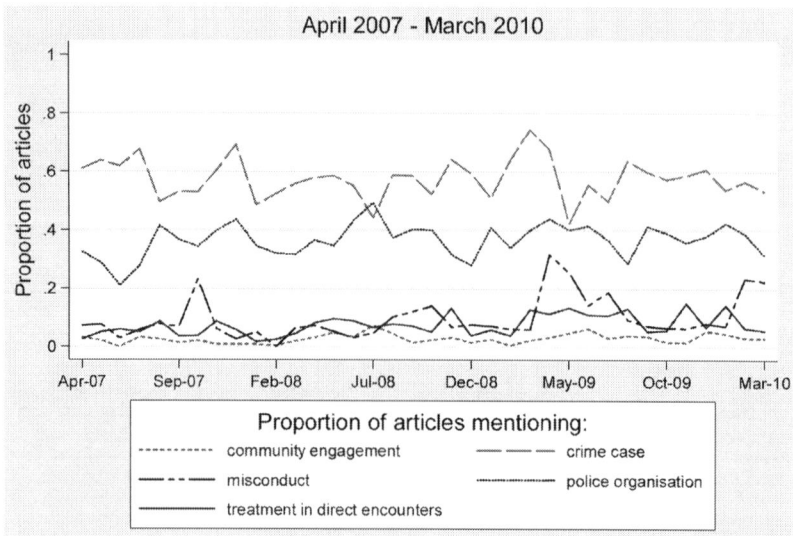

Figure 6.3 Topics in media coverage of the police over time.

on the police organisation. The evaluation of police effectiveness in handling criminal cases is mostly neutral (47 per cent) and relatively rarely depicts the police as incompetent or ineffective in handling cases (24 per cent). In contrast, the majority of articles that refer to the police as an organisation are critical (34 per cent) or ambiguous in their evaluation (37 per cent). The effectiveness of the police organisation as a whole is evaluated less positively than police effectiveness in specific crime cases. Only 8 per cent of the newspaper articles explicitly comment on how the police have treated a member of the public in a direct encounter. Of these articles, 90 per cent report disrespectful or discriminating behaviour by police officers; only 10 per cent explicitly mention fair and respectful treatment or the police being helpful to a member of the public. This means that a key driver of confidence, fair and respectful treatment, is reported in less than 1 per cent of the total number of articles on policing. Albeit cases of police misconduct receive greater attention (8 per cent of the total number of articles), they are infrequent and event-driven: 56 per cent of the articles reporting on misconduct were recorded in the months of the policing of the G20 protests and the subsequent investigations into potential police misconduct, the inquest into the shooting of de Menezes by police officers and calls for Sir Ian Blair to resign over this incident.

In summary, police effectiveness is routinely evaluated but police community engagement and fair treatment receive little media attention. Community engagement (that is, acts demonstrating that the police listen to the concerns of the local community, respond to them or show themselves transparent and accountable for what they are doing to address local issues) are mentioned in less than 3 per cent of the articles with, again, no time trend emerging. Less than 1 per cent of the articles mention fair (or unfair) treatment. This pattern is stable, with no trends emerging over the three-year period. There are two implications of this. First, because reporting on police fairness and engagement is rare, and because the bulk of media reporting focused on what is the weakest predictor of overall confidence in the police (Jackson and Bradford 2010), trust in police effectiveness, newspaper reporting is unlikely to have a strong impact on public confidence. Reporting on acts of police community engagement – as well as how the police treat members of the public in direct encounters – might be too few and far between to have an impact on public confidence in the police. Second, given that the media do not report on police community engagement and fair treatment, the police have to use means of direct communication to communicate engagement and procedural fairness to the individuals who do not come into regular contact with police officers (Hohl *et al.* 2010).

Descriptive analysis of newspaper profiles

The study considers five agenda-setting newspapers. Table 6.2 summarises the basic characteristics of the papers.

Focusing on police reporting, Figure 6.4 shows that compared to the other newspapers, the *Sun* and the *Mirror* publish, on average, the lowest absolute number of police headlines. That is not surprising given they are tabloids which

Table 6.2 Basic characteristics of newspapers.

Newspaper	Type	Political orientation
·The *Times*	Broadsheet	Right
The *Guardian*	Broadsheet	Left
The *Daily Mail*	Mid-market	Right
The *Sun*	Tabloid	Right
The *Mirror*	Tabloid	Left

generally contain much fewer articles than broadsheets. If we take into account the overall number of articles within one edition, the proportion of articles on policing is highest in the tabloids and lowest in the broadsheets (Reiner 2010). The *Daily Mail* has, on average, the highest level of police coverage and also the greatest variability over time, appearing to be more story-driven than the *Guardian* and *The Times* which have very similar levels of policing coverage and much lower variation in the number policing headlines per month.

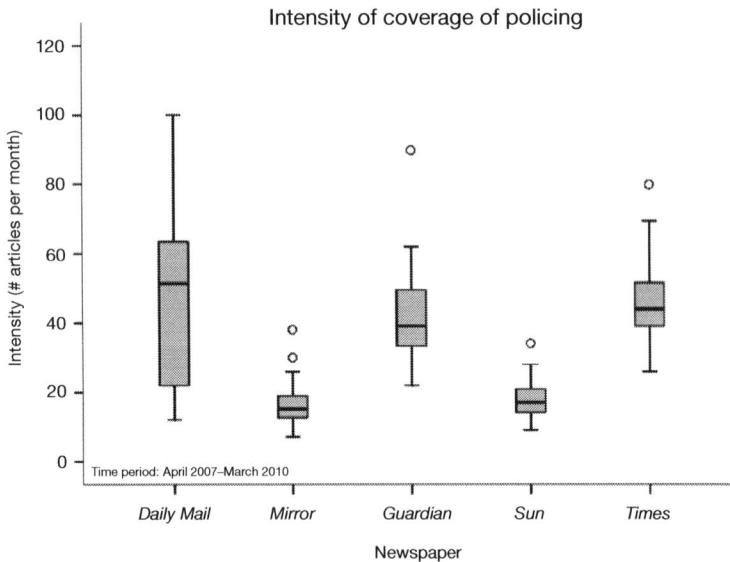

Figure 6.4 Number of policing-related articles per month: boxplot.

Note: On the outliers (circles), three of the five outliers are the month April 2009 (G20 protests), in *The Times* also the month October 2007 (de Menezes trail) and in the *Mirror*, August 2007 (various unrelated crime investigations).

The following newspaper profiles of policing coverage are based on Figure 6.5, Figure 6.6 and Table 6.3.

The Daily Mail

The *Daily Mail* had the highest intensity of policing coverage until December 2008, but coverage has been decreasing continuously since. Compared to the other newspapers, the *Daily Mail* reports less frequently on police misconduct, is more likely to relate crime statistics to policing, and criticises the police organisation more frequently than any other newspaper in the study. The number of negative articles exceeds the number of positive articles throughout the three-year period. Yet, during the G20 protests when police were heavily criticised for their policing tactics by other newspapers (in particular the *Guardian*), the *Daily Mail* remained sympathetic.

The Sun

In the *Sun*, policing coverage is overwhelmingly about investigations of ongoing crime cases. Like the *Mirror*, the proportion of articles featuring police misconduct is high and the proportion of articles on the police organisation comparatively low. The *Sun* is least critical of police practices, gives the most positive evaluation of police effectiveness in handling crime cases, and is the most supportive of the police. The tone of the *Sun* coverage remained, similar to the *Daily Mail*, supportive of police when the more left-wing papers the *Guardian* and the *Mirror* heavily criticised the police brutality towards G20 protesters. Yet, the overall police-sympathetic tone changed temporarily in relation to the allegations against Sir Ian Blair in 2008, and in October 2009 with reference to the case of Fiona Pilkington.

The Mirror

Characteristic of the *Mirror* is the relatively high proportion of articles on police misconduct and poor treatment of members of the public in the hands of police officers. In this regard *Mirror* coverage is akin to the other left-wing paper in the study, the *Guardian*. Compared to the other newspapers, the *Mirror* has the lowest frequency of reporting on the police organisation. *Mirror* coverage shows great event-driven volatility in how critical or supportive the tabloid is of the police. Critical coverage of the police temporarily spiked in relation to the de Menezes misconduct inquest and subsequent resignation of Sir Ian Blair, and in the aftermath of the G20 protests. Yet, the *Mirror* also praised the police in a large number of articles in January and February 2008 (Ipswich murder trial).

The Guardian

The *Guardian* comments on poor treatment by police in direct encounters more frequently than any other newspaper, and is least likely to pass a positive

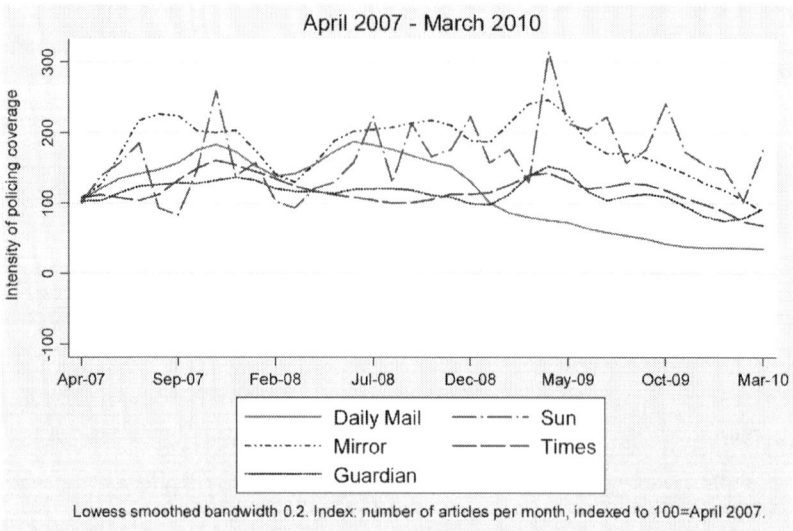

Figure 6.5 Intensity of policing coverage in different newspapers.

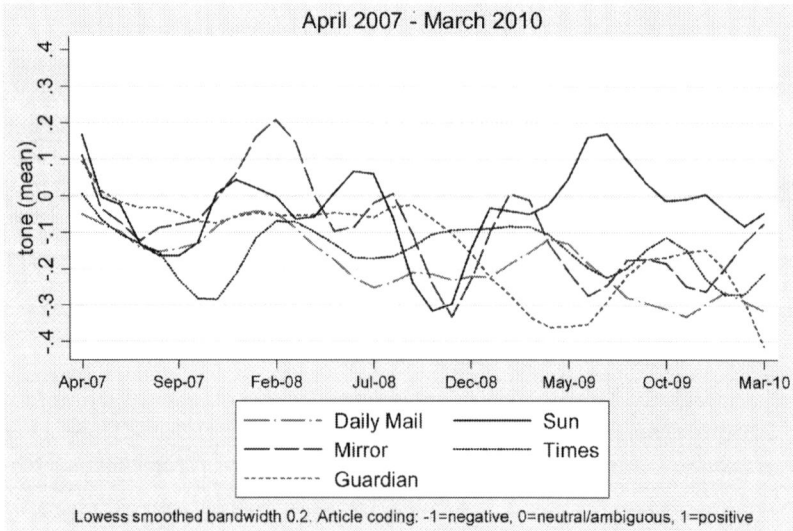

Figure 6.6 Development of newspaper tone of reporting on policing.

Table 6.3 Trends in the content of newspaper reports.

Percentage of articles	Daily Mail	Mirror	Guardian	Sun	Times	Mean
Specific crime case	52	62	65	60	52	57
Police organisation	43	25	40	28	46	39
Community engagement	4	2	3	2	3	3
Misconduct	5	15	7	15	7	8
Poor treatment	7	6	9	5	5	7
Fair and respectful treatment	2	0	0	1	0	1
Crime statistics	7	4	6	4	5	6
Evaluation crime case effectiveness						
• negative	29	26	22	16	23	24
• neutral	43	47	50	48	45	47
• positive	15	18	12	20	14	15
• ambiguous	13	9	16	16	17	15
Evaluation organisational effectiveness						
• negative	39	35	31	25	34	34
• neutral	13	15	18	15	19	16
• positive	9	19	9	22	13	12
• ambiguous	39	32	42	39	34	37
Overall tone						
• negative	28	26	22	22	27	25
• neutral	36	44	45	41	38	40
• positive	12	14	10	19	12	13
• ambiguous	24	16	24	18	22	22

judgement on how the police handle a specific crime case. Still, compared to the other newspapers, the *Guardian* reports comparatively neutrally. Since Sir Ian Blair started facing racism and nepotism allegations in summer 2008, the tone has become increasingly more critical. The *Guardian* had a particularly intense and critical coverage of the policing of the G20 protests (April 2009) and the police investigation of phone hacking of hundreds of public figures by the *News of the World* (February and March 2010), resulting in an extremely high ratio of negative to positive articles in those months and adding to the overall trend towards a more critical evaluation of the police.

The Times

The Times publishes the highest proportion of articles on the police organisation. On all other criteria considered in this study, *The Times*' coverage of policing is balanced and moderate, neither particularly critical nor particularly supportive. The intensity of policing coverage and overall tone are fairly consistent over the three-year period, with small spikes in coverage during prominent key events.

Descriptive analysis of confidence trajectories

Figure 6.7 plots the development of public confidence against the intensity of media reporting. We observe a slight dip in confidence in February 2008, which appears paradoxical given that the media coverage of police was largely due to the Ipswich murder trial, and included unusually positive reporting. We also observe a small temporary increase in confidence in the month after Sir Ian Blair's resignation (October 2008). However, these temporary changes are small. Overall, public confidence has been stable, albeit with a slight increase over the three-year period. But as discussed above, newspaper coverage of policing has varied greatly over the same period, with high-profile events and stretches of both high and low intensity of media coverage.

Virtually absent variation in public confidence over time, in the presence of significant variation in media coverage, provides some evidence against the hypothesis that changes in the intensity of media coverage have an impact on public opinion. In the descriptive analysis above, we have seen that media coverage does not only vary greatly over time, it also varies between newspapers. The five newspapers differ in their coverage of policing with regard to topics, tone and intensity of coverage. This is to be expected given that the newspapers selected for this study were chosen to represent a wide range of political leanings, world-views and readerships. Our selection also includes tabloids as well as broadsheets.

Perhaps, in averaging over newspaper readerships, we are masking covariation between media reporting and confidence within newspaper readerships. Figure

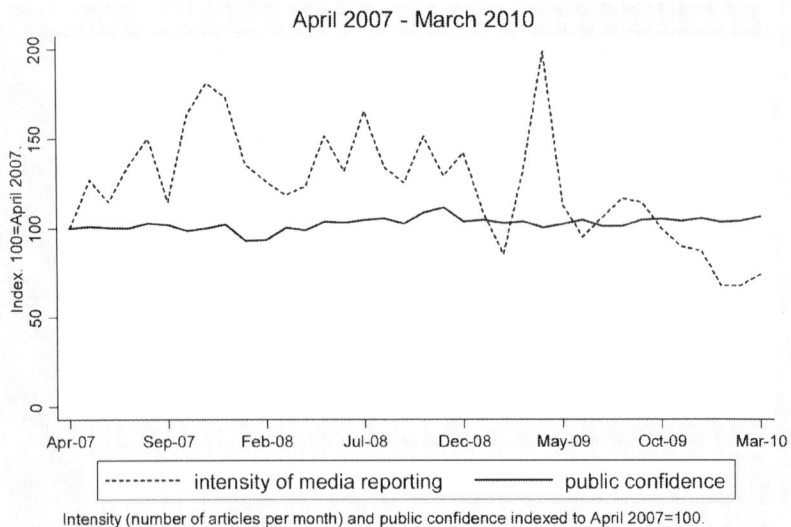

Intensity (number of articles per month) and public confidence indexed to April 2007=100.

Figure 6.7 Media coverage of and public confidence in the police.

6.8 shows the development of confidence for the different newspapers, and Table 6.4 tests whether the observed differences in confidence levels between newspapers are statistically significant in a simple linear regression model. Albeit statistically significant, the differences in confidence levels between newspapers are small. This is surprising given the amount of variability in policing coverage and world-views between the newspapers.

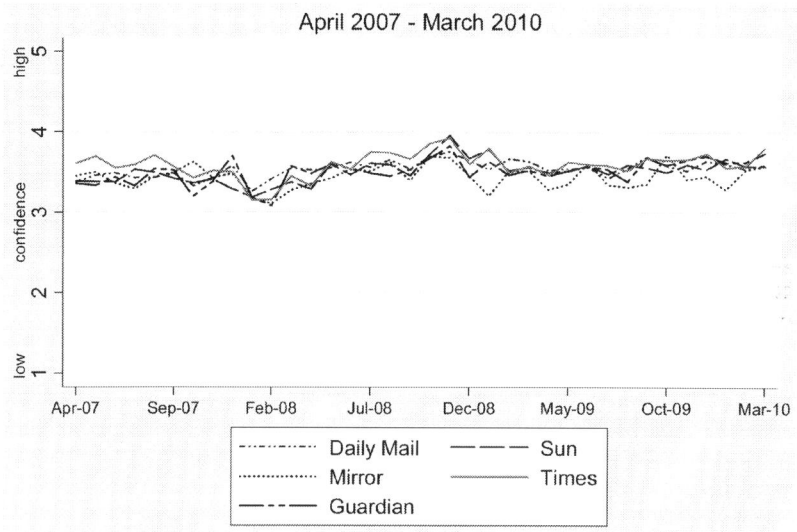

Figure 6.8 Confidence in the police by newspaper readership.

Table 6.4 Predicting confidence in the police by newspaper readership.

Response variable: confidence in the police	Coefficient
Time	0.02***
Time (squared)	0.00***
Daily Mail (ref.: *Sun*)	0.03**
Mirror (ref.: *Sun*)	−0.06***
Guardian (ref.: *Sun*)	0.01
Times (ref.: *Sun*)	0.07***
Intercept (i.e. mean *Sun*)	3.35***

Note: Sample size *n*=23,833
* significant at the 5% level, ** significant at the 1% level, *** significant at the 0.1% level.

The confidence trajectories of the five newspaper readerships are largely parallel. But at a few time points they appear out of synchronisation. For example, *Guardian* readers experienced a greater loss in confidence than readers of other newspapers in October 2007 when the police were questioned over the cost of the futile 'cash for honours' inquest and Sir Ian Blair was criticised for his bonus pay. The resignation of Ian Blair in October 2008 appears to have resulted in a small increase in confidence regain across newspaper readerships, yet not in *Mirror* readers. *Mirror* readers also showed a greater loss of confidence in April 2009 (G20 protests) than readers of the other four newspapers. In turn, the appointment of Sir Paul Stephenson in January 2009 appears to have restored confidence among *Daily Mail* and *Mirror* readers, but not among the readers of the *Guardian*, *The Times* or the *Sun*. These differences are small, yet might point towards different newspaper readerships being affected by different types of events and responding differently to the same event.

Perhaps it is not so much the intensity, but the contents of policing coverage that matters?

The effect of media reporting on public confidence in the police

Given the stability of patterns of media reporting (Figure 6.3) and public confidence (Figure 6.7) over this three-year period, the following regression analysis shifts the focus from an over-time perspective to how media reporting affects public levels of trust cross-sectionally, pooling data from all three years. To probe the hypotheses formulated above, the regression analysis tests the effect on public confidence in the police of reporting on police community engagement, police fairness (including the extreme case of its absence, misconduct) and police effectiveness. Given the observed differences between newspapers, regressions are run separately for each newspaper. Because the data are pooled across three years, a time variable is introduced that controls for any trending in public confidence that is due to something other than the explanatory variables in the model. Finally, to separate the impact of contents of media portrayals from a potential 'any publicity is good publicity' effect, the models control for intensity of media coverage (indexed to 1=April 2007 within each newspaper). The results are shown in Table 6.5.

The first hypothesis states that reporting on police activities that signals the police listen, understand and respond to the issues and concerns of the local community (engagement) has a positive impact on public confidence. Controlling for other characteristics of newspaper reporting, the results show a confidence-enhancing effect of reporting on community engagement in *The Times* readership. A 10-point increase in the percentage of articles reporting on community engagement is associated with a 0.37 point increase in confidence (measured on a five point scale).[3] To put this effect size into perspective, we need to remember that articles on community engagement are rare. *The Times* publishes, on average, a mere 1.3 articles a month mentioning an act of police community engagement. The effect of newspaper reporting on community engagement is not statistically significant in any other newspaper readership.

Table 6.5 Predicting confidence in the police by content of newspaper articles.

Response variable: *confidence in the police*	Daily Mail *Coefficient*	Sun *Coefficient*	Mirror *Coefficient*	Guardian *Coefficient*	Times *Coefficient*
Model 1					
Engagement	−1.96***	0.03	0.46	−0.71	2.70**
• engagement*trust	−0.88**	0.41*	0.19	−0.50	−0.48
Model 2					
Misconduct	−0.04	0.19*	0.13	0.27	−0.30
• misconduct*trust	0.03	0.03	−0.02	−0.36**	−0.24
Model 3					
Treatment					
• poor	−0.57*	−0.19	−0.19	−0.29	−0.35
• poor*trust	−0.38*	−0.13	−0.31*	−0.66***	−0.04
Model 4					
Treatment					
• good	0.67	0.91	−0.96	3.57	−0.89
• good*trust	0.05	0.45	1.55	2.23	−0.37

Notes
Coefficients for all other variables in the model (full model, table 4) not displayed. Descriptive statistics of variables in the model:
Confidence in the police: $1 = $ low, $5 = $ high, mean $= 3.54$
Motive-based trust: min. $= -3.71$, max $= 2.86$, mean $= -0.14$
Time: min $= 1$, max $= 36$; Intensity: Indexed to $1 = $ April 2007.
All other variables: Proportion of total number of articles mentioning the category, e.g. engagement.
* significant at the 5% level, ** significant at the 1% level, *** significant at the 0.1% level.

Up until now we have not considered the close relationship between confidence (an overall summary rating of the police) and specific dimensions of trust (particularly trust in police fairness and intentions). The results of a regression model include an interaction effect between reporting on community engagement and a measure of trust. The interaction effect is used to test whether the effect of media coverage on public confidence is contingent on the level of trust. In other words, are people who already trust the police more receptive to positive messages?

The effect of newspaper reporting about police community engagement on confidence in the police did indeed depend on the level of trust in the police. The greater a *Sun* reader's trust in the police, the greater the positive impact of reporting about community engagement on their confidence in the police. For *Daily Mail* readers, reporting about acts of community engagement has a negative effect on confidence, and the negative impact is larger the greater the *Daily Mail* reader's motive-based trust in the police. We can only speculate about potential explanations. Perhaps the reported acts of community engagement are at odds with either the image *Daily Mail* readers have of police – tough crime fighters rather than 'social workers' – and might have been directed to groups of the population that *Daily Mail* readers do not identify or sympathise with.

The first hypothesis is therefore supported with modifications: newspaper reporting on police community engagement has a positive impact on confidence in some members of the public, but no impact or even a negative impact on others. The effect on confidence in the police depends on which newspaper readership a respondent belongs to (no effect on *Mirror* and *Guardian* readers), and within some readerships also on the level of motive-based trust in police (*Sun* and *Daily Mail* readers). Such an interaction effect is also observed as we move to the second hypothesis.

The second hypothesis states that reporting on how the police treat members of the public in direct encounters has an impact on public confidence in the police. For *Guardian* and *Sun* readers, reporting on fair and respectful treatment has a small confidence-enhancing effect. Again, it is important to remember that explicit reporting on police officers treating people with fairness and respect is rare – it is mentioned in less than 1 per cent of the articles. Whether and to what extent reporting on poor treatment has a negative impact on confidence depends on the level of motive-based trust. Poor treatment shakes confidence in the police more in those whose confidence is tied to high levels of motive-based trust. Reporting on police misconduct only has a negative impact for *Guardian* readers, with the effect again being dependent on the level of motive-based trust. In contrast, reporting on police misconduct appears to enhance confidence for *Sun* readers (independent of their level of motive-based trust). Much of the reporting on misconduct between April 2007 and March 2010 pertained to the shooting of de Menezes, who police officers believed to be a potential terrorist, and the G20 protests. It might be speculated that this effect is explained by the police's seemingly 'tough' approach to threats to social order and potential terrorists, resonating with what *Sun* readers expect from police.

To summarise, the second hypothesis finds partial support. Fair treatment has a small positive effect on some readerships. The extent to which reporting on poor treatment has a negative effect on confidence depends on the level of trust. Effect sizes are small and only statistically significant in some of the readerships.

The third hypothesis states that reporting about police effectiveness should have a small positive impact on confidence. Across readerships, most reporting about police effectiveness has no statistically significant effect on confidence. A few regression coefficients are statistically significant, for example reporting that depicts the police as ineffective appears to have a positive impact on *Sun* readers, and coverage that is critical of the police organisation has a positive impact on readers of *The Times*. Overall, an inconsistent and inconclusive picture emerges. Interaction effects with motive-based trust were tested, but did not change the picture.

It follows that the findings are also inconclusive with regard to the fourth hypothesis. This postulated that, based on the confidence model, we would expect the effect of newspaper coverage of police community engagement and procedural justice to be greater than the effect of reporting on police effectiveness. We find evidence for effects of reporting about engagement and procedural fairness on confidence within some readerships (sometimes conditional on motive-based trust), yet effect sizes are small and such reporting is rare. Less than 3 per cent of articles on policing make reference to acts of police community engagement, less than 8 per cent explicitly mention how members of the public have been treated when in the hands of police officers.

In contrast, police effectiveness is frequently evaluated, yet reporting on the police's handling of a crime case or on the police organisation as a whole has no statistically significant effect in most readerships; the few statistically significant effects are small and produce an inconsistent and inconclusive picture.

Finally, the results provide evidence for an 'any publicity is good publicity' effect – higher intensity in policing coverage is associated with higher levels of confidence. Yet, with the exception of the *Daily Mail* readership, the effect ceases to be significant once all other characteristics of media coverage considered in this analysis are taken into account.[4]

Summary

In this chapter we have combined a content analysis of reporting on policing in five agenda-setting newspapers with a large-scale population representative survey. Over the three-year period (from April 2007 to March 2010), media coverage of policing varied greatly. There were periods of high as well as low intensity of press coverage as well as sharp peaks caused by high-profile events such as the 'cash for honours' inquest, the trial for misconduct in the shooting of Jean Charles de Menezes by police officers, the Sir Ian Blair scandals and resignation or the contested policing of the G20 protests. But this variability in media coverage is not matched by covariation in public confidence. Confidence was on a continuous trajectory of slight increase over the three-year period. While the five newspapers differ in world-views, political leaning and, as the analysis has shown, their coverage of policing, differences in confidence levels between newspaper readerships remained small throughout the three-year period.

The public's confidence in the police has been stable. It appears largely immune to the ups and downs of press reporting, and does not follow the dividing lines of the newspapers they read. Pooled across three years, there is however enough variation in the confidence variable to draw conclusions on the general patterns in the associations between press reporting and public confidence. We considered the impact of reporting about police community engagement, procedural fairness and police effectiveness on public confidence in the police. The findings suggest that reporting on police effectiveness does not have a statistically significant effect. But reporting on police community engagement and procedural fairness can have a statistically significant effect on public confidence. There are four major qualifications.

First, the effect sizes are small. Second, reports of community engagement and positive evaluations of procedural fairness are sparse – less than 3 per cent of articles mention acts of community engagement and less than 1 per cent explicitly mention police officers treating members of the public with dignity, fairness and respect. Incidents of police misconduct are relatively rare. But when they do occur, they get covered extensively. A total of 8 per cent of press reporting mentions a case of police misconduct; 7 per cent of articles explicitly mention members of the public being treated disrespectfully or unfairly in the hands of police officers. Reporting on engagement and fair treatment appears to be too infrequent to have a substantial effect on public confidence. And although most reporting is in relation to ongoing police investigations, there is no convincing evidence for an effect of evaluations of police effectiveness on trust. This might, at least in part, explain why this study keeps the tradition in media studies of finding little evidence for a media effect.

Third, the effect of reporting on community engagement and procedural fairness on public confidence is contingent on the level of motive-based trust. Yet a note of caution is required. While the distinction between trust and confidence is conceptually useful and fairly easy to make, the empirical separation is less clear. It is often difficult to determine whether a survey measure is tapping into one or another (Siegrist 2010). In this study, there is a close analogy between several of the items that compromise the motive-based trust indicator and the definition of the 'poor treatment' code in the media analysis; this might be reflected in the observed interference of motive-based trust in the relationship between reporting on procedural fairness and public confidence in the police.

Fourth, the observed media effects differ between readerships and are not statistically significant in all of them. This might suggest that different readerships are affected by different types of events and affected differently by the same type of event. *Mirror* and *Guardian* readers are mostly affected by reporting on police misconduct and poor treatment of citizens in direct encounters. But *Sun* readers' confidence is not negatively affected by reporting on misconduct: on the contrary, it appears to enhance it. At the same time, reporting on fair and respectful treatment and community engagement has, contingent on the level of motive-based trust, a confidence-enhancing effect. *Daily Mail* readers differ from all others in that they are negatively affected by reporting on police community engagement.

This complex picture may be a reflection of the diverse images of policing images current within the population. While levels of confidence in the police might be similar for different readerships, what the police mean to them might differ. Some of the findings described above correspond with some of the stereotypes of different newspaper readerships. The police might be a symbol for authoritarian values and the preservation of social order to *Sun* and *Daily Mail* readers, and within that frame of reference, reporting on misconduct might be interpreted as a sign of the police being 'tough' on potential terrorists (de Menezes) and 'hippie' protestors (G20). Police community engagement might be a signal of 'too soft' policing or of preferential treatment of groups some readers might disapprove of. In contrast, *Guardian* readers might see the police as a guardian of civil society that should respect civil rights and liberties. Their confidence in the police is shaken when these rights and liberties are violated, for example by police tactics used during the G20 protests or the scandals that surrounded Sir Ian Blair. The quantitative data used in this study can only hint at these ideas, and qualitative research using in-depth interviews and ethnographic approaches are required to describe them appropriately (see for example the work of Girling *et al.* 2000, or Loader and Mulcahy 2003).

Our work in this chapter has a number of limitations. The media measures have been assigned to respondents based on self-reported newspaper readership. We cannot verify whether respondents actually did read the newspaper they reported to read, and even if they did, whether they read the articles that referred to policing. A further practical limitation is the comparatively short three-year period covered in this study. Public confidence has been very stable over the past five years, and the picture might look very different if we consider long-term developments. Both public confidence and media images of the police have undergone dramatic changes since World War II (Reiner 2010). Finally, our work suffers from the notorious difficulties inherent in media studies: the omnipresence of the media, the near-impossibility of isolating and disentangling media effects and following from that, the near-impossibility of attributing causal effects to media exposure. This type of study can also only pick up short-term effects, with cumulative long-term effects often going undetected (Livingstone 1996). But our findings suggest that the media have, at most, only a minor influence on public confidence. The sources of trust and confidence thus seem to lie elsewhere.

7 The social ecology of trust in the police

In this chapter we consider the first step in a series of multilevel models of public trust in the police. Why do some people believe that the police are competent to do what they are expected to do, while others do not? Why do some people feel that the police share the interests and motives of individuals and communities, while others do not? Does trust in police effectiveness and police fairness and shared interests 'cluster' in neighbourhoods, whereby people who share the same locality tend to have similar levels of trust?

We find that neighbourhood context accounts for 8 per cent of the variation in public trust in police effectiveness and 9 per cent of the variation in public trust in police fairness and intentions. Introducing key compositional factors – most notably gender, age, ethnicity, employment status and residential characteristics – makes little difference to the neighbourhood clustering, suggesting that between-neighbourhood variation is not down to the different patterning in socio-demographic characteristics of residents of those neighbourhoods.

What explains these neighbourhood differences? Structural characteristics (concentrated disadvantage, residential stability and ethnic composition of a locality) and social characteristics (levels of collective efficacy, disorder and worry about crime in a neighbourhood) emerge as important. Low trust in the police tends to cluster in areas that are disadvantaged (and have high crime levels), have low residential stability and low collective efficacy, have high levels of disorder, and have high levels of fear of crime. Collective efficacy is an especially important predictor of trust in the police.

Structural characteristics of the neighbourhood

What do we mean by the social ecology of trust in the police? Analysing data from the Project on Human Development in Chicago Neighborhoods, Sampson and Bartusch (1998) constructed a 'satisfaction with police' scale from five measures, covering police engagement with the local neighbourhood, effectiveness in dealing with crime and disorder, and responses to crime victims. Decomposing variance within and between neighbourhoods – and incorporating individual and area effects at the correct level of influence – they found that concentrated disadvantage, ethnic concentration and crime levels accounted for a striking 82 per cent of the variation between neighbourhoods.

Once they accounted for the concentrated disadvantage and crime rates of a neighbourhood, they found that the previously important predictor of race was no longer substantively or statistically significant.[1] Sampson and Bartusch (1998: 800–1) concluded:

> Apparently, then, it is a neighbourhood context more than a race-specific attitude that explains estrangement from the police ... At the same time, inner-city 'ghetto' areas displayed elevated levels of legal cynicism, dissatisfaction with the police, and tolerance of deviance generally defined ... In support of contextual accounts of subculture (e.g., Anderson 1990, 1997; Sampson 1997), it thus appears that there is an ecological structuring to normative orientations –'cognitive landscapes' where crime and deviance are more or less expected and institutions of criminal justice are mistrusted. These differences are not large, but they are consistent nevertheless. We would thus offer the take-away message that normative orientations towards law and deviance are rooted more in experiential differences associated with neighbourhood context than in a racially induced subcultural system. Because race and neighbourhood are confounded, the tendency in the literature has been, incorrectly in our view, to attribute to African Americans a distinct culture of violence.

We apply a similar approach to our London data. As far as possible we replicate the neighbourhood-level measures of Sampson and Bartusch (see also Sampson and Groves 1989; Sampson *et al.* 1997), using Brunton-Smith's (2008; and Brunton-Smith and Sturgis 2011) factorial ecology approach. Generating comparable measures of (a) concentrated disadvantage, (b) ethnic concentration, and (c) residential stability, we combine multiple indicators of specific neighbourhood characteristics into a series of condensed measures (allowing us to mitigate concerns about multicollinearity). Principal components analysis – using oblique rotation – identifies shared neighbourhood-level factors that characterise the variance in the separate indicators. This approach is data-driven; it is based upon a formative model; and we conceptualise the construct as determined by the observations (see Edwards and Bagozzi 2000). Weighted factor scores are saved and included in the multilevel models.

We would like to thank Ian Brunton-Smith for data gathering, and for conducting the principal components analysis used for this study. With his permission we present the factor loadings. Table 7.1 shows that three factors were extracted that account for 83.5 per cent of the total variation in the items included in the analysis. The extracted factors largely mirror Sampson and Grove's (1989) classification. The first factor is clearly tapping into concentrated disadvantage, with the one exception being the high loading for the amount of Black people in the area. The second factor is residential stability, combining in-migration and out-migration (and also to some degree the amount of foreign born). The third factor is ethnic composition, with the exception of the amount of Black people in the area.

Table 7.1 Scaling structural characteristics of London neighbourhoods: principal components analysis.

	Component		
	1	*2*	*3*
Income support	0.92	0.05	0.11
Unemployed	0.90	0.14	0.30
Lone parent	0.89	−0.10	−0.08
Local authority housing	0.84	−0.07	−0.04
Black	0.83	0.11	0.25
In migration	−0.03	0.94	0.08
Out migration	0.01	0.93	0.11
Asian	0.00	−0.07	0.91
Foreign born	0.34	0.50	0.83

We also draw upon an LSOA-level measure of crime generated as part of the 2010 Index of Multiple Deprivation. Recorded crime figures (violence, burglary, theft and criminal damage) were taken and converted into the rate of crime per 1,000 at-risk population (the English Indices of Deprivation 2010). For violence, theft and criminal damage offences, the sum of the constituent notifiable offences from April 2008 to March 2009 was divided by the total resident population for mid-2008 (as well as the non-resident workplace population). For burglary, the notifiable offences from April 2008 to March 2009 was divided by the number of dwellings from the 2001 Census (as well as the number of business addresses).

Social characteristics of the neighbourhood

Collective efficacy is the first neighbourhood characteristic of a more social nature that we build a measure for. Collective efficacy is based largely on ties of trust and affect between local residents (Sampson *et al.* 1997). Collective efficacy implies both a joint understanding of the desirability or undesirability of certain actions and a shared willingness to engage in action oriented to prevent undesirable acts from occurring (Morenoff *et al.* 2001). Following Sampson *et al.* (1997) we treat collective efficacy as a combined property of the neighbourhood. We use a two-step procedure. First, we create a score for each individual. This score is based on their perceptions of social cohesion and informal social control in the neighbourhood.[2] Latent trait analysis (using full information maximum likelihood, in LatentGold 4.0) showed that a one-factor model fitted the data well.

Second, these individual scores are used to calculate an estimate of the average perception of social cohesion and informal social control among the people in each LSOA. The most obvious such estimate would be the average of the individual scores for the sample respondents from an area. However, if these sample means were then used as explanatory variables in regression models for various response variables, the estimates of regression coefficients would be biased, because of the measurement error due to the fact that the sample averages are not equal to the true averages across all the people who live in an area. The area-level estimates we use are obtained by starting with the within-area averages, but then shrinking them toward a common estimated average across all the areas, with the amounts of shrinkage derived from a joint model for the sample means across the areas (Kuha *et al.* 2011). This exercise is an instance of small-area estimation in survey analysis (Rao 2003). Using these estimates in subsequent modelling essentially removes the measurement-error bias in estimated regression coefficients.

The same procedure is used for perceived disorder, which is the second of our social characteristics of the neighbourhood. Calculating the neighbourhood-level (or cluster-level in multilevel modelling terminology) mean of perceived disorder, we construct a measure of some kind of consensual or shared perception of disorder (c.f. Sampson and Raudenbush 2004).[3] The third and final social characteristic is worry about crime – again, the cluster-level mean.[4]

Variation in trust in police effectiveness

Table 7.2 presents the intra-class correlations from five fitted multilevel models. The empty model, which includes no covariates, indicates that just under 8 per cent of the variation occurs between neighbourhoods (the rest is individual, that is, within-neighbourhood variation, plus random error). Grouping by neighbourhood thus conveys some information. People who live in the same neighbourhood share some tendency to judge the effectiveness of the police similarly.

The second model adds gender, age, ethnicity, work status, residential status, access to a vehicle and number of children as individual-level predictors. Fitting this compositional model is important because people are not randomly distributed across neighbourhoods. They select into neighbourhoods, and we do not want to attribute differences between neighbourhoods to neighbourhoods that are, in fact, a function of differential selection of individuals into localities (Sampson *et al.* 2002). We find that only 10 per cent of the neighbourhood-level

Table 7.2 Neighbourhood variation in trust in police effectiveness in London.

	ICC	*Variance explained (%)*
Empty model	0.08	
Compositional model	0.07	10
Adding structural characteristics	0.06	18
Adding social characteristics	0.05	38
Adding structural and social characteristics	0.05	41

Note: ICC=intra-class correlation

variation is explained (Table 7.2). While there may be other sources of selection bias,[5] much of the neighbourhood-clustering thus seems to be a function of ecological context, instead of any differential sample composition.

We then add, one at a time, each of the four measures of neighbourhood structural characteristics (not shown here). Importantly, the order in which they are added makes little difference to the estimated effect. There is one exception. When crime levels are added on their own, the coefficient is 0.008 ($p<0.001$). But in the model that also contains the other three structural characteristics, the coefficient is 0.004 ($p<0.001$). Adding all four structural characteristics (as well the individual-level predictors contained in the compositional model) indicates that 18 per cent of the neighbourhood-level variation can be explained by the factors in the fitted model.

Strikingly, when we add the social characteristics, we explain 38 per cent of the between-neighbourhood variation. Again, it does not matter which order each of these measures were introduced into the equation. For example, adding collective efficacy without worry and perceived disorder (and the structural characteristics) gives similar estimates to the model to the full model (that includes all the social characteristics).

Turning to Table 7.3 (model 4), neighbourhood levels of collective efficacy, perceived disorder and worry about crime are important predictors of trust. They are also more important than structural characteristics: the greater the level of collective efficacy, the higher the expected value of trust. Similarly, the greater the level of perceived disorder and worry about crime in the neighbourhood, the more likely it is that individuals in that community will have low levels of trust in police effectiveness. These are additive effects. So individuals who live in disorderly and fearful neighbourhoods that lack collective efficacy will be especially likely to lack trust in the police. Smaller effects are found for concentrated disadvantage (the more deprived the neighbourhood the less trust in the police) and residential stability (the more stable the neighbourhood the more trust in the police).

Turning to individual-level characteristics, we find that age has a significant non-linear effect (note that interaction effects between gender and age are not statistically significant). Trust is lowest among people aged between 45 and 64 and highest among those aged under 25 and over 85. People who describe themselves as 'Indian' or 'Pakistani' tend to have higher levels of trust than people who describe themselves as 'White British'. Conversely, people who describe themselves as 'Black or Black British: Caribbean' or 'Mixed: White and Black Caribbean' tend to have lower levels of trust than people who describe themselves as 'White British'. Finally, lower levels of trust in police effectiveness are associated with being a home owner, buying on a mortgage, renting from the council, having a car and having children.[6] Most of these statistical effects are small, however. The difference in the conditional mean level of trust in police effectiveness between the White British and Black Caribbean groups – to take one example – is only around 5 per cent of the total scale length.

Table 7.3 Explaining individual and neighbourhood variation in trust in police effectiveness

	Model 1			Model 2			Model 3			Model 4		
	Coefficient	S.E.	t-Ratio	Coefficient	S.E.	t-Ratio	Coefficient	S.E.	t-Ratio	Coefficient	S.E.	t-Ratio
Intercept	6.33	0.08	80.95***	6.32	0.08	80.70***	8.55	0.18	48.16***	8.64	0.19	46.04***
Person level (N = 38,346)												
Female	0.00	0.02	−0.26	−0.01	0.02	−0.36	0.00	0.02	0.11	0.00	0.02	0.06
Age	−0.21	0.03	−8.08***	−0.21	0.03	−7.96***	−0.21	0.03	−7.77***	−0.20	0.03	−7.70***
Age (squared)	0.02	0.00	7.13***	0.02	0.00	6.97***	0.02	0.00	6.75***	0.02	0.00	6.68***
Ethnicity (White British is the reference category):												
White – Irish	−0.16	0.05	−2.87**	−0.14	0.05	−2.61**	−0.14	0.05	−2.52*	−0.14	0.05	−2.54*
White – any other	0.06	0.03	1.94	0.08	0.03	2.68**	0.07	0.03	2.29*	0.07	0.03	2.46*
Mixed – White and Black Caribbean	−0.18	0.05	−3.71***	−0.17	0.05	−3.34***	−0.18	0.05	−3.56***	−0.17	0.05	−3.34***
Mixed – White and Black African	−0.11	0.06	−1.92	−0.09	0.06	−1.57	−0.10	0.06	−1.78	−0.09	0.06	−1.53
Mixed – White and Asian	−0.17	0.09	−1.95	−0.15	0.09	−1.76	−0.13	0.08	−1.59	−0.13	0.08	−1.58
Other mixed	−0.03	0.06	−0.57	−0.02	0.06	−0.34	−0.01	0.06	−0.17	−0.02	0.06	−0.33
Indian	0.05	0.04	1.22	0.09	0.04	2.37*	0.12	0.04	3.17**	0.13	0.04	3.36***
Pakistani	0.09	0.05	1.95	0.14	0.05	2.96**	0.18	0.05	3.78***	0.19	0.05	3.98***
Bangladeshi	−0.10	0.05	−2.05*	−0.04	0.05	−0.74	0.05	0.05	1.11	0.07	0.05	1.43
Other Asian or Asian British	−0.07	0.06	−1.12	−0.04	0.06	−0.63	−0.03	0.06	−0.46	−0.03	0.06	−0.42
Black or Black British – Caribbean	−0.28	0.04	−6.76***	−0.25	0.04	−6.01***	−0.27	0.04	−6.73***	−0.26	0.04	−6.34***
Black or Black British – African	0.00	0.03	−0.02	0.02	0.03	0.72	0.01	0.03	0.26	0.02	0.03	0.71
Other Black or Black British	−0.12	0.08	−1.44	−0.10	0.08	−1.27	−0.09	0.08	−1.16	−0.09	0.08	−1.13
Chinese	0.04	0.12	0.31	0.07	0.12	0.58	0.05	0.12	0.40	0.06	0.12	0.52
Other chinese or other ethnic group	0.16	0.09	1.70	0.20	0.09	2.11*	0.24	0.09	2.54*	0.25	0.09	2.64**
Work status (Working full time is the reference):												
Working part time, 8–29 hrs per/wk	0.01	0.03	0.22	0.01	0.03	0.18	0.01	0.03	0.35	0.01	0.03	0.32
Working part time (less than 8 hrs per/wk)	−0.03	0.10	−0.30	−0.04	0.10	−0.36	−0.05	0.10	−0.47	−0.05	0.10	−0.51
Not working	−0.09	0.04	−2.11*	−0.09	0.04	−2.21*	−0.10	0.04	−2.32*	−0.10	0.04	−2.41*
House person	0.14	0.03	4.40***	0.14	0.03	4.52***	0.12	0.03	3.85***	0.12	0.03	3.83***
Retired	0.07	0.04	1.85	0.07	0.04	1.93	0.07	0.04	1.93	0.07	0.04	1.93

continued overleaf

	Model 1			Model 2			Model 3			Model 4		
	Coefficient	S.E.	t-Ratio	Coefficient	S.E.	t-Ratio	Coefficient	S.E.	t-Ratio	Coefficient	S.E.	t-Ratio
Registered unemployed	0.04	0.04	0.92	0.04	0.04	0.98	0.02	0.04	0.43	0.02	0.04	0.37
Unemployed but not registered	-0.26	0.12	-2.25*	-0.27	0.12	-2.35*	-0.32	0.12	-2.74**	-0.32	0.12	-2.76**
Student/full time education	-0.09	0.04	-2.06*	-0.08	0.04	-1.96*	-0.09	0.04	-2.16*	-0.09	0.04	-2.18*
Working status (other)	-0.02	0.09	-0.19	-0.03	0.09	-0.36	-0.02	0.09	-0.22	-0.03	0.09	-0.36
Housing situation (Own property outright is the reference category):												
Buying on mortgage	0.25	0.03	8.94***	0.25	0.03	9.12***	0.23	0.03	8.50***	0.24	0.03	8.59***
Rented from council	0.07	0.03	2.49*	0.09	0.03	3.18***	0.10	0.03	3.58***	0.11	0.03	3.83***
Rented from housing association	0.41	0.04	11.33***	0.43	0.04	11.8***	0.38	0.04	10.55***	0.39	0.04	10.74***
Rented from private landlord	0.41	0.03	13.22***	0.42	0.03	13.5***	0.39	0.03	12.82***	0.40	0.03	12.92***
Tenure (other)	0.70	0.06	10.92***	0.71	0.06	11.19***	0.73	0.06	11.44***	0.74	0.06	11.59***
Household access to a car	-0.03	0.02	-1.56	-0.04	0.02	-2.16*	-0.05	0.02	-2.51	-0.05	0.02	-2.83**
Number of kids	-0.12	0.01	-11.02***	-0.12	0.01	-10.98***	-0.11	0.01	-10.32***	-0.11	0.01	-10.22***
Neighbourhood level (N = 4,747)												
Concentrated disadvantage				-0.07	0.01	-6.70***				-0.05	0.01	-4.97***
Residential stability				0.04	0.01	3.95***				0.04	0.01	4.16***
Immigrant concentration				-0.08	0.01	-7.65***				-0.01	0.01	-0.82
Crime				-0.04	0.02	-2.60**				-0.02	0.01	-1.60
Collective efficacy							0.18	0.02	-7.50***	0.20	0.03	-8.00***
Perceived disorder							-0.12	0.01	-11.92***	-0.12	0.01	-11.74***
Worry about crime							-0.18	0.01	-19.77***	-0.17	0.01	-18.13***
Variance explained	10%			18%			38%			41%		

Variance explained

Model 1	Model 2	Model 3	Model 4
0.10	0.18	0.38	0.41

Variance components

Between neighbourhoods	0.43
Within neighbourhoods	1.48

Note: unstandardised coefficients, * significant at the 5% level, ** significant at the 1% level, *** significant at the 0.1% level.

Variation in trust in police fairness and intentions

We next turn to the second element of trust in the police. As outlined in Chapter 5, trust in police fairness and intentions is reflected in this study by people's agreement or disagreement with statements such as 'they can be relied on to be there when you need them', 'they are dealing with the things that matter to people in this community', 'they would you treat you with respect if you had contact with them for any reason' and 'the police in this area treat everyone fairly regardless of who they are.'

Table 7.4 presents the intra-class correlations from five fitted models. An empty variance components model indicates that just over 9 per cent of the variation occurs between neighbourhoods (again, the rest is random error and within-neighbourhood variation). As with trust in effectiveness, conditioning on individual-level characteristics such as gender, age, ethnicity and work status makes little difference to the amount of estimated between-neighbourhood variance. And as with trust in effectiveness, adding social characteristics explains a good deal of the between-neighbourhood variation (76 per cent, including compositional effects).[7]

Table 7.5 presents the results from four models (comparable to Table 7.4 for trust in police effectiveness). The most striking finding is the effect of neighbourhood levels of collective efficacy. That the coefficient dwarfs that of any of the other estimated effects is an important finding. It suggests that people derive a sense of police fairness and shared interests in part from the strength of the norms that govern local community order. When informal social controls are strong, people seem to think that the police are fair and dependable (c.f. Jackson and Sunshine 2007). A moderate effect is also found for perceived disorder: the greater the level of perceived disorder in the neighbourhood, the more the trust among individuals in that neighbourhood. A small effect is found with worry about crime: the greater the level of worry about crime in the neighbourhood, the less the trust among individuals in that neighbourhood. Structural characteristics of the neighbourhoods are not significant predictors.

We also find a significant gender and age interaction. For females, trust is lowest among those aged between 25 and 54 and highest among those aged 15 to 17 and 75+. For males, there is a linear relationship between age and trust: the older the individual the higher the expected level of trust. Again, household access to a car is associated with less trust. Unlike trust in effectiveness,

Table 7.4 Neighbourhood variation in trust in police fairness and priorities in London.

	ICC	*Variance explained (%)*
Empty model	0.09	
Compositional model	0.09	5
Adding structural characteristics	0.08	10
Adding social characteristics	0.02	76
Adding structural and social characteristics	0.02	76

Note: ICC=intra-class correlation

Table 7.5 Explaining individual and neighbourhood variation in trust in police fairness and priorities.

	Model 1			Model 2			Model 3			Model 4		
	Coefficient	S.E.	t–Ratio	Coefficient	S.E.	t–Ratio	Coefficient	S.E.	t–Ratio	Coefficient	S.E.	t–Ratio
Intercept	5.26	0.10	51.66***	5.30	0.10	52.01***	-0.15	0.18	-0.85	-0.31	0.19	-1.63
Person level (N=37,711)												
Female	0.54	0.12	4.49***	0.54	0.12	4.43***	0.52	0.12	4.38***	0.52	0.12	4.38***
Age	0.07	0.04	2.02*	0.06	0.04	1.79	0.01	0.04	0.22	0.01	0.04	0.25
Age (squared)	0.00	0.00	-1.16	0.00	0.00	-0.94	0.00	0.00	0.44	0.00	0.00	0.40
Female*age interaction	-0.23	0.04	-5.22***	-0.23	0.04	-5.17***	-0.22	0.04	-5.06***	-0.22	0.04	-5.06***
Female*age (squared) interaction	0.02	0.00	5.72***	0.02	0.00	5.69***	0.02	0.00	5.61***	0.02	0.00	5.61***
Ethnicity (reference: White British)												
White – Irish	0.02	0.06	0.28	0.00	0.06	0.03	-0.03	0.06	-0.47	-0.02	0.06	-0.32
White – any other	0.16	0.03	5.15***	0.15	0.03	4.81***	0.12	0.03	3.96***	0.13	0.03	4.21***
Mixed – White and Black Caribbean	-0.11	0.05	-2.02*	-0.11	0.05	-2.06*	-0.14	0.05	-2.80**	-0.14	0.05	-2.72**
Mixed – White and Black African	0.06	0.06	1.03	0.07	0.06	1.08	0.01	0.06	0.20	0.02	0.06	0.26
Mixed – White and Asian	-0.25	0.09	-2.78**	-0.25	0.09	-2.83**	-0.22	0.09	-2.53*	-0.22	0.09	-2.48*
Other mixed	-0.30	0.06	-4.99***	-0.34	0.06	-5.54***	-0.36	0.06	-6.04***	-0.35	0.06	-5.83***
Indian	0.22	0.04	5.30***	0.22	0.04	5.32***	0.20	0.04	4.91***	0.21	0.04	5.18***
Pakistani	0.31	0.05	6.30***	0.31	0.05	6.30***	0.29	0.05	5.92***	0.30	0.05	6.15***
Bangladeshi	0.29	0.05	5.79***	0.29	0.05	5.82***	0.23	0.05	4.81***	0.25	0.05	5.03***
Other Asian or Asian British	0.09	0.07	1.39	0.09	0.07	1.38	0.09	0.06	1.44	0.10	0.06	1.58
Black or Black British – Caribbean	-0.16	0.04	-3.79***	-0.16	0.04	-3.69***	-0.16	0.04	-3.72***	-0.15	0.04	-3.55***
Black or Black British – African	0.17	0.03	4.93***	0.17	0.03	5.09***	0.13	0.03	4.07***	0.14	0.03	4.16***
Other Black or Black British	-0.06	0.09	-0.74	-0.07	0.09	-0.84	-0.09	0.08	-1.04	-0.08	0.08	-0.96
Chinese	0.42	0.12	3.45***	0.43	0.12	3.51***	0.38	0.12	3.15**	0.39	0.12	3.21***
Other Chinese or other ethnic group	0.18	0.10	1.80	0.17	0.10	1.76	0.22	0.10	2.28*	0.23	0.10	2.37*
Work status (reference: working full-time)												
Working part time (8–29 hrs per/wk)	-0.06	0.03	-1.77	-0.05	0.03	-1.58	-0.01	0.03	-0.20	-0.01	0.03	-0.24
Working part time (<8hrs per/wk)	-0.21	0.10	-2.08*	-0.21	0.10	-2.04*	-0.15	0.10	-1.45	-0.15	0.10	-1.44
Not working	-0.27	0.05	-6.08***	-0.27	0.05	-6.02***	-0.22	0.04	-5.00***	-0.22	0.04	-5.01***

	Model 1			Model 2			Model 3			Model 4		
	Coefficient	S.E.	t–Ratio	Coefficient	S.E.	t–Ratio	Coefficient	S.E.	t–Ratio	Coefficient	S.E.	t–Ratio
House person	−0.13	0.03	−3.81***	−0.12	0.03	−3.67***	−0.06	0.03	−1.82	−0.06	0.03	−1.78
Retired	−0.04	0.04	−1.17	−0.04	0.04	−1.05	−0.01	0.04	−0.12	0.00	0.04	−0.09
Registered unemployed	−0.28	0.05	−6.22***	−0.28	0.05	−6.16***	−0.21	0.04	−4.69***	−0.21	0.04	−4.63***
Unemployed but not registered	−0.29	0.12	−2.41*	−0.28	0.12	−2.30	−0.14	0.12	−1.15	−0.14	0.12	−1.17
Student/full time education	−0.12	0.05	−2.56**	−0.12	0.05	−2.60**	−0.10	0.05	−2.21*	−0.10	0.05	−2.15*
Working status (other)	−0.33	0.10	−3.37***	−0.33	0.10	−3.36	−0.14	0.10	−1.45	−0.14	0.10	−1.46
Housing situation (reference: own property outright)												
Buying on mortgage	0.02	0.03	0.57	0.01	0.03	0.46	0.01	0.03	0.21	0.01	0.03	0.31
Rented from council	−0.06	0.03	−2.09*	−0.08	0.03	−2.76**	−0.11	0.03	−3.61***	−0.10	0.03	−3.35***
Rented from housing association	−0.22	0.04	−5.77***	−0.23	0.04	−6.06***	−0.22	0.04	−5.80***	−0.21	0.04	−5.56***
Rented from private landlord	0.02	0.03	0.73	0.02	0.03	0.53	0.06	0.03	1.76	0.06	0.03	1.90
Tenure (other)	0.43	0.07	6.33***	0.41	0.07	6.14***	0.36	0.07	5.45***	0.36	0.07	5.51***
Household access to a car	−0.28	0.02	−14.10***	−0.27	0.02	−13.92***	−0.24	0.02	−12.57***	−0.24	0.02	−12.65***
Number of kids	0.12	0.01	10.76***	0.13	0.01	11.04***	0.12	0.01	11.11***	0.12	0.01	11.01***
Neighbourhood level (N=4,741)												
Concentrated disadvantage				0.00	0.01	−0.37				0.01	0.01	0.53
Residential stability				0.10	0.01	9.25***				−0.01	0.01	−1.07
Immigrant concentration				0.01	0.01	0.68				−0.02	0.01	−2.32*
Crime				−0.06	0.02	−3.38***				−0.03	0.01	−2.13*
Collective efficacy							0.94	0.02	42.50***	0.96	0.02	41.03***
Perceived disorder							0.12	0.01	12.57***	0.12	0.01	12.77***
Worry about crime							−0.05	0.01	−5.51***	−0.04	0.01	−4.49***

Variance components

Between neighbourhoods	0.49	
Within neighbourhoods	1.541	

Variance explained

Model 1	Model 2	Model 3	Model 4
1%	5%	73%	74%

Note: unstandardised coefficients, * significant at the 5% level, ** significant at the 1% level, *** significant at the 0.1% level.

however, differences between people from different ethnic groups (within the same neighbourhood) are more marked. Groups with higher levels of trust than those who describe themselves as 'White British' are 'White – any other', 'Indian', 'Pakistani', 'Bangladeshi', 'Black or Black British: African', 'Chinese' and 'Other Chinese or other ethnic group'. Groups with lower levels than 'White British' are 'Mixed – White and Black Caribbean', 'Mixed – White and Asian', 'Other mixed' and Black or Black British: Caribbean'. However, these effects are relatively small – especially compared to the effect of collective efficacy.

Summary

In this chapter we have shown that trust in the police clusters in the neighbourhoods in which people live. People who live in the same area tend to have somewhat similar levels of trust (at least compared to randomly selected individuals from across London). Some 8 per cent of the variation in trust in police effectiveness, and some 9 per cent of the variation in trust in police fairness and shared interests, can be explained by neighbourhood. These amounts of explained variation are comparable to those found in many studies of neighbourhood effects in other substantive fields (e.g. Brunton-Smith and Sturgis 2011).

We also found that socio-demographic factors like gender, age and ethnicity are less important than the nature of the neighbourhood. Trust in police is higher in areas that have relatively high levels of collective efficacy and relatively low levels of perceived disorder and worry about crime, and for trust in police fairness and shared interests, collective efficacy seems especially important. It seems that the quality of informal policing is linked to people's trust in the formal police organisation. Moreover, the greater the level of perceived disorder in the neighbourhood, and the greater the level of worry about crime, and for the lower the expected levels of public trust.

Structural characteristics are less important, although higher levels of trust are found in more disadvantaged and more residentially stable areas. It may not be so much the 'objective' condition of their neighbourhood that affects people's trust in police, but rather its (collectively) 'subjective' nature. Equally, while individual characteristics – age, gender, ethnicity – do play some role in influencing trust judgements, the wider social context in which people are embedded appears to be more important. This is not to say, of course, that individual experience does not influence trust in the police. And it is to this issue that we now turn.

8 One type of contact

Being approached by the police

Having shown the significance of neighbourhood context, we now turn to people's individual encounters with police officers. Focusing initially on police-initiated contact, we consider the stops, searches and arrests that our London respondents have experienced in the 12 months prior to their interview. We first examine who has which type of contact. We then model associations between (a) the judgements that individuals make about their experiences and (b) their level of trust in the police. Doing all this within a multilevel approach allows us to build on the models presented in Chapter 7. Alongside the main variables of interest – reflecting people's experience of police-initiated contact – we factor into our analytical model some key socio-demographic factors and some important features of the neighbourhood context.

In Chapter 4 we outlined some of the historical trends in public contacts with the police. We discussed the empirically supported idea that personal contact is an important determinant of people's perceptions of the trustworthiness of the police, as well as their confidence in the job that the police carry out. We showed that the relationship between contact with officers and confidence in the police has changed over time. Satisfactory contact had very little statistical effect on confidence in the earlier years of our BCS dataset, resulting in an almost totally asymmetrical pattern (c.f. Skogan 2006). Over time, however, there has been a significant change towards a more symmetrical picture (c.f. Tyler and Fagan 2008; Bradford *et al.* 2009a).

The findings we present in this chapter – and in Chapters 9 and 10 – take an important step towards testing Tyler's procedural justice model of cooperation (Tyler and Huo 2002; Tyler 2006a). Tyler's model places importance on the links between experience, motive-based trust and legitimacy. So the relationship between contact and trust in police fairness and intentions is of particular interest in the proceeding analysis. We examine the relationship between trust in the police and encounters with the officers, particularly whether people felt satisfied or dissatisfied with how they were treated.

Who has police-initiated contact?

Studies of police-initiated contact tend to concentrate on those marginalised, excluded and other groups often seen as 'police property'. Whether the emphasis is on ethnic minority groups (Brunson 2007; Carr *et al.* 2007; Sharp and Atherton 2007), young people (Loader 1996; McAra and McVie 2005), working-class communities (Choongh 1997) or protestors and political activists (Gorringe and Rosie 2009), these studies have taken the fact of a high level of contact between the police and the particular group as a (problematic) given.

Certain groups in society clearly do have higher odds than other groups of being stopped, searched, arrested or otherwise forced into contact with the police. Whether the unequal distribution of police attention is more or less inevitable (as it may be in the case of age, given the well-known age distribution of many types of offending behaviour) or deeply problematic (as in the continued over-representation of people from minority ethnic groups in most categories of police-initiated contact: see Bowling and Philips 2002, 2007), it is clear that certain groups and types of people are more likely to have this type of contact with the police.

Yet we know little about the relative weights of different socio-economic and other factors in influencing the odds of 'coming to the attention' of the police (although see FitzGerald *et al.* 2002). If it is still largely the case that the police deal primarily with the problems of the 'lower classes' or those with low social status (and/or that the police exist primarily to keep the same under observation and therefore control, see Choongh 1996; Waddington 1999), does it follow that police-initiated contact is heavily concentrated among such groups? Or does the spreading experience of crime (Garland 2001), and indeed policing, mean that a wider range of characteristics predict contact experiences?

We first consider police-initiated contacts. What are the factors that most strongly predict this type of contact with the police? Is it all about age, ethnicity and social class? Or are other factors in play? We draw on previous work that has highlighted the geographic as well as social distribution of differential experiences of the police (e.g. Sampson and Bartusch 1998; Reisig and Parks 2000; Schafer *et al.* 2003). A glance at the crime maps now produced by police forces across England and Wales reinforces the common-sense view that crime – or at least crime that is reported to the police – is not evenly distributed. On its own this might predict greater chances of contact with the police among those living in 'high crime' areas. Add to the mix the traditional police emphasis on 'policing' some social groups in order to 'protect' others (leaving the former over-policed and under-protected, and the latter, arguably, over-protected and under-policed), and we would appear to have a recipe for a profoundly unequal distribution of contact with officers, both geographically and socially.

Thus far, however, these relationships have been more assumed than investigated in depth in the UK. A key element to the analysis in this chapter is multi-level modelling, which helps explain both individual and area-level variance in rates of police-initiated contact across London.

Being stopped by the police

Given our interest in the relationship between area-level characteristics and experiences of the police, it would be convenient to draw a distinction between (a) police stops that occurred close to where people live and (b) police stops that occurred further away. The METPAS allows this distinction to be made. The survey asks respondents whether the stop they have experienced occurred 'in the local area' or 'elsewhere in London'. However, a less welcome feature of the METPAS is that it reports comparatively low rates of contact with the police. Only 2 per cent of the sample reported a car or foot stop, compared with around 10 per cent in most sweeps of the BCS. The reasons for this are unclear. The structure of the METPAS sample does not depart significantly from the demographic make-up of the London population as a whole (if it did, we might immediately suspect non-response bias).[1] But, addressing this issue is beyond the scope of this book. It does mean, though, that it was preferable to use an indicator that combined 'local' and 'London-wide' stops.

We should say, however, that we are not concerned with overall rates of contact. We are interested in those characteristics that are associated with a greater or lesser chance of contact. As long as there is no systematic variation in recall rates across population categories – and there is no obvious reason to think that there is – the estimates displayed below should not be biased by the relatively low rates of contact reported in the METPAS. Importantly, to test the robustness of our findings, in Chapter 9 we also draw upon data from the BME sample.

We first address the question of who is stopped and/or searched by the police in London. For now we combine being stopped and being searched, principally because of numbers. Some 778 individuals reported being stopped by the police and 220 individuals reported being searched and/or arrested. Because we want to examine the effect of various socio-demographic factors on the odds of experiencing this type of contact with the police (all the while conditioning on the neighbourhood in which people live), it is helpful to maximise variation on the outcome variable across important sub-populations.

To anticipate the main results, area-level characteristics are not generally important predictors of experiencing a stop (a finding that was replicated in further analysis, not presented here, that looked at local stops and stops that occurred elsewhere in London separately[2] – contact the lead author for details). With the exception of residential stability – that is, the speed with which people move in and out of a neighbourhood – it does not seem that the nature of the area in which someone lives has much of an association with their odds of being stopped by the police; personal characteristics instead appear to be key. The lack of association between local crime rates and experiences of police stops is at first glance perplexing. However, beyond the basic observation that there is no necessary one-to-one link between the level of recorded crime and police activity, there are two further plausible explanations.

The difficulty of obtaining survey responses from those individuals most likely to experience police stop and/or stop-and-search activity is one explanation – this is likely to be a key factor. The other is the tension inherent in a number of inter-related factors that relate to the way police stop-and-search activity is directed. The MPS continues to have faith in stop-and-search as a crime-prevention strategy, which would predict differential odds of being stopped across areas with different levels of crime; but it is in fact a relatively ineffectual practice when it comes to actually apprehending offenders, which might imply it is not being used in the right places. Furthermore, stop activity has a strong symbolic element, and may be high in areas that are not particularly high in crime, such as some parts of central London; but it can also be highly targeted at small 'high-crime' hot-spots embedded in wider areas with much lower levels of reported offending, such as transport hubs. Both factors may confound the area-level data we have available.

A combination of all these factors, and many more, might be behind the lack of significant associations between area-level measures and the odds of being stopped reported in Table 8.1, and should caution against an over-interpretation of the data reported here.

Who is stopped and/or searched by the police?

We estimate two multilevel binary logistic models. Given the level of debate around ethnic disproportionality in police stop-and-search activity (EHRC 2010), we first include only ethnicity as a covariate. This allows consideration of the bivariate association between ethnicity and the odds of being stopped and/ or searched by the police (Table 8.1). Because of the low numbers of people who were approached by the police, we use an aggregated categorisation of ethnicity (seven categories). Later analyses – modelling trust in the police – return to the full categorisation.

Model 1 ignores the neighbourhood in which individuals live, while model 2 partitions the variance appropriately. Surprisingly, it does not matter whether one compares individuals who live in the same neighbourhood (addressing whether their odds of being stopped and/or stopped and searched differ according to

Table 8.1 Who is stopped and/or searched by the police in London? A focus on ethnicity.

	Model 1			Model 2		
	Odds ratio	95% confidence interval		Odds ratio	95% confidence interval	
Ethnicity (reference: White British) Mixed	1.64***	1.27	2.12	1.67***	1.29	2.18
Indian	2.11***	1.58	2.80	2.10***	1.57	2.81
Pakistani /Bangladeshi	1.48**	1.11	1.97	1.46*	1.09	1.96
Black Caribbean	1.87***	1.40	2.50	1.88***	1.40	2.52
Black African	2.20***	1.75	2.78	2.22***	1.75	2.81
Other	1.47***	1.18	1.83	1.49***	1.19	1.86
Between neighbourhoods variance				−0.87		
Within neighbourhoods variance				0.65		
ICC				0.11		

Note
* significant at the 5% level, ** significant at the 1% level, *** significant at the 0.1% level.
ICC=intra-class correlation

ethnicity) or one compares individuals who are assumed to be randomly sampled across London (modelling the odds across these sub-populations). Modelling within-neighbourhood variation makes little difference (comparing model 2 to model 1). Being of any of the ethnic minority groups is associated with higher odds of being stopped compared to being 'White British'.

We next add a range of socio-demographic covariates into the fitted model (Table 8.2). Adding the compositional (socio-demographic) and area-level (structural characteristics and crime levels) factors helps to explain 29 per cent of the area-level variation. The results can be summarised as follows:

- Women are much less likely than men to report having been stopped or searched in the past year (an adjusted odds-ratio of 0.20 means that the odds of a female being stopped are 80 per cent less than the adjusted odds of a male being stopped);
- The younger you are, the more likely you are to be stopped or searched by the police, and the odds of experiencing a stop/search decrease increasing rapidly with age;
- Individuals from all ethnic minority groups but the Pakistani' and 'Bangladeshi' group have higher odds of being stopped/searched than those from the 'White British' group;
- Access to a car predicts higher probability of being stopped or searched.

Overall, a familiar picture emerges. The METPAS findings resonate strongly with other work in this area (see, for example, FitzGerald *et al.* 2002). Being young, male, Black, 'mixed' race and having a car are all characteristics associated with a higher likelihood of being stopped by the police. Some elements of Table 8.2 will be less familiar, however. People who owned their home outright are more likely to be stopped than other people, for example. Most surprising is a lack of evidence for the effect of structural characteristics of the neighbourhood in which individuals live.[3] Only residential stability is significant in any of the models. Neighbourhood levels of crime, disadvantage and immigrant concentration do not predict the odds of being stopped by the police. One interpretation of this might be that while the police may behave differently in different areas, it is the characteristics of individuals who live there, not the areas, that provoke or trigger foot or car stops.

The experience of police stops is concentrated heavily among men, the young, and those from certain ethnic minority groups. But the extent of the variation by ethnic group is less than might be expected, given the enormous ethnic disparities in stop-and-search rates reported by other studies (see, for example, Miller 2010; EHRC 2010). Part of this difference is likely to be due to the introduction of statistical controls. Based on raw METPAS data (not reported here, please contact the first author for more details), Black Caribbean Londoners are around 2.5 times more likely to report being stopped than their 'White British' counterparts. This is a figure not so dissimilar from that reported in previous studies. We might also note that the Equality and Human Rights Commission (2010) report, for example, compares stop-and-search data with population estimates. Since the

Table 8.2 Who is stopped and/or searched by the police in London? Explaining individual and neighbourhood variation.

	Odds Ratio	95% confidence interval	95% confidence interval
		lower bound	upper bound
Person level (N=39,553)			
Female	0.20***	0.12	0.31
Age	0.62***	0.58	0.66
Age squared	1.12*	1.03	1.23
Ethnicity (reference: White British)			
Mixed	1.38*	1.05	1.82
Indian	1.44*	1.06	1.96
Pakistani /Bangladeshi	0.91	0.67	1.25
Black Caribbean	1.64**	1.21	2.23
Black African	1.83***	1.42	2.35
Other	1.28*	1.01	1.62
Work status (reference: working full-time)			
Working part time (8– 29 hrs/wk)	2.04***	1.60	2.62
Working part time (less than 8hrs/wk)	1.70	0.77	3.74
Not working	0.90	0.58	1.42
House person	0.58*	0.38	0.89
Retired	0.83	0.56	1.22
Registered unemployed	1.19	0.82	1.71
Unemployed but not registered	1.62	0.79	3.34
Student/full time education	0.83	0.63	1.10
Working status (other)	2.01*	1.00	4.05
Housing situation (reference: own property outright)			
Buying on mortgage	0.60***	0.46	0.78
Rented from council	0.53***	0.39	0.71
Rented from housing association	0.56**	0.38	0.80
Rented from private landlord	0.35***	0.26	0.47
Tenure (other)	0.80	0.50	1.29
Household access to a car	1.36**	1.12	1.65
Number of kids	1.13**	1.03	1.24
Neighbourhood level (N=4,748)			
Concentrated disadvantage	0.98	0.90	1.06
Residential stability	0.77***	0.71	0.84
Immigrant concentration	1.02	0.95	1.10
Crime	1.05	0.93	1.18
	Variance components		Variance explained
Between neighbourhoods	−1.23		29%
Within neighbourhoods	0.54		

Note: * significant at the 5% level, ** significant at the 1% level, *** significant at the 0.1% level.

stop/search data must contain a significant amount of double counting (the same individual being stopped more than once), this methodology may both over- and under-estimate the extent of the disproportionality in stop/search: over-estimate, in the sense that it is likely to be very specific types of people who are singled out for this type of police attention (for example, young Black Caribbean men living in certain parts of London), while others from the same group – older Black Caribbean women – are much less likely to be stopped. Under-estimation is likely because at the same time the grossly disproportionate experience of those who are frequently stopped will be occluded (since the stop rate is calculated over the whole population). Our survey data is not necessarily subject to the same problems, certainly in relation to over-estimation, but the METPAS is in this instance most useful for looking at the broad distribution of the experience of police stops. A definitive mapping of this type of experience is beyond its capability.

On another level, our findings are more nuanced. A relatively wide range of characteristics are associated with higher probabilities of contact with the police that cannot be neatly corralled by the idea that the police deal primarily with the poor, the excluded and the disenfranchised. To take just two examples, people on low incomes are less likely to own cars, and they use them less when they do own them (Sustainable Development Commission 2011). Yet, all else being equal, car access is a strong predictor of experiencing a police stop. People who own their own homes are more likely to report being stopped than those with other housing tenures. Perhaps one message here is that almost everyone may have direct personal experience of interaction with officers – for all that street and car stop activity is undeniably concentrated on specific social groups. Such experiences may prove a vital influence on their trust in the police. We thus turn to a detailed consideration of the estimated effects of contact on expected levels of trust.

The association between police-initiated contact and trust

Previous research has established that being stopped by the police – whether in a car or on foot – can be a key moment in an individual's sense of trust in the police (FitzGerald *et al.* 2002; Rosenbaum *et al.* 2005; Skogan 2006; Tyler and Fagan 2008; Bradford *et al.* 2009a). As the procedural justice model and other accounts of the relationship between police and public attest (see, for example, Tyler and Huo 2002; Waddington 1999), the way police officers treat people powerfully communicates their own trustworthiness. Procedural justice expresses the extent to which officers view the individual concerned as worthy of respect, dignity and inclusion within the social group the police represent. Police officers can, of course, communicate quite the opposite, being particularly important – and fraught with potential difficulty – in those moments when police use their power to intrude into and disrupt people's lives.

A significant body of US-based research suggests that police often behave differently and 'treat people differently' depending upon the characteristics of area in which the encounter is taking place (e.g. Mastrofski *et al.* 2002; Terrill and Reisig 2003). We add to this literature by locating individuals within the area in which they live. Chapter 9 narrows the focus to a particular group of people – young men from minority ethnic groups living in highly diverse London boroughs – many of whom may have highly problematic relationships with the police. Is the pattern of associations between contact and trust, found across London as a whole, replicated among this sample?

In this chapter we concentrate on the 'general' population, and add to the literature by exploring the effect of positive and negative encounters. The overall negative relationship between recent contact with the police and trust and confidence is well-established (see, for example, Skogan 1994; FitzGerald *et al.* 2002; Flatley *et al.* 2010). On average, trust in the police is lower among those who have had recent contact with officers, something largely due to an asymmetry in the effect of contact on trust (Skogan 2006). Drawing on data from the 1992 British Crime Survey (and from studies conducted in a range other cities), Skogan demonstrated a marked variation in the impact of contact on public confidence in the effectiveness and community engagement of the police. As discussed in Chapter 4, positively assessed encounters failed to result in improvements in confidence; while negatively assessed encounters were strongly linked to lower confidence. In general, it seems, the impact of contact is damaging at worst, negligible at best.

Why would well-received encounters with the police fail to have a knock-on effect on public trust in the police, while poorly received contacts do have an effect? Skogan (2006) points to Weitzer and Tuch's (2004) suggestions that, in their dealings with the police, people either dismiss good experiences as exceptions to the norm, or treat good service as a given, reacting therefore only to bad. Pre-existing ideas shape how experiences are interpreted. The social, cultural and emotional 'baggage' bought to an encounter with the police may strongly influence the lessons, in terms of police trustworthiness, that are drawn from them. Positive encounters may not lead to improved overall assessments because they are either expected (by those with previously positive views about the police) or viewed as one-off occurrences (among those with previously negative views). By contrast, unsatisfactory contacts could challenge previously positive views and reinforce previously negative ones. Waddington (1999) probes this issue more deeply. Because the police patrol the boundaries of inclusion and exclusion, contact is inherently status-challenging (c.f. Smith 2007). The best that can be expected of any encounter is confirmation of individual's social standing. But there are many possibilities for police behaviour to undermine this status, resulting in resentment and consequently damaging opinions of the police.

In short, there are suggestions in the policing literature that any contact with the police might be unsettling, disturbing and potentially endangering to trust and confidence. 'The empirical message is, unfortunately: "You can't win, you can just cut your losses." No matter what you do, it only counts when it goes against you.' (Skogan 2006: 119). Yet it may be premature to reach this conclusion. Recent panel studies (Tyler and Fagan 2008; Gau 2010; Myhill and Bradford 2011) have shown that well-received contacts can have a positive effect on opinions, although police-initiated contact appears to be the 'hardest', most asymmetric case. Tyler's procedural justice model further suggests that the experience of procedurally fair policing can have a positive effect on trust in almost any circumstance. And as we saw in Chapter 4 (see also Bradford *et al.* 2009a), while asymmetry certainly exists, it is not as severe as Skogan suggests. Well-handled interactions (that are perceived to be a positive experience) may, in some circumstances, be linked with higher levels of trust.

Because the METPAS is a cross-sectional survey that interviews respondents at one point in time only, it cannot be used to replicate the panel studies that have provided us with the best evidence so far of the potential effect of personal experience on trust in the police. Using cross-sectional data, we can only uncover evidence of the association between contact and trust. But the METPAS is suited for addressing a second set of problems: those concerning the interrelationships between trust in the police, contact experiences and the places in which people live.

There is certainly some evidence to suggest that police behave differently in different areas. Whether it is a result of police cultures that separate members of the public into 'deserving' and 'undeserving' categories based in part on where they live (Reiner 2000), or the interaction between neighbourhood context and the personal characteristics of the people officers encounter (Terrill and Reisig 2003), or simply the operational exigencies involved in policing high- or low-crime areas, there seems little doubt that the police can and often do treat people differently depending on where they encounter them (Mastrofski *et al.* 2002).

Recall that we saw above that this does not seem to translate directly into different types of 'stop' experiences in different types of area. However, we might still expect that police behaviour is 'worse' in high-crime or more disadvantaged areas, perhaps because officers conflate the perceived characteristics of the area with those of the individuals they encounter (Werthman and Piliavin 1967; Smith 1986). On the other hand, police may be less ready to use force or other oppressive behaviour in areas characterised – or thought to be characterised – by high levels of poverty, since they expect 'bad behaviour' in such areas and are cynical about the possibility of affecting change within them (Klinger 1997). It is thus important to adjust for the neighbourhood context.

In Chapter 7 we presented evidence for significant area-level variation in public trust in the police. As we have already discussed, this finding resonates with US-based work showing that area-level characteristics can be important influences on opinions of the police. Sampson and Bartusch (1998) found strong associations between both the violent crime rate and concentrated disadvantage and 'satisfaction' with the police in their Chicago data. Interested in explaining the strong correlation between race and opinions of the police in the city, they concluded that 'estrangement from the police' (ibid: 800) among Blacks was caused primarily by neighbourhood context rather than race-specific attitudes. In a slightly later study Reisig and Parks (2000), using data from two different cities, found that 'cognitively and emotionally-based response to neighbourhood conditions appeared to be the most important determinants of individual attitudes toward the police' (ibid: 625), although they note that personal experience with the police was also an important factor. Both these studies (along with a number of others – see for example Weitzer 2000) propose that the area in which people live can be an important influence on their opinions of the police.

Variation in trust in police effectiveness

The next step is to use multilevel modelling to investigate the association between recent experience of a car-stop or street-stop and trust in the police. Table 8.3 shows the results of a series of multilevel linear regression models predicting trust in police effectiveness. We first find that area-level variation in experiences of police-initiated contact does not explain the variation in trust in police effectiveness described in Chapter 8 (model 6 in Table 8.3): the area-level variation does not seem to be even partly due to variation in experiences of police-initiated contact across people living in different areas. The other important findings are summarised below:

- Contact with officers has, overall, a negative statistical effect on this component of trust. All else being equal, the use of stops as a police tactic is associated with lower average levels of trust in police effectiveness among those who experience them (model 2). Similarly, the overall statistical effect of being searched and/or arrested is negative (model 4).
- Adding satisfaction with the stop (model 3), we find that unsatisfactory stops are strongly associated with lower levels of trust. Even those who are 'fairly satisfied' with the way the police acted have, on average, less trust in police effectiveness than those who did not experience a stop at all. However, being 'very satisfied' with the police is associated with a small but significant increase in this component of trust.
- For those searched and/or arrested, the METPAS allows assessment of the effect of individual's judgements of officer's fairness (model 5). Searches/ arrests experienced as unfair, or only somewhat fair, are strongly associated with lower levels of trust in police effectiveness. Those experienced as fully procedurally fair are not associated with higher levels of trust. It seems that, in relation to trust in police effectiveness at least, the best the police might hope for is to 'manage' such encounters, rather than expect the use of procedural justice to enhance trust.

Again, the importance of neighbourhood social characteristics is underlined. Even controlling for people's contact with the police, low trust in police effectiveness is associated with living in areas that are disorderly, that lack shared values and shared commitment to act on these values, and are (collectively) worried about crime.

Variation in trust in police fairness and intentions

What of the association between contact experiences and trust in police fairness and intentions? Thus far in this chapter we have considered trust in police effectiveness. Fitting comparable models, but this time explaining variation in the other aspect of trust (trust in procedural fairness and intentions), we find first that police-initiated contact does not explain any of the neighbourhood-level variation in trust in police fairness/intentions (see model 6 in Table 8.3). As before, area-level

Table 8.3 Police-initiated contact and trust in police effectiveness.

	Model 1	Model 2	Model 3	Model 4	Model 5	Model 6
	Coefficient	Coefficient	Coefficient	Coefficient	Coefficient	Coefficient
Intercept	1.47***	1.47	1.46***	1.47***	1.47***	1.46***
Person level (N=38,346)						
Female	0.00	−0.01	−0.01	0.00	−0.01	−0.01
Age	−0.20***	−0.21***	−0.22***	−0.22***	−0.22***	−0.22***
Age (squared)	0.02***	0.02***	0.02***	0.02***	0.02***	0.02***
Ethnicity (reference: White British)						
White – Irish	−0.14*	−0.13*	−0.14**	−0.14*	−0.14*	−0.14**
White – any other	0.07*	0.07*	0.07*	0.07*	0.07*	0.07*
Mixed – White and Black Caribbean	−0.17***	−0.16**	−0.16**	−0.16**	−0.16**	−0.16**
Mixed – White and Black African	−0.09	−0.09	−0.08	−0.09	−0.09	−0.08
Mixed – White and Asian	−0.13	−0.13	−0.13	−0.13	−0.13	−0.13
Other mixed	−0.02	−0.02	−0.01	−0.02	−0.02	−0.01
Indian	0.13***	0.13***	0.13***	0.13***	0.13***	0.13***
Pakistani	0.19***	0.19***	0.19***	0.19***	0.18***	0.19***
Bangladeshi	0.07	0.07	0.07	0.07	0.07	0.06
Other Asian or Asian British	−0.03	−0.02	−0.03	−0.03	−0.03	−0.03
Black or Black British – Caribbean	−0.26***	−0.25***	−0.25***	−0.25***	−0.25***	−0.24***
Black or Black British – African	0.02	0.03	0.03	0.03	0.03	0.03
Other Black or Black British	−0.09	−0.09	−0.09	−0.09	−0.10	−0.09
Chinese	0.06	0.07	0.05	0.07	0.06	0.06
Other Chinese or other ethnic group	0.25**	0.25**	0.24**	0.25**	0.25**	0.24**
Work status (reference: working full-time)						
Working part time (8–29 hrs/wk)	0.01	0.02	0.02	0.01	0.02	0.02
Working part time (less than 8 hrs/wk)	−0.05	−0.05	−0.04	−0.05	−0.05	−0.04
Not working	−0.10	−0.10*	−0.10*	−0.10*	−0.10*	−0.10*
House person	0.12***	0.12***	0.12***	0.12***	0.12***	0.12***
Retired	0.07	0.07	0.07	0.07	0.07	0.07
Registered unemployed	0.02	0.02	0.02	0.02	0.02	0.02
Unemployed but not registered	−0.32**	−0.31**	−0.30**	−0.31**	−0.30**	−0.29*
Student/full time education	−0.09*	−0.10*	−0.09*	−0.09*	−0.09*	−0.09*
Working status (other)	−0.03	−0.03	−0.04	−0.03	−0.03	−0.03
Housing situation (reference: own property outright)						
Buying on mortgage	0.24***	0.23***	0.23***	0.24***	0.23***	0.23***
Rented from council	0.11***	0.11***	0.11***	0.11***	0.11***	0.11***
Rented from housing association	0.39***	0.39***	0.39***	0.39***	0.39***	0.39***
Rented from private landlord	0.40***	0.39***	0.38***	0.39***	0.39***	0.38***
Tenure (other)	0.74***	0.74***	0.73***	0.74***	0.74***	0.74***

Continued overleaf

	Model 1	Model 2	Model 3	Model 4	Model 5	Model 6
	Coefficient	*Coefficient*	*Coefficient*	*Coefficient*	*Coefficient*	*Coefficient*
Household access to a car	−0.05**	−0.05**	−0.05**	−0.05**	−0.05**	−0.05**
Number of kids	−0.11***	−0.11***	−0.11***	−0.11***	−0.11***	−0.11***
Stopped by the police in past 12 months		−0.36***				
Very or completely dissatisfied with the police during the encounter			−1.40***			−0.94***
Fairly dissatisfied with the police during the encounter			−1.51***			−1.33***
Fairly satisfied with the police during the encounter			−0.35**			−0.33**
Very satisfied with the police during the encounter			0.27**			0.28**
Searched or arrested by the police in past 12 months				−0.68***		
No procedural justice in the search or arrest					−1.82***	−1.10***
Some procedural justice in the search or arrest					−0.66**	−0.32
Procedural justice					−0.06	−0.05
Neighbourhood level (N=4,747)						
Concentrated disadvantage	−0.05***	−0.05***	−0.05***	−0.05***	−0.05***	−0.05***
Residential stability	0.04***	0.04***	0.04***	0.04***	0.04***	0.04***
Immigrant concentration	−0.01	−0.01	−0.01	−0.01	−0.01	−0.01
Crime	−0.02	−0.02	−0.02	−0.02	−0.02	−0.02
Collective efficacy	−0.20***	−0.19***	−0.20***	−0.20***	−0.20***	−0.20***
Perceived disorder	−0.12***	−0.12***	−0.12***	−0.12***	−0.12***	−0.12***
Worry about crime	−0.17***	−0.17***	−0.17***	−0.17***	−0.17***	−0.17***
Between neighbourhoods variance	0.32	0.32	0.32	0.32	0.32	0.32
Within neighbourhoods variance	1.47	1.47	1.46	1.47	1.47	1.46

Note: unstandardised coefficients, * significant at the 5% level, ** significant at the 1% level, *** significant at the 0.1% level.

variation in this component of trust does not seem to be even partly due to variation in experiences of police-initiated contact across people living in different areas.

Turning to the association between contact and trust in police fairness and intentions, Table 8.4 shows that, holding constant a wide range of potentially confounding variables at both the individual and area level, we find that the overall association between being stopped by officers and trust in police fairness and intentions is again negative. Probing slightly more deeply, the results here echo those presented in Bradford *et al.* (2009a), in that the association between contact and this aspect of trust is slightly less asymmetrical than was the case for trust in effectiveness. Similar results to trust in police effectiveness are found with regard to being searched and/or arrested: being treated with

Table 8.4 Police-initiated contact and trust in police fairness and priorities.

	Model 1	Model 2	Model 3	Model 4	Model 5	Model 16
	Coefficient	Coefficient	Coefficient	Coefficient	Coefficient	Coefficient
Intercept	−0.31	−0.28	−0.19	−0.23	−0.18	−0.15
Person level (N=37,711)						
Female	0.52***	0.50***	0.46***	0.45***	0.42***	0.43***
Age	0.01	0.00	−0.02	−0.02	−0.03	−0.03
Age (squared)	0.00	0.00	0.00	0.00	0.00	0.00
Female age interaction	−0.22***	−0.21***	−0.20***	−0.20***	−0.19***	−0.19***
Female age (squared) interaction	0.02***	0.02***	0.02***	0.02***	0.02***	0.02***
Ethnicity (reference: White British)						
White – Irish	−0.02	−0.02	−0.03	−0.02	−0.02	−0.03
White – any other	0.13***	0.13***	0.13***	0.13***	0.13***	0.13***
Mixed – White and Black Caribbean	−0.14**	−0.14**	−0.13*	−0.14**	−0.13**	−0.13*
Mixed – White and Black African	0.02	0.02	0.03	0.02	0.02	0.03
Mixed – White and Asian	−0.22*	−0.22*	−0.21*	−0.22*	−0.22*	−0.21*
Other mixed	−0.35***	−0.35***	−0.34***	−0.35***	−0.35***	−0.34***
Indian	0.21***	0.21***	0.21***	0.21***	0.21***	0.21***
Pakistani	0.30***	0.30***	0.30***	0.30***	0.30***	0.30***
Bangladeshi	0.25***	0.25***	0.24***	0.24***	0.24***	0.24***
Other Asian or Asian British	0.10	0.10	0.10	0.10	0.10	0.10
Black or Black British – Caribbean	−0.15***	−0.15***	−0.13**	−0.15***	−0.14**	−0.13**
Black or Black British – African	0.14***	0.14***	0.15***	0.14***	0.15***	0.15***
Other Black or Black British	−0.08	−0.08	−0.08	−0.09	−0.09	−0.08
Chinese	0.39**	0.39**	0.37**	0.40***	0.38**	0.37**
Other Chinese or other ethnic group	0.23*	0.23*	0.22*	0.23*	0.23*	0.22*
Work status (reference: working full-time)						
Working part time (8–29 hrs/wk)	−0.01	−0.01	−0.01	−0.01	−0.01	−0.01
Working part time (<8hrs/wk)	−0.15	−0.14	−0.14	−0.15	−0.15	−0.14
Not working	−0.22***	−0.22***	−0.22***	−0.22***	−0.22***	−0.22***
House person	−0.06	−0.06	−0.06	−0.06	−0.06	−0.06
Retired	0.00	0.00	0.00	0.00	−0.01	0.00
Registered unemployed	−0.21***	−0.21***	−0.20***	−0.20***	−0.20***	−0.20***
Unemployed but not registered	−0.14	−0.14	−0.11	−0.13	−0.12	−0.11
Student/full time education	−0.10*	−0.10*	−0.09*	−0.10*	−0.09	−0.09
Working status (other)	−0.14	−0.14	−0.15	−0.14	−0.14	−0.15
Housing situation (reference: own property outright)						
Buying on mortgage	0.01	0.01	0.00	0.01	0.01	0.00
Rented from council	−0.10***	−0.10***	−0.10***	−0.10***	−0.10***	−0.10***
Rented from housing association	−0.21***	−0.21***	−0.21***	−0.21***	−0.21***	−0.21***
Rented from private landlord	0.06	0.06	0.05	0.06	0.05	0.05
Tenure (other)	0.36***	0.36***	0.37***	0.37***	0.37***	0.37***

Continued overleaf

	Model 1	Model 2	Model 3	Model 4	Model 5	Model 16
	Coefficient	*Coefficient*	*Coefficient*	*Coefficient*	*Coefficient*	*Coefficient*
Household access to a car	−0.24***	−0.24***	−0.24***	−0.24***	−0.24***	−0.24***
Number of kids	0.12***	0.12***	0.12***	0.12***	0.12***	0.12***
Stopped by the police in past 12 months		−0.20***				
Very or completely dissatisfied with the police during the encounter			−2.37***			−1.89***
Fairly dissatisfied with the police during the encounter			−1.11***			−0.94***
Fairly satisfied with the police during the encounter			−0.04			−0.02
Very satisfied with the police during the encounter			0.66***			0.65***
Searched or arrested by the police in past 12 months				−0.72***		
No procedural justice in the search or arrest					−2.28***	−1.04***
Some procedural justice in the search or arrest					−0.90***	−0.43
Procedural justice in the search or arrest					0.25	0.10
Neighbourhood level (N=4,741)						
Concentrated disadvantage	0.01	0.01	0.01	0.01	0.01	0.01
Residential stability	−0.01	−0.01	−0.01	−0.01	−0.01	−0.01
Immigrant concentration	−0.02*	−0.02*	−0.02*	−0.02*	−0.02*	−0.02*
Crime	−0.03*	−0.03*	−0.03*	−0.03*	−0.03*	−0.03*
Collective efficacy	0.96***	0.96***	0.95***	0.96***	0.95***	0.95***
Perceived disorder	0.12***	0.12***	0.12***	0.12***	0.12***	0.12***
Worry about crime	−0.04***	−0.04***	−0.04***	−0.04***	−0.04***	−0.04***
Between neighbourhoods variance	0.23***	0.23***	0.23***	0.23***	0.23***	0.23***
Within neighbourhoods variance	1.53***	1.53***	1.52***	1.53***	1.53***	1.52***

Note: unstandardised coefficients, * significant at the 5% level, ** significant at the 1% level, *** significant at the 0.1% level.

procedural justice is not associated with any higher or lower expected levels of trust, compared to not being stopped and/or arrested.

The positive estimated effect of stops that were well-handled by officers is important, and further underlined by an examination of single versus multiple police stops. Consider the possibility that the effects of being stopped only once in the past year may be different to the effect of being stopped multiple times. A total of 40,178 individuals had not been stopped (whether on foot or in their car) by the police; 503 individuals had been stopped once; 162 individuals had been stopped twice; 70 individuals had been stopped 3 to 9 times; and 43 individuals had been stopped 10 times or more. Further analysis showed that for people who had experienced multiple stops, being stopped by the police has a more negative effect (and the effects are more asymmetrical), compared to people who have had just one stop (Table 8.5).

Table 8.5 The effect of multiple encounters with the police.

	Stopped only once in the past year			Stopped more than once in the past year		
	Coefficient	95% confidence interval		Coefficient	95% confidence interval	
Very or completely dissatisfied with the police during the last encounter	−1.81***	−2.37	−1.25	−2.71***	−3.15	−2.28
Fairly dissatisfied with the police during the last encounter	−0.68*	−1.26	−0.10	−1.64***	−2.27	−1.01
Fairly satisfied with the police during the last encounter	0.22	−0.05	0.49	−0.63**	−1.04	−0.23
Very satisfied with the police during the last encounter	0.71***	0.47	0.94	0.54**	0.19	0.89

Note: * significant at the 5% level, ** significant at the 1% level, *** significant at the 0.1% level.

Summary

The findings presented in this chapter replicate those of other studies. It seems that contact with the police may often damage trust. While there is certainly an asymmetry in the effect of contact on confidence, this is not total, and 'very satisfactory' contacts, in particular, are associated with higher levels of trust. By placing the individuals who experience contacts with police within the areas in which they live, we are able to home in more precisely on the relationship between contact and confidence, thus reducing the risk that the observed association between experience and opinion is due to extraneous factors (such as the differential distribution of police activity across London).

Comparing back to the models shown in Chapter 7, it is worth noting that including contact experiences does little to alter the coefficients of the other variables. Contact experiences do little to explain variation in trust by ethnic group or, in particular, area characteristic. What this means precisely is difficult to say, although it certainly suggests that people who live in high collective-efficacy areas do not trust the police more because they have better quality – or simply fewer – contacts with officers.

Finally, again as found by previous studies (e.g. Bradford *et al.* 2009a), we note that trust in fairness and/or intentions appears to be more open to positive change. While even 'fairly satisfactory' contact is associated with lower trust in police effectiveness this is not the case for fairness and/or intentions, where a rather large degree of symmetry is apparent. Again we find an indication that procedural justice can increase public trust – a point we pick up later in the book when we connect trust in police fairness to institutional legitimacy and public cooperation.

9   A focus on a special population

Young males from Black and Minority Ethnic groups

This chapter moves away from our representative sample of Londoners. We examine the experience of police stops – as well as the correlations between how these encounters were experienced and subsequent trust in the police – among a particular collection of individuals. Focusing on young men from ethnic minority groups who live in diverse and mainly inner-London areas, we draw on a survey conducted in four London boroughs in the summer of 2010. The nature of the sampling precludes this survey from being seen as representative of the broader population. But it does provide a rich set of data concerning the knowledge, experiences and opinions of the police among a group (or set of groups) often believed to have very different views of the police than those from less disadvantaged or excluded groups.

The survey fielded many of the METPAS measures, but it also contained a number of additional questions around stop-and-search activity, as well as more precise measures of the experience of police procedural justice and trust in police procedural justice. Rates of contact are, unsurprisingly, higher than in the general population survey of London. Some 21 per cent of respondents reported being stopped by the police in the past year; 9 per cent reported having been searched and/or arrested (not necessarily as a result of being stopped). Individuals who reported being stopped by the police in the past year were asked why they were stopped. Respondents could give multiple answers, and Table 9.1 shows that the three most commonly cited reasons (aside from 'other') are 'because the police thought I had drugs', 'because of my appearance', and 'just for a chat'.

Respondents were also asked whether the officer(s) treated them in a procedurally fair manner during the encounter: were they given a reason for being stopped; were they told what was going to happen next; were they treated with respect; and were the police justified in stopping them. Given controversy over stop-and-search powers, it is indeed surprising how many individuals in our sample thought that the police acted in procedurally fair ways (Table 9.2). Around three-quarters (76 per cent) thought that they were given a reason for why they had been stopped (albeit that 40 per cent answered 'yes, to some extent'). Two-thirds (66 per cent) said that they were told what was going happen next (35 per cent said 'yes, to some extent') and said that they were treated with respect (38 per cent said 'yes, to some extent'). Strikingly, over one-half (58 per cent) said they thought the police were justified in stopping them.

Table 9.1 Why did people think they were stopped by the police? A focus on the booster sample.

	Not been stopped	*Stopped*
Reason for being stopped	808 (79%)	209 (21%)
Because they thought I had drugs		53
Other		48
Because of my appearance		30
Just for a chat		24
To inspect my vehicle		21
Because I matched the description of a suspect		20
Because of my race		19
To request my licence/tax disc/other documentation		15
Because they thought I had a weapon		13
Because of my religion		10
Because I was speeding		10
On suspicion that I had committed another traffic offence		9
Because they thought I had stolen property		6
To give advice/information		5
Because they thought I had the tools to commit a crime		5
Because they thought I had committed a crime		4

Note: respondents could choose multiple reasons. Total reasons chosen = 292.

Table 9.2 Perceptions of the procedural fairness of police treatment when stopped.

Do you feel that ...	*Not at all*	*Not really*	*Yes, to some extent*	*Yes, fully*	*Total*
you were given a reason for why you had been stopped?	12	38	82	73	205
you were told what would happen next?	26	45	71	63	205
you were treated with respect?	29	46	79	52	206
the police were justified in stopping you?	42	44	71	46	203

Recall that 9 per cent of the respondents reported being searched and/or arrested by the police over the past 12 months. These individuals were asked about police behaviour. Similar answer patterns are found. Individuals are least likely to think that the police were justified in searching and/or arresting them, even though just over one-third said that they were. Again around two-thirds of individuals said that they were given a reason why they had been stopped and/ or searched. Around two-thirds were told what would happen next (Table 9.3).

Table 9.3 Perceptions of the procedural fairness of police treatment when searched and/or arrested.

Do you feel that ...	Not at all	Not really	Yes, to some extent	Yes, fully	Total
you were given a reason for why you had been searched and/or arrested?	13	15	32	32	92
you were told what would happen next?	12	16	37	32	92
you were treated with respect?	16	20	35	21	92
the police were justified in searching and/or arresting you?	27	18	27	19	91

In the analyses presented below, we add experiences of stop-and-search into our fitted models, separately predicting (a) trust in police effectiveness, (b) trust in police procedural justice and (c) trust in police fairness and intentions. We create new variables that indicate whether someone had (i) been stopped and felt that they experienced no procedural justice from the officer(s) in question, (ii) been stopped and felt that they experienced some procedural justice from the officer(s) in question, and (iii) been stopped and felt that they had experienced procedural justice from the officer(s) in question.

As outlined above, there are four aspects to our measure of the perceived procedural justice of the encounter: that the respondent was given a reason; told what would happen next; were treated with respect; and that they saw the stop as justified in some way. A mean value was taken from the four variables among those who had been stopped (and separately, searched and/or arrested), where 'not at all'=0, 'not really'=1, 'yes, to some extent'=2, and 'yes, fully'=3. No procedural justice was defined as an average between 0 and 1.5, some procedural justice was defined as an average between 1.6 and 2, and procedural justice was defined as an average between 2.1 and 3.

Those who were stopped by the police during the past 12 months were also asked two further questions. First, what was their 'overall opinion of the police' prior to the experience? Second, what was their opinion of the police 'as a result of this experience'? Table 9.4 shows that around half of the 210 individuals said that they had 'mixed' opinions of the police prior to being stopped. Most of these individuals reported that they thought that their opinion was unchanged as a result of their experience. Of the one-quarter of individuals who had a 'generally low' opinion of the police prior to being stopped, most reported having a 'worse opinion' as a result of the experience or their opinion being 'unchanged'.

Vicarious experience of the police

So far in this book we have shown that direct encounters with the police are strong predictors of trust in the police. Especially important is whether people

Table 9.4 Perceptions of the effect of being stopped by the police.

Overall opinion of the police as a result of this experience ...	Overall opinion of the police prior to this experience				
	Generally high	Generally low	Mixed	No opinion	Total
unchanged	13	26	75	18	132
better opinion	2	5	11	0	18
worse opinion	3	20	14	1	38
Don't know	1	1	3	17	22
Total	19	52	103	36	210

are satisfied with how the police treat them. Yet indirect encounters with the police may be just as important. Experience of the police is unlikely to be limited to direct personal contacts. People will often see officers interacting with other people (perhaps their friends and family) in the areas in which they live, and vicarious experiences have been shown to be an important predictor of public opinions of the police in the US (Miller *et al.* 2004; Rosenbaum *et al.* 2005). Our survey contained a number of question aimed at investigating these issues. Respondents were asked whether they had ever seen police officers being rude or violent, or whether anyone in their household had seen these behaviours.

Table 9.5 shows that most people had not personally seen a police officer talk to someone in a rude manner or use unjustified physical force. Still, around one-fifth of respondents said that they had. Similarly, one-fifth of respondents said that someone in their household had witnessed such police behaviour.

Table 9.5 Vicarious experience of police misconduct.

Percentages	Never	Once	Twice	Three times or more
Have you personally ever seen an MPS officer talk to anyone in a manner that was rude?	77%	10%	4%	10%
Have you personally ever seen an MPS officer use physical force against anyone, which you thought was unjustified?	81%	9%	3%	6%
Apart from your own experiences, has anyone in your household ever seen an MPS officer talk to anyone in a manner that was rude?	79%	4%	2%	3%
Apart from your own experiences, has anyone in your household ever seen an MPS officer use physical force against anyone, which you thought was unjustified?	82%	3%	1%	2%

Variation in trust in police effectiveness

Armed with these insights into the experiences of our special population, we now turn to the modelling of trust among our BME sample. An important preliminary step is to add the indirect experience variables one at a time. Adding these factors allows us to assess whether controlling for some experiences means other experiences lose substantive and/or statistical significance (because the experiences cluster among individuals and are mutually predictive of trust). Not shown here – but please contact the first author for more details – we find that when each individual indirect experience is added on their own, they are separately predictive of lower trust. Seeing a police officer talking to someone in a rude manner, seeing a police officer using unjustified physical force, having someone in the household who has seen an officer talking to someone in a rude manner, and having someone in the household who has seen an officer using unjustified physical force – when considered separately, these are all associated with lower trust in police effectiveness. But once the four experiences are added in one model, personally having seen a police officer using unjustified physical force is the only factor that explains variation. This is therefore included in the proceeding models.

Table 9.6 shows the results of a series of models in which the outcome variable is trust in police effectiveness. Note that there are no statistically significant differences in trust comparing different ethnic groups (also note that age, housing status, work status and borough were also added, and were generally insignificant predictors). Experiencing a police stop is again associated with a lower level of trust in police effectiveness (model 3). The association between having been searched and/or arrested and lower trust in police effectiveness was even stronger (model 5). Probing slightly more deeply, it is obvious that a perceived lack of police fairness is behind the overall association. Looking at the stop data (model 4), stops experienced as procedurally unfair has a very strong and substantively large negative association with trust. Stops with 'some' procedural fairness has a slightly weaker but still substantial negative impact. But 'fair' stops have no significant statistical effect on trust in police effectiveness.

Searches and/or arrests demonstrate a similar pattern. Note that these results imply total asymmetry. Only those stops experienced in a very positive way are not associated with more negative views and these are, themselves, not associated with greater trust. We can only speculate on the reasons for this. It might be that experience of multiple stop-and-searches, at both an individual and group level, has severely undermined the potential for positive police behaviour (that is, treating people fairly) to enhance trust.

Variation in trust in police procedural justice

As with trust in police effectiveness, we add indirect experience variables one at a time. This allows us to assess whether controlling for some experiences means other experiences lose substantive and/or statistical significance. Not shown here – but again, please contact the first author – we find that when each individual indirect experience is added on their own, they are separately predictive of lower

Table 9.6 Explaining variation in police effectiveness in the booster sample.

	Model 1	Model 2	Model 3	Model 4	Model 5	Model 6
	Coefficient	Coefficient	Coefficient	Coefficient	Coefficient	Coefficient
Intercept	2.54	1.81	2.05	2.64	2.75	2.72
Ethnicity (reference: White and Black Caribbean)						
White and Black African	−0.84	−0.95	−0.82	−0.94	−0.84	−0.92
White and Asian	−1.12	−1.13	−1.07	−1.10	−1.08	−1.09
Any other mixed background	0.22	0.17	0.22	0.11	0.17	0.12
Indian	0.18	0.02	0.13	0.09	0.17	0.11
Pakistan	0.03	−0.17	−0.04	−0.06	0.03	−0.04
Bangladeshi	−0.06	−0.28	−0.14	−0.19	−0.08	−0.18
Any other Asian background	0.09	−0.06	0.09	−0.02	0.08	−0.01
Caribbean	−0.46	−0.65	−0.53	−0.53	−0.44	−0.50
African	−0.06	−0.14	−0.05	−0.12	−0.05	−0.10
Any other Black background	0.55	0.64	0.66	0.55	0.56	0.55
Chinese	0.61	0.49	0.60	0.49	0.58	0.51
Any other ethnic group	−0.71	−0.78	−0.67	−0.78	−0.70	−0.76
Seen a police office act in a violent manner	−0.46***			−0.40***	−0.40***	−0.38***
Stopped by the police, experienced no procedural justice		−1.25***		−0.89**		−0.73*
Stopped by the police, experienced some procedural justice		−0.94**		−0.75*		−0.65
Stopped by the police, experienced strong procedural justice		−0.28		−0.01		−0.13
Searched/arrested by the police, experienced no procedural justice			−0.88		−0.53*	−0.24
Searched/arrested by the police, experienced some procedural justice			−0.57		−0.35	−0.18
Searched/arrested by the police, experienced strong procedural justice			−0.05		0.07	0.14
R-squared	9%	7%	7%	10%	10%	10%
N	974	974	974	974	974	974

Note: unstandardised coefficients,* significant at the 5% level, ** significant at the 1% level, *** significant at the 0.1% level.

trust. This is the same pattern found in trust in police effectiveness, but unlike trust in police effectiveness, when we add all four variables into the model, they are each a statistically significant additive predictor. Of particular note is the finding that having someone in the household who has seen an officer use unjustified physical force is associated with higher levels of trust, conditioning on the other three experiences (as well as age, ethnicity, work status, home status and borough). We proceed in our analyses with one variable from each of the personal and household experiences, for the sake of parsimony. We pick unjustified violence.

Table 9.7 shows the results of our modelling of trust in police procedural justice. Again we find few differences in levels of trust comparing our different ethnic groups. Once we control for stop-and-searches, having personally seen a police officer act in a violent manner is more important than having someone in the household having seen a police officer act in a violent manner. In the final model (model 6), we find that trust is on average lower among those people who were searched and arrested and felt that the officer treated them with no procedural justice. The effect of being stopped in the street is negative in model 2, but it loses some significance once other experiences are taken into account.

A note on variation in trust in police fairness and intentions

Recall that the METPAS did not field strong measures of trust in police procedural justice. In order to draw comparisons to the METPAS, we conduct the above analyses on trust in police fairness and intentions in the booster sample. We find that the findings lie somewhere between trust in police effectiveness in the booster and trust in police procedural justice. For example, the effects of police stops are somehow mid-way between the two.

Summary

This chapter – in common with other studies – has shown that the potential for stop-and-search contacts damaging trust in the police is strong and consistent. By contrast, the possibility of positive encounters of this type enhancing trust is weaker. Unlike the general METPAS sample, people in the BME sample almost always reacted badly to police-initiated contact.

When it comes to trust in the police it is not so much *who* you are but *where* you are and *what you experience* that seem to be important factors. While the patterns of social change sketched out in Chapters 3 and 4 may have undermined previous types of social stratification that influenced experiences and opinions of the police, it would foolish to suggest these no longer exist at all. Naturally, they may simply have changed form, shifting into new structures that are poorly captured by quantitative variables such as 'ethnic group'. More appositely, however, we might note that (sub)cultural factors are likely to continue playing a key role, for some groups at least. Among young men from ethnic minority groups, for example, it may be that being stopped by the police has achieved such social and cultural resonance that trust is almost certain to be damaged

Table 9.7 Explaining variation in police procedural justice in the booster sample.

	Model 1	Model 2	Model 3	Model 4	Model 5	Model 6
	Coefficient	Coefficient	Coefficient	Coefficient	Coefficient	Coefficient
Intercept	7.40***	5.97**	6.49**	7.53***	7.76***	7.71***
Ethnicity (reference: White and Black Caribbean)						
White and Black African	−1.08	−1.22	−1.04	−1.21	−1.08	−1.12
White and Asian	−0.71	−0.67	−0.42	−0.65	−0.49	−0.45
Any other mixed background	−0.23	−0.26	−0.22	−0.38	−0.31	−0.31
Indian	1.23**	0.97*	1.16**	1.09*	1.22**	1.17**
Pakistan	0.50	0.19	0.44	0.38	0.54	0.50
Bangladeshi	0.67	0.32	0.56	0.48	0.63	0.56
Any other Asian background	0.73	0.52	0.79	0.57	0.76	0.70
Caribbean	−0.20	−0.54	−0.27	−0.30	−0.12	−0.16
African	0.25	0.16	0.33	0.18	0.32	0.30
Any other Black background	−0.78	−0.56	−0.56	−0.76	−0.77	−0.79
Chinese	0.90	0.70	0.89	0.71	0.86	0.80
Any other ethnic group	0.09	−0.06	0.17	−0.03	0.16	0.11
Seen a police office act in a violent manner	−0.77***			−0.68***	−0.63***	−0.61***
Someone in the household seen a police officer act in a violent manner	−0.10*			−0.07	−0.07	−0.06
Stopped by the police, experienced no procedural justice		−2.10***		−1.42***		−0.64
Stopped by the police, experienced some procedural justice		−1.61***		−1.24***		−1.04**
Stopped by the police, experienced strong procedural justice		−0.73*		−0.25***		−0.44
Searched/arrested by the police, experienced no procedural justice			−2.18***		−1.57***	−1.29***
Searched/arrested by the police, experienced some procedural justice			−0.76**		−0.40	−0.15
Searched/arrested by the police, experienced strong procedural justice			−0.19		0.01	0.20
R-squared	27%	22%	24%	28%	29%	30%
N	958	958	958	958	958	958

Note: unstandardised coefficients,* significant at the 5% level, ** significant at the 1% level, *** significant at the 0.1% level.

irrespective of how the officers behave. Perhaps being consistently affected, and disadvantaged, by excessive police attention has created a distinct orientation toward the police among this group that places them apart from the majority.

The policy implications are clear. If police wish to enhance public trust within a section of the community with whom they have historical problematic relationships they should attempt to minimise stop-and-search activity. Equally, in as much as some such activity will always be necessary, much more effort is needed to manage such encounters in a suitable way. Police stops constitute only a small proportion of all contacts between police and public, however, and it is to the more numerous categories of public-initiated contact that we now turn.

10   Another type of contact
Reporting crime

In Chapters 8 and 9 we showed that police-initiated contacts – such as street-stops – seem to have a negative impact on both trust in police effectiveness and trust in police fairness and intentions. Some encounters were judged positively by the individuals involved, and in our general population survey of Londoners, positively received stop encounters are linked to higher average levels of trust (Chapter 8). Importantly, this does not seem to be the case for a special population of young males from Black and Minority Ethnic groups (Chapter 9), suggesting that these encounters are more fraught and more adversarial than the sorts of interactions that the average person in London tends to have with officers.

Looking across the literature, there is a good deal of evidence that personal contact with officers – particularly when people are stopped by the police – powerfully affects an individual's trust in the police (Skogan 2006; Tyler and Fagan 2008; Bradford *et al.* 2009a; Myhill and Bradford 2011; Mazerolle *et al.* 2012). But police-initiated contacts are only one type of contact that people have with the police. The most common form of contact between police and public is one in which a member of the public has approached the police for assistance or advice, or to exchange information. For instance, the British Crime Survey regularly reports that more than twice as many people experience contact with the police after initiating it themselves than do so via a police-initiated encounter. While many of these contacts will be entirely mundane – asking directions, making some other enquiry or simply passing the time of day   others will be made at difficult or stressful moments for the individual concerned. They may have been the victim of a crime; they may have seen something they found distressing; they may have been caught up in events that effectively force them into contact with the police; and in a small minority of cases matters of life and death will be at stake.

Just as police-initiated contacts provide a moment in which trust in the police is tested, so do the more numerous public-initiated contacts. When considering such contacts, many of the points raised in Chapters 8 and 9 resurface, not least because research has consistently found an association between recent self-initiated contact with the police with trust or confidence in the police. Because of the asymmetry in the effect of contact on trust, the net effect seems to be negative. And again it appears that, on average, personal experience damages trust in police. Equally, there is much to suggest that the police 'service' received by those who initiate contact with officers will vary according to the area in which they live.

There may, however, be some important differences between the two types of police–public encounters. Recent studies have started to delve deeper into the relationship between self-initiated contact and trust in the police. Using METPAS data, Bradford *et al.* (2009a) found that satisfactory self-initiated contact did have a small but significant positive association with trust in police fairness and community engagement. Using panel data, Myhill and Bradford (2011), found that the relationship between contacts initiated by victims of crime and, in particular, those initiated by individuals for reasons other than victimisation, were rather *symmetrical* in their effect on overall confidence in the police.

What aspects of contact are most important to people? A significant body of research on and around the notion of procedural justice highlights the critical role of fairness and the transparency of the procedures used by officers. For example, a study of Londoners conducted ten years ago found that the main cause of dissatisfaction with police contacts among crime victims was the perceived lack of fairness, interest and effort on the part of officers, rather than lack of a 'result' (Fitzgerald *et al.* 2002). This is consistent with the findings of a number of US studies (e.g. Tyler 2001; Engel 2005; Tyler and Fagan 2008; see also Mastrofski *et al.* 1996, 2002; McCluskey *et al.* 1999; McCluskey 2003). Members of the public appear to prioritise behaviours such as dealing with matters promptly, listening to those involved, following correct procedure and, in some sense, offering some concrete help (even if this does not end in a 'result'). These behaviours communicate both the seriousness with which the situation is taken, and therefore of the status of those involved, *and* the competence of the police, its ability to do the job with which it is tasked. According to Skogan (2006: 104):

> One consistent finding is that victims are less 'outcome'-oriented than they are 'process'-oriented – that is, they are less concerned about someone being caught or (in many instances) getting stolen property back, than they are in how promptly and responsibly they are treated by the authorities. Police are judged by what physicians might call their 'bedside manner'. Factors like how willing they are to listen to people's stories and show concern for their plight are very important, as are their politeness, helpfulness and fairness. Rapid response has positive effects as well.

The importance of procedural justice in victims' encounters with the police is underlined by Elliott *et al.*'s (2011) study. Interviewing around 100 victims of crime in Australia, they found support for the importance of participation in the process, quality of interpersonal treatment, neutrality of decision-making and trustworthiness in outcome acceptance and legitimacy. They also employed qualitative probing to explore the meaning that individuals attached to different aspects of procedural justice, and analysis of open-ended elaboration supported the validity of a group value model (Lind and Tyler 1988; Tyler and Lind 1992): namely that procedural justice communicates to individuals value and status in society.

Research on the experience of Victim Support services among crime victims also underlines the importance of the procedural aspects of individual's treatment by criminal justice authorities (Bradford 2011a). Because Victim Support is a charity that offers emotional and practical help to those affected by crime, it is well placed to offer them a voice, explain to them what is going on, and give them a sense that they are valued recipients of the 'services' of the criminal justice system. Satisfaction with Victim Support services is linked to both a more favourable opinion of the way the police handled the case and to higher levels of trust in the criminal justice system as a whole (ibid.). Because Victim Support has no role in the detection and sanctioning of crimes, these effects are by definition independent of the actual outcome of the case. The findings once again affirm that it is the process through which people are treated that is key.

In this chapter we examine the association between self-initiated contact with police and levels of trust. As with prior chapters, we use multilevel modelling to unpack individual and area-level effects. Considering the association between this type of contact and trust, we examine whether variation in contact across London can explain any of the area-level variation in trust, and we estimate the effect of victimisation itself on trust in the police. It is a consistent, if arguably counter-intuitive, finding of research into public opinions of the police that the mere fact of victimisation is not very strongly associated with variation in judgements. As might be expected, there is usually some link between victimisation, trust and (lower) confidence (e.g. Bradford *et al.* 2009a; Walker *et al.* 2006). But much of the association seems explained not by the mere fact of victimisation but to what happened after in terms of police response. The reason for this apparently strange aspect of the public trust in the police is in fact probably simple – people do not blame the police for crime (Walker *et al.* 2006; c.f. Jackson and Bradford 2009), nor do they necessarily expect the police to solve all the crimes that are brought to their attention (Myhill and Bradford 2011). As previous work suggests, it is rather disorder and possibly anti-social behaviour that are more important to people when they think of the links between policing, crime and order (Jackson *et al.* 2009).

We add to this literature by capitalising on the size of the METPAS dataset. Looking at the associations between trust and victimisation across a whole range of crime types, we do not expect to find consistent links between being a victim of crime and lower trust in the police. But it might be that the general picture masks effects from specific types of victimisation. By adding victimisation to the models of trust, we are also able to investigate the possibility that some of the area-level variation in trust described in Chapter 7 is explained by variation in the experience of crime victimisation.

Finally, we look again at the effect of vicarious experience on trust in the police. A number of studies have found the effects of second-hand experiences to be powerful predictors of trust in the police (e.g. Rosenbaum *et al.* 2005). But what is the effect of vicarious victimisation? Does hearing about friends, family or neighbours' experiences of crime affect people's trust in the police?

Victimisation, public-initiated contacts and trust in police effectiveness

Variation in trust in police effectiveness

Table 10.1 takes the model of trust in police effectiveness developed in Chapter 5 and adds victimisation and public-initiated contacts. We present here an edited version of the table (the full model can be obtained from the first author). We should note at the outset that the effect of adding the different experiences is more incremental than is shown in Table 10.1. One at a time we added victimisation, satisfaction with the police when they came to hear about the victimisation, whether someone in the family or household has been a victim, satisfaction with the police about a crime that they have witnessed, and satisfaction with the police when they have contacted them for information. Importantly, we found that the effects of the socio-demographics barely changed as the model was built up. However, the effects of the contact variables tended to decrease slightly. This suggests that experiences with the police do tend to cluster within individuals.

Table 10.1 Explaining variation in police effectiveness in London: adding victimisation and police-initiated contact.

	Model 1	Model 2	Model 3
	Coefficient	Coefficient	Coefficient
Intercept	8.80***	8.85***	8.81***
Person level (N=38,346)			
Very or completely dissatisfied with the police during a stop encounter	−0.78***	−0.76***	−0.61**
Fairly dissatisfied with the police during a stop encounter	−1.19***	−1.09***	−1.00***
Fairly satisfied with the police during a stop encounter	−0.10	−0.14	−0.11
Very satisfied with the police during a stop encounter	0.38***	0.35***	0.35***
No procedural justice during search/arrest (explained reasons, explained procedure, treated with respect)	−0.91***	−0.86***	−0.75**
Some procedural justice during search/arrest (explained reasons, explained procedure, treated with respect)	−0.05	−0.07	0.03
Procedural justice during search/arrest (explained reasons, explained procedure, treated with respect)	0.00	−0.04	−0.04
Victimisation in past 12 months: Car theft or things stolen from a car	−0.10	−0.04	0.03
Damage to a car	−0.36***	−0.31***	−0.22***
Bike stolen	−0.26***	−0.26***	−0.18**
Burglary or attempted burglary	−0.16*	−0.12	−0.03
Vandalism or things stolen from their garden	−0.44***	−0.40***	−0.29***
Mugging	−0.12	−0.07	0.01
Pickpocket	−0.17	−0.19*	−0.14

	Model 1	Model 2	Model 3
	Coefficient	Coefficient	Coefficient
Violent crime	−0.39***	−0.31**	−0.26**
Attempted violence	0.03	0.02	0.15
Harassment	−0.56***	−0.44***	−0.24***
Domestic violence	0.13	0.07	0.08
Hate crime	−0.09	−0.02	−0.02
Other victimisation	−0.46***	−0.37***	−0.22*
Police came to hear about victimisation: Completely dissatisfied (ref: no contact)		−1.53***	−1.28***
Very dissatisfied		−1.31***	−1.11***
Fairly dissatisfied		−0.98***	−0.82***
Neither satisfied nor dissatisfied		−0.37***	−0.30**
Fairly satisfied		−0.11	−0.12
Very satisfied		0.46***	0.47***
Completely satisfied		0.84***	0.57***
Heard about someone in neighbourhood being victim			−0.44***
Someone in family been a victim			−0.23***
Contacted the police about a crime you witnessed: Completely dissatisfied (ref: no contact)			−1.25***
Very dissatisfied			−0.92***
Fairly dissatisfied			−0.34
Neither satisfied nor dissatisfied			−0.52**
Fairly satisfied			−0.15
Very satisfied			0.03
Completely satisfied			0.77***
Contacted the police for information: Completely dissatisfied (ref: no contact)			−0.93***
Very dissatisfied			−1.08***
Fairly dissatisfied			−0.98***
Neither satisfied nor dissatisfied			−0.31***
Fairly satisfied			−0.05
Very satisfied			−0.07
Completely satisfied			0.76***
Neighbourhood level (N=4,747)			
Concentrated disadvantage	−0.05***	−0.05***	−0.05***
Residential stability	0.04***	0.04***	0.05***
Immigrant concentration	−0.01	−0.01	−0.01
Crime	−0.02	−0.03	−0.02
Collective efficacy	−0.22***	−0.23***	−0.23***
Perceived disorder	−0.11***	−0.11***	−0.10***
Worry about crime	−0.17***	−0.17***	−0.17***
Between neighbourhoods	0.32***	0.32***	0.31***
Within neighbourhoods	1.45***	1.45***	1.43***

Note: unstandardised coefficients,* significant at the 5% level, ** significant at the 1% level, *** significant at the 0.1% level.

Several findings in Table 10.1 are of note. First, we asked respondents about their experience of crime over the past 12 months of interview, ranging from property to personal, including identity-based victimisation. Having been a victim of property crime, violent crime, harassment or 'other' is associated with lower levels of trust in police effectiveness. These associations appear to be robust to reactions to the way the police dealt with the matter (see model 2), although the effect of victimisation does decrease once we take into account satisfaction with 'the way the police handled the matter. These findings seem to complicate the idea – described above – that there are only rather weak associations between victimisation and trust in the police.

Second is the extent of the symmetry in association between self-initiated contact and this type of trust. All else being equal, those who had satisfactory contacts as victims[1] are considerably more likely to report higher trust in police effectiveness than those with no such contact. Those with unsatisfactory contact are much less likely to do so. While the extent of this symmetry is not replicated across contacts initiated by witnesses, or to ask the police for information, even here 'complete' satisfaction is quite strongly associated with higher odds of trusting the police to be effective.

Third, the statistical effects of vicarious victimisation – hearing about someone in the neighbourhood being victimised, or having a family member fall victim to crime – are as large as being directly victimised oneself. The relevance to trust in the police of stories and experiences that circulate in people's communities and circles of friends and families is again underlined.

Variation in trust in police fairness and priorities

Table 10.2 shows results from a series of models predicting trust in police fairness and intentions. There are some interesting differences between these models and those predicting trust in police effectiveness shown in Table 10.1. First, the associations between victimisation and trust are weaker. Only the experience of damage to one's car and harassment are consistently associated with lower trust in police fairness and intentions. Given the strength of the association between this component of trust and overall measures of confidence, this finding may explain why studies looking at the latter find only weak associations between victimisation and confidence in the police. Indeed, it is hardly surprising that the experience of victimisation does not, at least in any straightforward way, lead to a feeling that the police are unfair; although it might affect people's sense that the police are engaged with and act on things that are important to them.

Second, the statistical effects of public-initiated contact on this component of trust are even less asymmetrical than is the case for trust in police effectiveness. While the symmetry is by no means total, even in regard to witness and 'information' contacts, positive contacts are quite strongly associated with higher levels of trust. In Chapter 4 we suggested that the effect of contact on trust and confidence may have become more symmetrical over time. It certainly seems, on the basis of Table 10.2, that for at least some types of contact and some components

Table 10.2 Explaining variation in police fairness and priorities in London: adding victimisation and police-initiated contact.

	Model 1	Model 2	Model 3
	Coefficient	*Coefficient*	*Coefficient*
Intercept	−0.09	−0.02	
Person level (N=37,711)			
Very or completely dissatisfied with the police during a stop encounter	−1.78 ***	−1.74 ***	−1.59 ***
Fairly dissatisfied with the police during a stop encounter	−0.83 ***	−0.70 **	−0.63 **
Fairly satisfied with the police during a stop encounter	0.12	0.07	0.08
Very satisfied with the police during a stop encounter	0.71 ***	0.66 ***	0.58 ***
No procedural justice during search/arrest (explained reasons, explained procedure, treated with respect)	−0.95 ***	−0.87 ***	−0.74 **
Some procedural justice during search/arrest (explained reasons, explained procedure, treated with respect)	−0.26	−0.29	−0.09
Procedural justice during search/arrest (explained reasons, explained procedure, treated with respect)	0.13	0.06	0.06
Victimisation in past 12 months: car theft or things stolen from a car	−0.05	0.02	0.06
Damage to a car	−0.24 ***	−0.19 ***	−0.14 **
Bike stolen	0.00	0.00	0.01
Burglary or attempted burglary	−0.06	−0.05	0.00
Vandalism or things stolen from their garden	−0.20 ***	−0.16 **	−0.10
Mugging	−0.08	−0.03	0.01
Pickpocket	0.18	0.15	0.16
Violent crime	−0.28 **	−0.21 *	−0.18
Attempted violence	0.14	0.13	0.25 *
Harassment	−0.59 ***	−0.45 ***	−0.30 ***
Domestic violence	0.28 *	0.18	0.14
Hate crime	−0.28 *	−0.20	−0.20
Other victimisation	−0.36 ***	−0.29 **	−0.15
Police came to hear about victimisation: completely dissatisfied (ref: no contact)		−1.88 ***	−1.50 ***
Very dissatisfied		−1.62 ***	−1.30 ***
Fairly dissatisfied		−1.36 ***	−1.16 ***
Neither satisfied nor dissatisfied		−0.65 ***	−0.58 ***
Fairly satisfied		0.06	0.03
Very satisfied		0.74 ***	0.61 ***
Completely satisfied		1.34 ***	1.04 ***
Heard about someone in neighbourhood being victim			−0.10 ***
Someone in family been a victim			−0.18 ***
Contacted the police about a crime you witnessed: Completely dissatisfied (ref: no contact)			−1.67 ***
Very dissatisfied			−1.52 ***
Fairly dissatisfied			−0.74 ***
Neither satisfied nor dissatisfied			−0.89 ***
Fairly satisfied			−0.06

Continued overleaf

	Model 1	Model 2	Model 3
	Coefficient	*Coefficient*	*Coefficient*
Very satisfied			0.22
Completely satisfied			0.65 ***
Contacted the police for information: Completely dissatisfied (ref: no contact)			−1.64 ***
Very dissatisfied			−1.18 ***
Fairly dissatisfied			−1.48 ***
Neither satisfied nor dissatisfied			−0.76 ***
Fairly satisfied			0.03
Very satisfied			0.60 ***
Completely satisfied			0.76 ***
Neighbourhood level (N=4,741)			
Concentrated disadvantage	0.01	0.01	0.01
Residential stability	−0.01	−0.01	0.00
Immigrant concentration	−0.02 *	−0.02 *	−0.01
Crime	−0.03 *	−0.03 *	−0.03 *
Collective efficacy	0.93 ***	0.92 ***	0.91 ***
Perceived disorder	0.13 ***	0.12 ***	0.12 ***
Worry about crime	−0.04 ***	−0.04 ***	−0.03 ***
Between neighbourhoods	0.25 ***	0.25 ***	0.25 ***
Within neighbourhoods	1.52 ***	1.50 ***	1.48 ***

Note: unstandardised coefficients,* significant at the 5% level, ** significant at the 1% level, *** significant at the 0.1% level.

of trust, it is entirely possible for individuals to come away from encounters with officers with their trust in the police enhanced.

Finally, vicarious experiences are less important predictors of trust in police fairness and/or intentions than they are for trust in police effectiveness. There is still, however, a relatively strong association between hearing about crime second-hand and lower levels of trust – stronger, now, than that between actually experiencing a crime and trust.

Crime and public-initiated contact

Trust in police effectiveness and fairness and/or intentions appears to be influenced in subtly but importantly different ways by experiences of victimisation and of self-initiated contacts. The experience of being a victim of crime has a rather more consistent association with assessments of police effectiveness than with views about fairness and/or intentions. For some types of crime, at least, victimisation is linked on average to less favourable views about how effective the police are. In a sense this is reassuring – we might expect to find *some* association between experiences of crime and opinions of the police. Indeed, for some people it is likely that continued exposure to crime and repeated victimisation seriously undermines their trust in the police – their sense that it is effective in its core tasks and, indeed, that it understands and acts on their concerns. The findings reported above, however, concur with other studies in that – for most people, most of the time – direct experience of crime is not a particularly strong predictor of trust in the police.

Vicarious victimisation, by contrast, *is* a consistent predictor of lower levels of trust. While we do not have the data to explore this issue further, there are two possible explanations. It may be that stories about police behaviour in relation to the victimisation of friends, families and neighbours are key. As with personal contact, perhaps the effect of vicarious experiences is asymmetrical, leading to a net negative effect. People may pay less attention to positive stories about the police than they do to negative accounts. But it might also be that while specific instances of victimisation do not have a major impact on trust, a pervasive sense of crime, based in part on hearing about instances of victimisation within one's local area or social circle, does have such an effect. A general unease about crime may well undermine trust in the effectiveness of the police and the sense that it has its priorities right. More work is required on this issue, although at first glance a combination of both factors seems likely.

Self-initiated contact is again a consistent predictor of both components of trust. Yet the asymmetry of this effect is greater in relation to trust in police effectiveness than in relation to trust in fairness and/or intentions. Indeed, in the latter case the statistical effect of those contacts experienced by victims of crime approaches symmetry. As Bradford *et al.* (2009a) speculate, perhaps trust in police effectiveness can *only*, in most circumstances, be undermined by personal experience. After all, such experiences are often likely to arise because something has 'gone wrong': a crime committed or disorder experienced. Further, despite any effort the police make it is often unlikely that a firm outcome will be reached. So while people may be satisfied with what officers did, perhaps they are less likely to think the police as a whole effective. By contrast, the police can demonstrate fairness – or unfairness – whatever the outcome of an encounter, and success or failure in this regard will adhere to the organisation they represent.

Final words on Part 3

In Part 4 we turn to legitimacy, so this is a good time to make a few concluding comments on trust in the police. Chapters 5 to 10 built up a model of public trust in the police using the METPAS data. We also addressed the experiences and attitudes of young men from various Black and Minority Ethnic groups in London. The METPAS data allowed us to partition the variance into individual and neighbourhood levels. In trust in police effectiveness, an empty model indicated that 8 per cent of the variation was clustered at the neighbourhood level (Table 10.3 summarises the degree to which certain predictors help explain this clustering). The biggest factor is the social character of that neighbourhood. More important than contact with the police and structural characteristics of the neighbourhood (such as disadvantage and deprivation) in explaining neighbourhood variation is the level of disorder, fear of crime and whether residents share values and are willing are to act upon those values (to exert subtle, informal social controls on individuals).

Turning to trust in police fairness and intentions, an empty model indicates that 9 per cent of the variation was clustered at the neighbourhood level (Table 10.4). Even more than trust in police effectiveness, the biggest factor is the social character of that neighbourhood. Of particular importance is whether residents share values and are willing are to act upon those values (to exert subtle, informal social controls on individuals).

Finally, the evidence so far supports Tyler's procedural justice model of policing. We have focused on individual links between contact with officers and trust in the police as an institution. Do the police have the right intentions? Are the police competent to do what they are tasked to do in society? Trust refers to people's ideas about the performance of the police, but it also implies their understandings of the extent to which the police take into account their interests and act according to motives that are appropriate to their position in society. If they want to be trusted by members of the public, the police must demonstrate to people that they are trustworthy to act in ways that reflect effectiveness, fairness

Table 10.3 Neighbourhood variation in trust in police effectiveness: a summary so far.

	ICC	Variance explained (%)
Empty model	0.08	
Compositional	0.07	10
Structural characteristics	0.06	18
Social characteristics	0.05	38
Structural and social characteristics	0.05	41
Adding police-initiated contact	0.05	41
Adding victimisation and public-initiated contact	0.04	43

Note: ICC=intra-class correlation

Table 10.4 Neighbourhood variation in trust in police fairness and priorities: a summary so far.

	ICC	Variance explained (%)
Compositional	0.09	
Structural characteristics	0.09	5
Social characteristics	0.08	10
Structural and social characteristics	0.02	76
Adding police-initiated contact	0.02	76
Adding victimisation and public-initiated contact	0.03	71

Note: ICC=intra-class correlation

and a certain responsiveness to local needs, values and priorities (c.f. Stoutland 2001; Jackson and Sunshine 2007; Jackson and Bradford 2010).

Trust in the police is rooted not only in the contact that individuals have with the police (particularly the procedural justice demonstrated by officers in those encounters), but also in the particular neighbourhood social context in which an individual lives (particularly levels of collective efficacy, that is, the extent to which people share values and are willing to act according to those values for the collective good). Our findings thus support key aspects of Tyler's framework (Sunshine and Tyler 2003a). But they also open up new avenues on the social ecology of police–public relations (c.f. Sampson and Bartusch 1998; Kirk and Matsuda 2011; Kirk and Papachristos 2011). Let us turn, now, to police legitimacy.

Part 4

Why do people grant the police legitimacy?

In Part 4 we shift from public beliefs about the effectiveness, fairness and intentions of the police to the recognition and justification of power. Putting Tyler's procedural justice model of policing further to the test, we examine whether contact, trust and neighbourhood context predict felt obligation *to* police power and moral alignment *with* police power. We start with a definition, assessing in Chapter 11 the meaning and measurement of police legitimacy. Do police have the right to dictate appropriate behaviour? Do citizens feel a corresponding duty to obey? Are individuals willing to assist officers, to defer to their directives, to report crimes, identifying suspects and giving evidence in court?

In Chapter 12 we turn to variation in legitimacy across individuals and neighbourhoods. Addressing structural and social characteristics of the neighbourhood – as well as individual-level contact and victimisation experience – we assess the social ecology of police legitimacy. Incorporating neighbourhood structural and social characteristics into the multilevel model, we examine whether felt obligation and moral alignment are – above and beyond any influence of trust in the police as an organisation – also a function of deprivation, residential stability and so forth. Structural disadvantage and the problems faced by people living in high-crime areas may exert an influence on obligation and moral alignment. The social context of civility, cohesion, collective efficacy and felt threat of crime may shape obligation. Perhaps the associations between contact, trust and legitimacy even 'go away' once we adjust for important neighbourhood influences?

Throughout we add trust to the fitted models. We thus examine whether trust in police acts as a mediator in the association between certain prior factors and legitimacy. We address whether the effects of neighbourhood context and police contact on legitimacy are direct (that is, they bypass trust), indirect (that is, they flow through trust), or both. What happens if the effect of neighbourhood – for example, living in a deprived area with low levels of collective efficacy – on legitimacy is mediated through trust? If the context shapes trust which then shapes legitimacy, we might conclude that legitimacy is being damaged via a specific sense of police neglect: namely, that the police seem (partly because of the neighbourhood in which an individual lives) less trustworthy to do their job effectively, less trustworthy to treat people fairly, and less trustworthy to take into account the interests and motives of citizens.

So, let us consider first the nature of police legitimacy.

11 What is police legitimacy?

At its most general, legitimacy is a kind of auxiliary process that explains the stability of 'any structure at any level that emerges and is maintained by other basic social processes' (Zelditch 2001: 40). Any social structure must, by definition, be in some sense legitimate if it is to function and be viable in the long term (Tyler 2006b). Institutions, practices and arrangements must, in order to develop, operate and reproduce effectively, be seen as right and proper by those who are subject to them.[1]

Legitimacy is a vital component of social institutions, practices and arrangements, not just in the long run for the very survival of institutions, but also on a day-to-day basis. Applied to the criminal justice system, the concept of legitimacy concerns notions of power, authority and justification. As the right to rule and the recognition by the ruled of that right (Beetham 1991; Coicaud 2002), the legitimacy of justice institutions is bound up with the right to be recognised, to have remit over a certain area of life (Habermas 1979), to command and to be obeyed (Weber 1978; Tyler 1990). People defer to – and cooperate with – legitimate legal authorities because they feel it is the right thing to do (Sunshine and Tyler 2003a, 2003b).

Police legitimacy

Legitimacy is the foundation of police authority (Tyler 2011a, 2011b). A legitimate police force demonstrates to citizens (a) why its access to and exercise of power is rightful, and (b) why those subject to its power have a corresponding duty to obey (Tyler 2006a). For Tyler, legitimacy is primarily the feeling of obligation to voluntarily defer to the police (Tyler 2006a, 2006b). Such deference is not due to fear of sanction, nor is it due to personal morality regarding the law. Importantly, it extends instead out of a responsibility to obey the authority of legal rules and law enforcement agents. Legitimacy results from the authorisation of authorities to determine appropriate behaviour; this authorisation removes the need to activate one's own moral principles. We obey an authority because *that* is the right thing to do.[2]

Legitimacy activates self-regulatory mechanisms; Kelman and Hamilton (1989) refer to legitimacy as 'authorization'. A person authorises an authority to determine appropriate behaviour within some situation, and then feels obligated to follow the directives or rules that authority establishes. According to these authors, the authorisation of actions by legitimate authorities

> seem[s] to carry automatic justification for them. Behaviourally, authorization obviates the necessity of making judgments or choices. Not only do normal moral principles become inoperative, but – particularly when the actions are explicitly ordered – a different type of morality, linked to the duty to obey superior orders, tends to take over.
>
> (Kelman and Hamilton 1989: 16)

The authorisation of the police emanates from relations between subordinates and authorities in social groups, with identification with authority generating the belief that the police are justified in expecting feelings of obligation and responsibility from citizens.

But police legitimacy may be instantiated not only in obedience as prerogative; it may also be partly based in the belief that the police broadly share one's moral values (c.f. Tankebe 2009: 1280–1). Hough *et al.* (2010) and Jackson *et al.* (in press) argue that a sense of shared moral values and subsequent group identity is part of the conferred right of the police to possess the right to govern. The idea that legitimacy has a normative, ideological or moral element is a position most forcibly outlined by Beetham (1991). Using as his starting point a critique of Weber, Beetham argues that the idea that legitimacy is purely a *belief* of the governed is not a tenable position, particularly when it is understood that such beliefs have no necessary connection to subjective or objective needs or preferences. Instead Beetham holds that those granting legitimacy always do so on the basis that it is an expression of common shared values. He suggests three dimensions which must each be fulfilled for a power to be considered legitimate: its conformity to a set of rules; the justifiability of these rules in terms of shared beliefs; and the expressed consent of those governed or otherwise affected by the power.

This approach has recently been applied to police legitimacy. Jackson *et al.* (2011) argue that three interlinked elements to legitimacy combine to form the belief that the police are 'appropriate, proper and just':

1   Obligation to obey and expressed consent: this is measured by asking people whether they would obey the directives of the police, *even if they disagreed with the specific directives*. A legitimate authority garners obedience from subordinates. People confer authority to the police and feel a corresponding duty to obey their instructions and fulfil the responsibilities that the police demand.
2   Moral alignment: this is measured by asking people whether they think the police are acting and making decisions in ways that accord with the values and morals of themselves and their community. This is not the recognition of power; the police are legitimised on the basis of consent and shared goals.
3   Legality: this is measured by asking people whether they believe that the police follow their own rules. A legitimate authority exercises that authority

according to established principles. People see the police as working under the rule of law – i.e. that the rules that govern conduct apply to all.

These dimensions are represented, first, by the extent to which the exercise of police power is perceived to adhere to the rules laid down for its use (which may not be rules in a legal sense but rather operate on a different basis, for example, morally); second, that these rules should be held as justifiable by those policed, that is, they should express some basic, common shared values; and third, that the legitimacy of the police will be expressed by the actions of those policed, in as much as they defer to police authority, comply with instructions and so on.

No one element is prioritised, but all must be present in the relationship between police and policed for the police to be legitimate. Legitimacy properly understood is not simply the right to be recognised as the appropriate institution with authority over a particular aspect of social life or set of problems (Habermas 1979), or 'largely unquestioned acceptance of authority' (Barker 2001: 33), although both are important. And if moral alignment is an important predictor of cooperation it follows that people cooperate with the police when this is an act consistent with their own moral values (c.f. Tyler and Blader 2005; de Cremer *et al.* 2010). Institutions can encourage cooperation by activating the ethical motivations that lead people to adhere to group rules and to act on behalf of the group (Tyler 1990; Tyler and Huo 2002). Moral alignment would thus provide an important additional normative force (beyond felt obligation to obey) that aids their efforts. Demonstrating that they are aligned with the values of individuals and communities, the police show their allegiance to the concept of 'policing by consent'; that is, that officers work closely with citizens to regulate social order.

Measuring legitimacy in the London survey

Police legitimacy may thus be partly present when people believe the police have authority (generating a corresponding duty to obey) but also present when people believe that the police act in accordance with a broad sense of shared moral values (generating a sense of justified power). Conferring legitimacy on an institution is to grant them the right to exist, the right to determine behaviour and the right to exert power. Legitimacy may not just be about feeling an obligation to obey, it is also a stance or act based on the expression of basic shared values. The belief that the police have an appropriate sense of right and wrong moves us from simple de facto 'recognition' of authority and minimal feelings of obligation (which may reflect an instrumental fear that if one did not obey officers, one would face particular consequences) toward a sense of shared moral purpose (rather than the interests of those who hold power). Rightly understood, authority is the restriction of behaviour for the sake of the collective good, and this collective good is defined according to shared moral values.

We assess the dimensionality and reliability of multiple indicators of felt obligation, moral alignment and intentions to cooperate. The first quarter of the 2009/2010 METPAS (n=5,120) fielded measures of legitimacy and cooperation with the police. Obligation to obey is measured using three questions (scale from 1 to 4, where 1='strongly agree' and 4='strongly disagree'):

- You should do what the police tell you to do even when you do not like the way they treat you;
- You should accept the decisions made by police, even if you think they are wrong;
- You should do what the police tell you to do even if you disagree.

Figure 11.1 presents the (weighted) frequencies. Around two-thirds of respondents agree with the three linked sentiments. Slightly more individuals agree with the statement that 'you should do what the police tell you to do even if you disagree'.

Moral alignment with the police was measured using three questions (scale from 1 to 4, where 1='strongly agree' and 4='strongly disagree'). These questions were designed to reflect the belief that the police share the values of the individual (and perhaps, by extension, the community), as demonstrated by how they act and the strength of social controls. The three items are:

- My own feelings about what is right and wrong usually agree with the law;
- The police can be trusted to make decisions that are right for people in my neighbourhood;
- The police usually act in ways that are consistent with my own ideas about what is right and wrong.

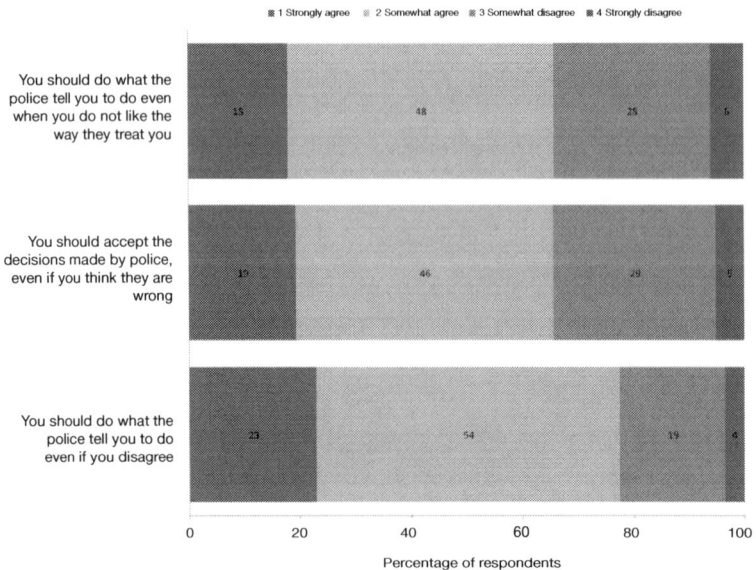

Figure 11.1 Felt obligation to obey the police in London.

Figure 11.2 presents the (weighted) frequencies. Similar proportions agree with each statement: somewhere between 85 per cent and 87 per cent.

Intention to cooperate with the police was measured using three questions (scale from 1 to 4, where 1='very likely' and 4='not at all likely'):

1   If the situation arose, how likely would you be to call the police to report a crime you witnessed?
2   If the situation arose, how likely would you be to report suspicious activity near your house to the police?
3   If the situation arose, how likely would you be to provide information to the police to help find a suspected criminal?

Figure 11.3 presents the (weighted) frequencies. Similar proportions agree with each statement. Just over half of respondents saying they were 'very likely' to do each of the behaviours.

As with trust, we use latent-variable modelling as the method for scaling. We test a series of statistical models to investigate the dimensionality of legitimacy and cooperation (using MPlus 5.2). These models specify legitimacy and cooperation in one of three different ways:

•   Model 1: one single underlying 'thing': spans felt obligation to obey the police, moral alignment with the police, and willingness to cooperate with the police and courts;

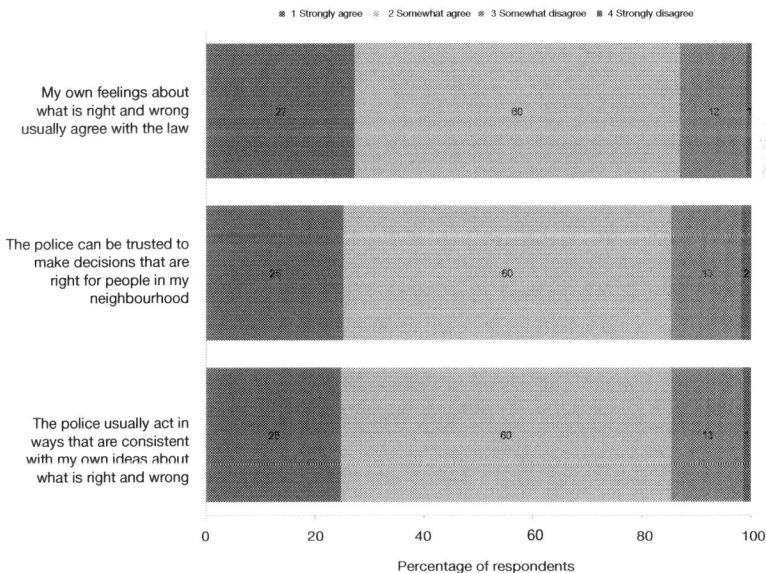

Figure 11.2 Moral alignment with the police in London.

156   *Why do people grant the police legitimacy?*

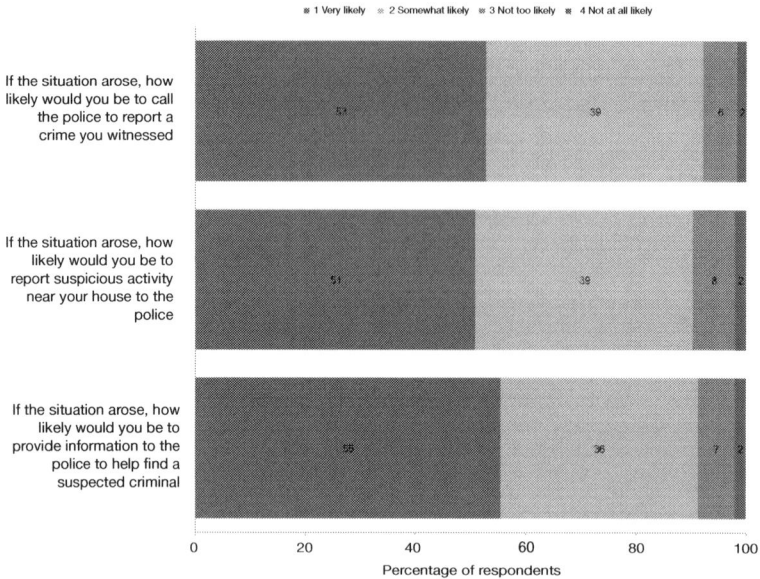

Figure 11.3 Willingness to cooperate with police in London.

- Model 2: two underlying 'things': (1) felt obligation to obey the police and moral alignment with the police; and (2) willingness to cooperate with the police and courts;
- Model 3: three underlying 'things': (1) felt obligation to obey the police; (2) moral alignment with the police; and (3) willingness to cooperate with the police and courts.

We also test a fourth model that includes not only obligation, moral alignment and cooperation, but also the three dimensions of trust. This allows us to test the empirical distinctiveness of trust, legitimacy and cooperation.

Results from the four models are shown in Table 11.1. Both exact and approximate-fit statistics suggest that model 1 and model 2 fit the data poorly. But model 3 fits well. People seem to distinguish between obligation to obey, moral alignment and willingness to cooperate; they are not merely reflections of one underlying construct. Model 4 also fits well, showing the distinctiveness of trust, legitimacy and cooperation.

Looking at the correlations between constructs from model 4, we see an especially high correlation between procedural fairness and shared interests ($r=0.92$), as well as a strong correlation between obligation to obey and moral alignment ($r=0.64$).

Figure 11.4 presents the factor loadings for model 3. The findings indicate that the scales have adequate reliability and the structure of the measurement model

Table 11.1 Fit statistics for one-, two- and three-factor confirmatory factor analysis solutions.

Model		χ^2	df	p	RMSEA	CFI	TLI
M1	One-factor	5,312	6	<0.0005	0.419	0.915	0.901
M2	Two-factors	3,551	6	<0.0006	0.342	0.943	0.934
M3	Three-factors	323	14	<0.0007	0.066	0.995	0.998
M4	Six-factors (with trust)	3,836	284	<0.0008	0.049	0.947	0.939

has some validity. This conclusion is strengthened by the fact that the factor loadings (validity coefficients) of the trust in effectiveness indicators are all statistically significant and of considerable magnitude.

Measuring legitimacy in the BME booster

The survey of young males from ethnic minority groups in London asked three questions about obligation to obey (note that the wording is slightly different, compared to the METPAS measures), one question about moral alignment and one question about the legality of the police. Figure 11.5 shows the topline findings. More people agreed with the statement 'you should obey the directives of the police if you consider their actions lawful' than the other statements (only 5 per cent disagreed). Of the three obligation questions, the one that people disagreed with the most was 'people like me have no choice but to obey the directives of the police' (28 per cent disagreed). Only 17 per cent disagreed with the moral alignment statement ('the police usually act in ways that are consistent with my own ideas of what is right and wrong'), and only 22 per cent disagreed with the legality statement ('when the police deal with people in my neighbourhood, they always behave according to the law').

Summary

In this chapter we have defined legitimacy as including not just felt obligation to obey but also a sense of moral alignment with the police (c.f. Hough *et al.* 2010; Jackson *et al.* in press). While legitimacy is conferred by citizens as well as systems (Hinsch 2008; Jackson *et al.* 2011), we focus in this book on the legitimacy that emanates from members of the public across London. We assume that police legitimacy is a latent property: it is the right to rule, the right to dictate appropriate behaviour and the justification of power. We cannot measure these 'things' directly, but we can access some of the structures of public opinion that help sustain and reproduce them. In our study, legitimacy is reflected in two sub-dimensions – obligation and moral alignment, and our analysis of the METPAS data suggests that these two sub-dimensions are analytically distinct (and they are empirically distinct from intentions to cooperate). They are also adequately measured by the multiple indicators at our disposal.

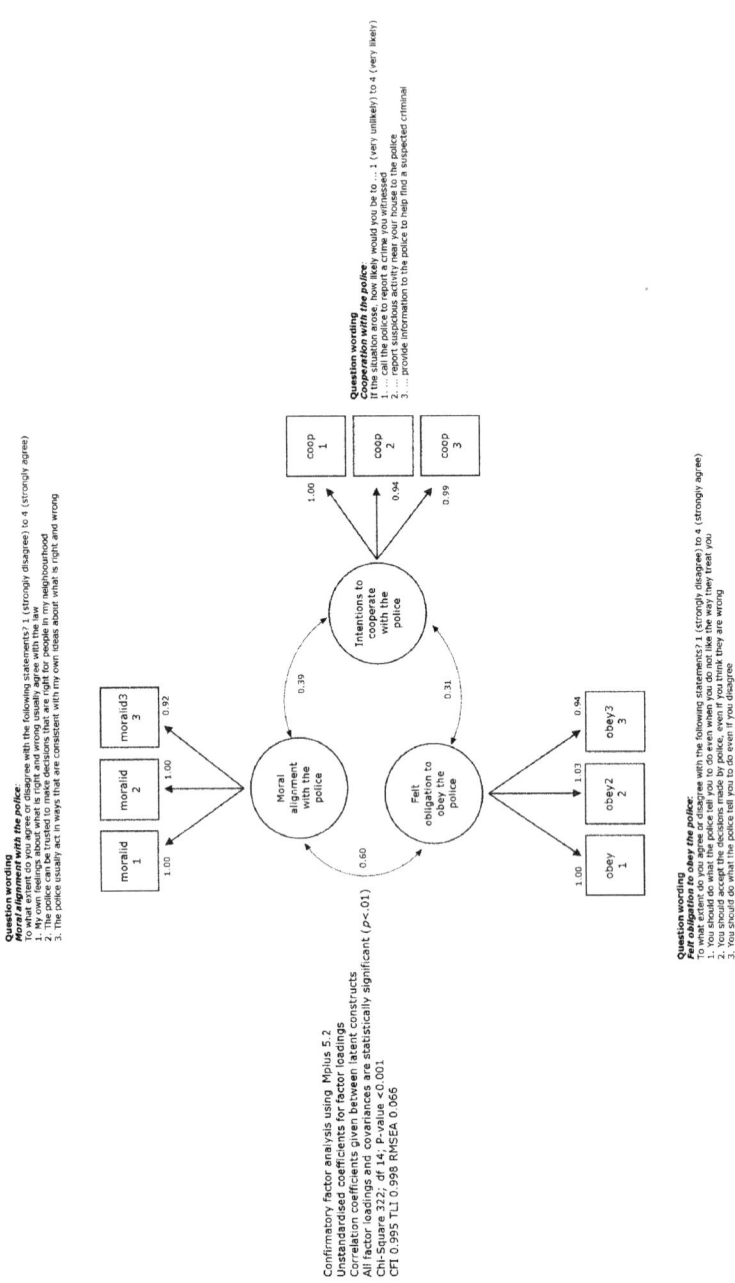

Question wording
Moral alignment with the police:
To what extent do you agree or disagree with the following statements? 1 (strongly disagree) to 4 (strongly agree)
1. My own feelings about what is right and wrong usually agree with the law
2. The police can be trusted to make decisions that are right for people in my neighbourhood
3. The police usually act in ways that are consistent with my own ideas about what is right and wrong

Question wording
Cooperation with the police:
If the situation arose, how likely would you be to ... 1 (very unlikely) to 4 (very likely)
1. ... call the police to report a crime you witnessed
2. ... report suspicious activity near your house to the police
3. ... provide information to the police to help find a suspected criminal

Confirmatory factor analysis using Mplus 5.2
Unstandardised coefficients for factor loadings
Correlation coefficients given between latent constructs
All factor loadings and covariances are statistically significant (*p*<.01)
Chi-Square 322; df 14; P-value <0.001
CFI 0.995 TLI 0.996 RMSEA 0.065

Question wording
Felt obligation to obey the police:
To what extent do you agree or disagree with the following statements? 1 (strongly disagree) to 4 (strongly agree)
1. You should do what the police tell you to do even when you do not like the way they treat you.
2. You should accept the decisions made by police, even if you think they are wrong
3. You should do what the police tell you to do even if you disagree

Figure 11.4 Measuring moral alignment, felt obligation and intentions to cooperate with the police: confirmatory factor analysis from the METPAS sample.

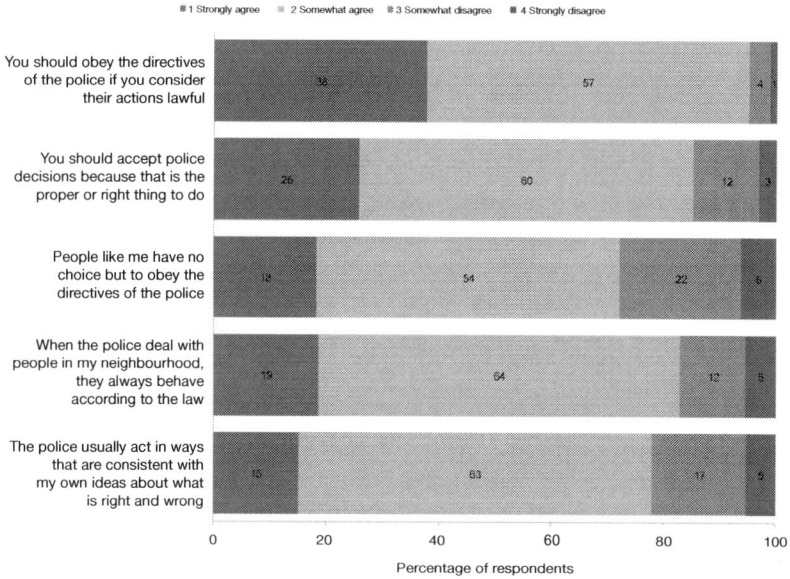

Figure 11.5 Willingness to cooperate with the police in the booster sample.

Our findings can be considered in the light of two recent US-based methodological studies (Reisig and Parks 2004; Gau 2011). Reisig and Parks (2004) examined scales of 'procedural justice' (analogous to our trust in police procedural fairness, for example, 'the police treat citizens with respect'), 'distributive justice' (e.g. 'the police enforce the law consistently when dealing with all people'), 'trust in the police' (e.g. 'the police can be trusted to make decisions that are right for your community') and 'obligation to obey' (analogous to our felt obligation, e.g. 'you should accept police decisions even if you think they are wrong'). They found that the scales generally worked well.[3] In similar methodological work, Gau (2011) provided evidence that 'trust in the police' and 'obligation to obey' should not be combined into one legitimacy scale. Importantly, she found that 'trust in the police' had considerable overlap with 'procedural justice' scales.

In this study we do not elide concepts of trust and legitimacy. We do not treat items like 'the police can be trusted to make decisions that are right for my community' as measures of people's recognition or justification of police power. Instead, we treat such items as beliefs about police competence and whether the police seem to have the right intentions towards citizens. When such items refer to the police understanding and responding to the needs of the community, we regard them as measures of 'trust in shared interests'. When such items refer to the police being fair, we regard them as measures of 'trust in police fairness' (in the METPAS) or 'trust in police procedural fairness' (in the BME survey). When such items refer to the police being effective, we regard them as measures of 'trust in police effectiveness'.

Our confirmatory factor analyses confirm the empirical distinctiveness of trust, legitimacy and cooperation. They also confirm the distinctiveness of obligation to obey and moral alignment (two sub-dimensions of police legitimacy). Gau (2011: 496) concludes that there is a strong 'need for further psychometric testing to determine just what, exactly, procedural justice and police legitimacy are and, just as importantly, are not'. Our approach is one way forward for police legitimacy research because it makes clear distinctions between trust and legitimacy, and it differentiates between the recognition of police power (consent to authority) and the justification of police power (shared values).

But analysis of concepts and measures are not enough. We want to use the data to shed light on variation in legitimacy. So let us turn to explaining heterogeneity in our two sub-dimensions of police legitimacy across individuals and neighbourhoods in London.

12 The social ecology of police legitimacy

Numerous studies – mostly conducted in the US – have treated trust, legitimacy, cooperation and compliance as individual attributes and psychological mechanisms (for example, Tyler and Huo 2002; Sunshine and Tyler 2003a; Tyler 2006a, 2006b; Tyler and Fagan 2008; Bradford *et al.* 2009a; Murphy *et al.* 2009; Jackson *et al.* 2011; Murphy and Cherney 2012). Thus far, however, no study has addressed the importance of neighbourhood context on police legitimacy, leaving an important gap in the literature on the possibly socially situated nature of this phenomenon. Might police legitimacy be shaped by the context and culture that is rooted at the level of the neighbourhood?

Yet, the utility of a sociological approach to people's attitudes towards the law has been amply demonstrated in the US literature. Exploring not police legitimacy but related public attitudes, a series of studies have linked neighbourhood characteristics to normative orientations to the law in Chicago. Focusing on public satisfaction with policing and legal cynicism (that is, the belief that the norms and rules enshrined in the laws of a society are not personally binding), the argument emanating from the work of Sampson and Bartusch (1998), Kirk and Matsuda (2011) and Kirk and Papachristos (2011) is, first, that concentrated disadvantage, segregation and institutional neglect breeds a more general sense of cynicism and distance from society. Second, aggressive policing clusters in certain neighbourhoods, generating antagonism among some of the residents. Third, neighbourhood residents talk and interact, and a sub-culture of legal cynicism and distrust in policing emerges partly as a result. Legal cynicism and satisfaction with policing is said to be shaped by sub-culture and contact that is 'augmented and solidified through communication and social interaction among neighbourhood residents' (Kirk and Papachristos 2011: 3).

Integrating psychological and sociological levels of analysis, we combine our earlier focus on individual-level correlations (between contact, trust, legitimacy and cooperation) with a new assessment of neighbourhood effects. We begin our empirical analysis of police legitimacy with a consideration of neighbourhood context. Examining whether residential stability, population homogeneity and economic conditions explain variation in Londoners' recognition and justification of police power (i.e. legitimacy), we hypothesise that intense disadvantage generates feelings of social segregation and isolation. In turn, this may encourage the belief that institutions have little influence over local life, combining with the declining significance of conventional norms to create alienation. In the void created, other norms and modes of conduct may develop – thereby eroding the sense that the police are a legitimate source of governance and appropriate conduct (Anderson 1999).

We also hypothesise that social characteristics of the neighbourhood are important. When subtle, informal social controls are strong, observers may conclude that the police are competent (Reiner 2010), that they have their best interests at heart (Jackson and Sunshine 2007), and that the legitimacy of formal agents of social controls is strong. People may invest greater legitimacy in the police when they live in a neighbourhood that already exerts strong normative pressures on the social value of regulation, orderliness and law-abidingness; conversely, poor social conditions may encourage the feeling that police power is not justified.

The first step in our modelling of police legitimacy is to address whether obligation to obey and moral alignment clusters at the neighbourhood level. As with trust, we show that neighbourhood is important; this emerges from our test of an empty model with no covariates. As with trust, we introduce key compositional factors – most notably gender, age, ethnicity, employment status and residential characteristics. We find that individual-level factors explain less of the neighbourhood clustering than the structural and social characteristics of the community. Of special importance here is the role of neighbourhood levels of collective efficacy in explaining the degree of people's moral alignment with the police. In a final step we add trust in the police to the fitted model.

We should note at the threshold, that we focus not on Lower Super Output Areas (LSOAs) but on a larger geographical unit of neighbourhood, Middle Super Output Areas (MSOAs). This means that our 4,500 individuals are clustered in 900 neighbourhoods rather than 2,500, thus increasing the within-cluster sample size. Please contact the first author for LSOA models, which show few substantive differences.

Obligation to obey the police

We begin by addressing variation in Londoners' feelings of obligation to the police. Table 12.1 presents the intra-class correlations (ICC) from five models. The first model is empty: it includes no covariates. Fitting this model indicates that 30 per cent of the variation occurs between neighbourhoods (the rest is random error and within-neighbourhood variation), indicating a strikingly large amount of neighbourhood homogeneity. It is noteworthy that this amount of clustering is much larger than it is for trust in police effectiveness (8 per cent of the variation is clustered at the neighbourhood level) and trust in police fairness and intentions (9 per cent of the variation is clustered at the neighbourhood level). It is also much larger than most neighbourhood effects studies in other substantive areas (for example, Brunton-Smith and Sturgis 2011).

The compositional model adds (as individual-level predictors) gender, age, ethnicity, work status, residential status, household vehicle access and number of children (Table 12.1). The ICC is hardly reduced (from 30 per cent to 29 per cent).

Consistent with our findings on trust in the police, neighbourhood clustering seems to be a function of ecological context rather than differential sample composition within localities.

The next step is to explain the noticeably large amount of between-neighbourhood variation. As with trust in the police (Chapter 7) we address whether particular (measurable) properties of neighbourhoods explain why residents of given localities view the police as more or less legitimate. Adding one at a time each of our four structural characteristics variables, we introduce concentrated disadvantage, residential stability, ethnic composition and levels of crime into the model. Building up the structural characteristics, Table 12.2 shows that the effects of concentrated disadvantage and ethnic composition do not change when the other characteristics are added to the equation (note that no individual-level predictors are included in the fitted models). The effects of residential stability and crime levels do, however, change. The effect of residential stability moves from 0.13** to 0.02. The effect of crime levels moves from 0.09 to –0.01. Table 12.2 shows that including all four structural characteristics variables into the model helps explain (with the compositional variables) 7 per cent of the between-neighbourhood variation.

Table 12.1 Neighbourhood variation in obligation to obey the police in London.

	ICC	Variance explained (%)
Empty model	0.30	
Compositional	0.29	2
Structural characteristics	0.28	7
Social characteristics	0.25	17
Structural and social characteristics	0.23	24
Structural and social characteristics and individual-level trust in the police	0.22	27

Note: ICC=intra-class correlation

Table 12.2 Explaining neighbourhood variation in obligation to obey the police: structural characteristics.

	Model 1	Model 2	Model 3	Model 4	Model 5
	Coefficient	*Coefficient*	*Coefficient*	*Coefficient*	*Coefficient*
Concentrated disadvantage	0.26***				0.21***
Residential mobility		0.13*			0.02
Ethnic composition			0.28***		0.24***
Crime levels				0.09	–0.01

Note: unstandardised coefficients,* significant at the 5% level, ** significant at the 1% level, *** significant at the 0.1% level.

Building up the social characteristics model in the same way, we find that the effects of collective efficacy and worry about crime are reduced once all three are added to the model (Table 12.3). Collective efficacy moves from 0.81*** to 0.52*** and worry about crime moves from –0.26*** to 0.10. At the neighbourhood level, then, it seems that day-to-day issues of disorder and social bonds are more important explanations of police authority than worry about crime. Together the social characteristics explain 17 per cent of the neighbourhood-level variation (Table 12.3).

Adding all the social and structural characteristics into the fitted model allows us to explain 24 per cent of the neighbourhood-level variation. Interestingly, adding individual-level trust in the police makes little difference to the explained neighbourhood variance. It follows that the composition of trust in the police in neighbourhoods does not explain the clustering of obligation to obey the police (conditioning on social and structural neighbourhood characteristics).

Table 12.4 presents full findings from our hierarchical multilevel linear modelling of obligation to obey the police.[1] Few of the individual-level socio-demographic characteristics are significant predictors of felt obligation to obey the police (holding constant the neighbourhood in which individuals reside). Notable exceptions include:

- The older an individual is, the more they feel obligated to obey the police;
- Those who identified themselves as 'Pakistani', 'Bangladeshi' or 'Chinese' feel stronger obligation (the effect was particularly strong for Bangladeshis and Chinese) than those who identified themselves as being 'White British';
- Those who indicated they were a 'house person' or 'retired' feel greater obligation than those who identified themselves as 'working full-time'.

Of the structural characteristics of the neighbourhood, high levels of concentrated disadvantages and high levels of ethnic diversity are associated with greater levels of felt obligation. The direction of the effect of concentrated disadvantage is surprising. One might expect more deprived areas to be policed more aggressively, and thus be implicated in decreased obligation to obey the police. For example Sampson and Bartusch (1998) found that poor neighbourhoods tended to exhibit greater legal cynicism and less satisfaction with the police. Yet,

Table 12.3 Explaining neighbourhood variation in obligation to obey the police: social characteristics.

	Model 6	Model 7	Model 8	Model 9
	Coefficient	*Coefficient*	*Coefficient*	*Coefficient*
Collective efficacy	0.81***			0.52 ***
Perceived disorder		–0.48***		–0.40 ***
Worry about crime			–0.26***	0.10

Note: unstandardised coefficients,* significant at the 5% level, ** significant at the 1% level, *** significant at the 0.1% level.

Table 12.4 Explaining individual and neighbourhood variation in obligation to obey the police.

	Model 1		Model 2		Model 3		Model 4		Model 5	
	Coefficient		Coefficient		Coefficient		Coefficient		Coefficient	
Intercept	5.03***	-0.22	5.05***	-0.22	5.26***	-1.03	6.34***	-1.06	6.83***	-1.05
Person level (N=4,048)										
Female	-0.02	-0.07	-0.01	-0.07	-0.02	-0.07	-0.01	-0.07	-0.01	-0.07
Age	0.15***	-0.03	0.15***	-0.03	0.14***	-0.03	0.15***	-0.03	0.13***	-0.03
Ethnicity (ref.: White British)										
White – Irish	0.07	-0.21	0.04	-0.21	0.08	-0.21	0.04	-0.20	-0.01	-0.20
White – any other	0.37**	-0.11	0.29*	-0.12	0.34**	-0.11	0.23*	-0.11	0.17	-0.11
Mixed – White and Black Caribbean	-0.05	-0.24	-0.13	-0.24	0.03	-0.24	-0.07	-0.24	-0.01	-0.23
Mixed – White and Black African	-0.31	-0.30	-0.34	-0.30	-0.28	-0.30	-0.32	-0.30	-0.25	-0.29
Mixed – White and Asian	-0.22	-0.41	-0.19	-0.41	-0.26	-0.40	-0.21	-0.40	-0.23	-0.39
Other mixed	0.00	-0.22	-0.09	-0.22	0.07	-0.21	-0.04	-0.21	0.04	-0.21
Indian	0.17	-0.16	0.11	-0.16	0.21	-0.16	0.18	-0.16	0.00	-0.15
Pakistani	0.55**	-0.20	0.47*	-0.20	0.66***	-0.20	0.58**	-0.20	0.44**	-0.19
Bangladeshi	1.15***	-0.19	1.07***	-0.19	1.29***	-0.19	1.23***	-0.19	1.15***	-0.18
Other Asian or Asian British	0.34	-0.24	0.28	-0.24	0.36	-0.24	0.30	-0.24	0.26	-0.23
Black or Black British – Caribbean	-0.30	-0.17	-0.37*	-0.17	-0.30	-0.17	-0.40*	-0.17	-0.42*	-0.16
Black or Black British – African	0.33*	-0.14	0.27	-0.14	0.36*	-0.14	0.28	-0.14	0.19	-0.14
Other Black or Black British	-0.21	-0.31	-0.29	-0.31	-0.14	-0.31	-0.25	-0.31	-0.13	-0.30
Chinese	0.91*	-0.38	0.89*	-0.38	0.90*	-0.37	0.88*	-0.37	0.78*	-0.36
Other Chinese or other ethnic group	-0.09	-0.54	-0.15	-0.54	-0.02	-0.54	-0.06	-0.54	-0.32	-0.52
Work status (ref: working full-time)										
Working part-time (8–29 hrs/wk)	-0.09	-0.13	-0.10	-0.13	-0.08	-0.13	-0.09	-0.13	-0.03	-0.12
Working part-time (<8hrs/wk)	-0.55	-0.34	-0.52	-0.34	-0.47	-0.34	-0.44	-0.33	-0.44	-0.33
Not working	0.30	-0.17	0.30	-0.17	0.34	-0.17	0.35*	-0.17	0.33*	-0.17
House person	0.34*	-0.13	0.33*	-0.13	0.31*	-0.13	0.29*	-0.13	0.21	-0.13
Retired	0.35**	-0.13	0.35**	-0.13	0.34**	-0.13	0.36**	-0.13	0.26*	-0.13

continued overleaf

	Model 1		Model 2		Model 3		Model 4		Model 5	
	Coefficient		Coefficient		Coefficient		Coefficient		Coefficient	
Registered unemployed	-0.34	-0.19	-0.33	-0.19	-0.34	-0.19	-0.33	-0.19	-0.35	-0.18
Unemployed but not registered	0.27	-0.41	0.24	-0.41	0.28	-0.41	0.25	-0.41	0.21	-0.40
Student/full time education	0.25	-0.16	0.27	-0.16	0.26	-0.16	0.28	-0.16	0.19	-0.15
Working status (other)	-0.22	-0.35	-0.27	-0.35	-0.14	-0.35	-0.19	-0.35	-0.20	-0.34
Housing situation (reference: own property outright)										
Buying on mortgage	0.07	-0.12	0.04	-0.12	0.04	-0.12	-0.01	-0.12	0.05	-0.11
Rented from council	0.17	-0.12	0.10	-0.12	0.23	-0.12	0.13	-0.12	0.21	-0.12
Rented from housing association	0.04	-0.17	-0.02	-0.17	-0.01	-0.17	-0.13	-0.17	-0.05	-0.16
Rented from private landlord	0.08	-0.13	0.05	-0.13	0.09	-0.13	0.03	-0.13	0.05	-0.13
Tenure (other)	0.04	-0.29	0.02	-0.29	0.08	-0.29	0.04	-0.29	0.05	-0.28
Household access to a car	-0.15	-0.08	-0.10	-0.08	-0.18	-0.08	-0.12	-0.08	-0.11	-0.08
Number of kids	-0.01	-0.08	-0.01	-0.08	0.00	-0.08	0.00	-0.08	-0.04	-0.08
Trust in police effectiveness									-0.01	-0.03
Trust in police fairness and intentions									0.32***	-0.02
Neighbourhood level (N=881)										
Concentrated disadvantage			0.22***	-0.06			0.30***	-0.06	0.29***	-0.06
Residential stability			0.04	-0.06			0.02	-0.05	0.02	-0.05
Immigrant concentration			0.20***	-0.06			0.22***	-0.05	0.21***	-0.05
Crime			0.00	-0.06			0.02	-0.06	-0.01	-0.06
Collective efficacy					0.36**	-0.14	v0.28*	-0.14	-0.07	-0.14
Perceived disorder					-0.43***	-0.07	-0.47***	-0.06	-0.49***	-0.06
Worry about crime					-0.12	-0.07	-0.22**	-0.07	-0.22**	-0.07

	Variance components
Between neighbourhoods	1.29
Within neighbourhoods	1.99

	Variance explained				
	Model 1	Model 2	Model 3	Model 4	Model 5
	2%	7%	17%	24%	27%

Note: unstandardised coefficients, * significant at the 5% level, ** significant at the 1% level, *** significant at the 0.1% level.

we find that felt obligation is higher (on average) in more deprived areas, conditioning on key social characteristics such as collective efficacy and disorder in the neighbourhood. Importantly, the positive correlation between obligation and concentrated disadvantage is present in a model that includes disadvantage as the only predictor. At this juncture we can only speculate as to why this is. Perhaps there is more aggressive policing in deprived areas which translates into a greater sense of police authority? Perhaps more aggressive policing generates not only more visible signs of power but also a greater need for authority when social order seems to be under threat?

The positive effect of neighbourhood ethnic diversity on obligation to obey the police may also be a little surprising. According to some commentators, ethnically diverse communities tend to be lacking in trust, with low levels of social cohesion, and with disputes regarding the equitable provision of public goods (Alesina and Ferrera 2000; Costa and Kahn 2003; Goodhart 2004; Phillips 2005). A number of recent academic studies – most prominently Putnam (2007) – have lent support to this perspective, indicating an apparently negative link between the ethnic diversity of local communities and the extent to which residents express trust in, and a sense of cohesion with, one another. But there is emerging, contradictory evidence that links ethnic diversity to more positive, more pro-social behaviours and attitudes. For example, Sturgis *et al.* (2012) found that Londoners were substantially more likely than citizens in the rest of the UK to report friendship ties and meaningful social contact with people from different ethnic groups. They also found that neighbourhood ethnic diversity was positively correlated with perceived social cohesion in London. Our findings build upon this work. We find that people who live in neighbourhoods with a high proportion of immigrants (and which tend to be ethnically diverse) also tend to feel a greater sense of obligation to obey the police. Immigration and the ethnic diversity it brings therefore seems to strengthen commitment to group authorities, not undermine it.

Turning next to the effect of the social characteristics of the neighbourhood, we find that individuals who live in areas with strong collective efficacy, low levels of neighbourhood disorder, and low levels of fear of crime also tend to feel obligated to obey the police (Table 12.4). These are additive effects: they build on one another. And contrary to the finding that individuals in more deprived neighbourhoods tend to invest more legitimacy in the police, we find that neighbourhoods that lack subtle, informal social controls, that are disorderly, and that contain worried residents, also tend to have lower levels of police legitimacy.

Is this because social and structural qualities of the neighbourhood influence trust in the police with a knock-on effect on felt obligation? It may be that people who live in deprived, ethnically diverse, cohesive and seemingly safe neighbourhoods feel more obligated to obey the police, because, for whatever reason, they trust the police more. A sense of police fairness and shared motives may generate connections to institutions, whereby they internalise the value of obeying authority (c.f. Tyler 2006a, 2006b).

Looking at the effect of trust in Table 12.4 (model 5), we find that trust in police fairness and intentions is an important predictor of felt obligation. And consistent with Tyler's procedural justice model, effectiveness is much less important than fair procedures and shared interests. What is critical is the way that the police treat people, then, as well as the extent to which the police understand and respond to community needs and problems. Taking into account people's trust in the fairness and shared priorities of the police, we find that the previously large effect of collective efficacy is now rendered not statistically significant. Collective efficacy seems to exert an influence on felt obligation to obey the police through the mediating process of trust in police fairness and intentions. The effects of neighbourhood disorder, immigrant concentration and worry about crime do not change: neighbourhood levels of disorder and worry about crime thus seem to exert a direct effect on felt obligation.

In summary, a core aspect of police legitimacy – namely, felt obligation to obey the police – is strongly related to trust in police fairness and/or shared priorities (not trust in police effectiveness) and neighbourhood levels of concentrated disadvantage, immigrant concentration, disorder and worry about crime. The strong effect of collective efficacy on obligation is almost entirely mediated by individual trust in police fairness and/or shared priorities, suggesting that people infer aspects of the trustworthiness of the police from a particular aspect of their social environment. Few individual characteristics are significant predictors, with the exception of the following groups feeling greater obligation: 'Pakistani', 'Bangladeshi' and 'Chinese' (compared to 'White British'); older people (compared to younger people); and those not working or retired (compared to working full-time).

Moral alignment with the police

We next turn to the other aspect of police legitimacy. Considering the sense of shared values and moral purpose with the police, our analyses follow the same structure as for obligation to obey. Table 12.5 presents the intra-class correlations from five models. The empty model shows that 30 per cent of the variation occurs between neighbourhoods; the compositional model indicates that the socio-demographic makeup of neighbourhoods explains only 2 per cent of between-area variance.

Table 12.5 Neighbourhood variation in moral alignment with the police in London.

	ICC	Variance explained (%)
Empty model	0.30	
Compositional	0.29	2
Structural characteristics	0.29	4
Social characteristics	0.19	38
Structural and social characteristics	0.18	40
Structural and social characteristics and individual-level trust in the police	0.16	48

Note: ICC=intra-class correlation

Adding each of the four structural neighbourhood characteristics variables one at a time, none (on its own) is a significant predictor of moral alignment with the police. Put all this together, and ethnic composition becomes a positive and significant predictor. As with obligation to obey, the more ethnically diverse the neighbourhood, the more people in that neighbourhood grant legitimacy to the police. But the effect is relatively small. And placing all four structural characteristics into the model (along with the compositional-style individual-level predictors) means that we can explain only 4 per cent of the neighbourhood-level variation (Table 12.6). Structural characteristics of the neighbourhood seem relatively unimportant in explaining moral alignment with the police.

Turning to social characteristics of the neighbourhood, we find that the effects of collective efficacy, perceived disorder and worry about crime are all reduced once the three factors are included in the model (Table 12.7). Collective efficacy moves from 1.47*** to 1.04***, perceived disorder moves from −0.69*** to −0.47*, and worry about crime moves from −0.29*** to 0.06. At the neighbourhood level, then, it seems that day-to-day issues of disorder and informal social controls are more important explanations of police legitimacy than worry about crime.

Table 12.6 Explaining neighbourhood variation in moral alignment with the police: structural characteristics.

	Model 1	Model 2	Model 3	Model 4	Model 5
	Coefficient	Coefficient	Coefficient	Coefficient	Coefficient
Concentrated disadvantage	0.07				0.03
Residential mobility		0.09			0.05
Ethnic composition			0.17		0.15**
Crime levels				0.02	−0.03

Note: unstandardised coefficients,* significant at the 5% level, ** significant at the 1% level, *** significant at the 0.1% level

Table 12.7 Explaining neighbourhood variation in moral alignment with the police: social characteristics.

	Model 6	Model 7	Model 8	Model 9
	Coefficient	Coefficient	Coefficient	Coefficient
Collective efficacy	0.15***			1.04***
Perceived disorder		−0.69***		−0.47***
Worry about crime			−0.29***	0.06

Note: unstandardised coefficients,* significant at the 5% level, ** significant at the 1% level, *** significant at the 0.1% level.

Together the social characteristics (and compositional effects) explain 38 per cent of the neighbourhood-level variation. The addition of structural characteristics to this model only shifts the amount of neighbourhood-level variation explained to 40 per cent. Clearly, social characteristics are the most important predictors of neighbourhood-level variation in the fitted model. Importantly, adding individual-level trust in the police makes only a small difference to the explained neighbourhood variance. As with obligation to obey the police, the composition of trust in the police in the neighbourhood helps explain only a small amount of the clustering of moral alignment with the police (conditioning on social and structural neighbourhood characteristics).

Model 5 of Table 12.8 puts all this together. Adding the social and structural characteristics into one model, we find that ethnic composition remains significant and concentrated disadvantage becomes significant. As with felt obligation, high levels of concentrated disadvantage are associated with greater levels of moral alignment. By comparison, social characteristics play a stronger role. The effect of neighbourhood collective efficacy is of special note. Even taking into account trust in police fairness and/or intentions (a strong predictor of moral alignment), collective efficacy is important. The effect is similar to that of neighbourhood disorder (again model 5): the stronger the social control, order and trust in a neighbourhood, the more individuals feel morally aligned with their police.

As with obligation to obey, we find that taking into account of levels of trust in fairness and/or shared priorities has a striking impact on the effect of collective efficacy on police legitimacy. Once trust is added to the equation, the effect size for collective efficacy is halved. Again this suggests that collective efficacy exerts an influence on legitimacy through the mediating process of trust in police fairness and intentions. As with felt obligation to obey the police, neighbourhood disorder is a predictor of moral alignment. None of the effect is mediated through individual-level trust in the police.

Compared to obligation to obey the police, there are a few more significant individual-level socio-demographic predictors for moral alignment (model 3). A strong sense of moral alignment with the police is associated with:

- being older;
- compared to being 'White British', identifying oneself as being 'Indian', 'Pakistani', 'Bangladeshi' or 'Chinese', and not identifying oneself as being 'Mixed – white and Asian', 'Other mixed' or 'Black or Black British – African';
- being a 'house person' rather than 'working full-time'.

Summary

So what does all this mean for the social ecology of police legitimacy? The work of Sampson and Bartusch (1998), Kirk and Matsuda (2011) and Kirk and Papachristos (2011) suggests that neighbourhood disadvantage, ethnic concentration and population instability all create the conditions in which the law exerts seemingly little power and little influence over individuals in Chicago. Residents

Table 12.8 Explaining individual and neighbourhood variation in moral alignment with the police.

	Model 1		Model 2		Model 3		Model 4		Model 5	
	Coefficient	S.E.	Coefficient	S.E.	Coefficient	S.E.	Coefficient	S.E.	Coefficient	S.E.
Intercept	6.01***	-0.21	6.02***	-0.21	2.67**	-0.88	3.06***	-0.93	2.73**	-0.87
Person level (N=4,048)										
Female	-0.05	-0.07	-0.05	-0.07	-0.06	-0.07	-0.05	-0.07	-0.06	-0.06
Age	0.08**	-0.03	0.08**	-0.03	0.07*	-0.03	0.07**	-0.03	0.05	-0.03
Ethnicity (ref.: White British)										
White – Irish	-0.17	-0.19	-0.19	-0.19	-0.18	-0.19	-0.19	-0.19	-0.26	-0.18
White – any other	0.31**	-0.11	0.27*	-0.11	0.25*	-0.11	0.18	-0.11	0.09	-0.10
Mixed – White and Black Caribbean	-0.22	-0.23	-0.27	-0.23	-0.14	-0.22	-0.20	-0.22	-0.09	-0.21
Mixed – White and Black African	-0.62**	-0.28	-0.63*	-0.28	-0.58*	-0.28	-0.61*	-0.28	-0.49	-0.26
Mixed – White and Asian	-0.74	-0.38	-0.72	-0.38	-0.83*	-0.38	-0.80*	-0.37	-0.81*	-0.35
Other mixed	-0.23	-0.20	-0.28	-0.20	-0.17	-0.20	-0.22	-0.20	-0.13	-0.19
Indian	0.66***	-0.15	0.62***	-0.15	0.71***	-0.15	0.70***	-0.15	0.43**	-0.14
Pakistani	0.49**	-0.18	0.44*	-0.18	0.64***	-0.18	0.61***	-0.18	0.40*	-0.17
Bangladeshi	0.72***	-0.18	0.67***	-0.18	0.90***	-0.18	0.86***	-0.18	0.78***	-0.17
Other Asian or Asian British	0.06	-0.22	0.02	-0.22	0.05	-0.22	0.03	-0.22	-0.06	-0.21
Black or Black British – Caribbean	-0.10	-0.16	-0.13	-0.16	-0.10	-0.16	-0.16	-0.16	-0.17	-0.15
Black or Black British – African	0.20	-0.13	0.18	-0.13	0.22	-0.13	0.17	-0.13	0.06	-0.13
Other Black or Black British	-0.19	-0.30	-0.24	-0.30	-0.15	-0.29	-0.21	-0.29	-0.05	-0.28
Chinese	0.37	-0.35	0.36	-0.35	0.36	-0.35	0.34	-0.35	0.25	-0.33
Other Chinese or other ethnic group	0.08	-0.51	0.02	-0.51	0.12	-0.50	0.09	-0.50	-0.22	-0.48
Work status (ref.: working full-time)										
Working part-time, 8–29 hrs/wk	-0.08	-0.12	-0.08	-0.12	-0.07	-0.12	-0.08	-0.12	-0.02	-0.11
Working part-time (<8 hrs/wk)	-0.51	-0.32	-0.49	-0.32	-0.31	-0.31	-0.29	-0.31	-0.30	-0.29
Not working	0.04	-0.16	0.04	-0.16	0.09	-0.16	0.11	-0.16	0.07	-0.15

continued overleaf

	Model 1		Model 2		Model 3		Model 4		Model 5	
	Coefficient	S.E.	Coefficient	S.E.	Coefficient	S.E.	Coefficient	S.E.	Coefficient	S.E.
House person	0.34**	-0.12	0.33**	-0.12	0.31*	-0.12	0.30*	-0.12	0.19	-0.12
Retired	0.31*	-0.12	0.31*	-0.12	0.31*	-0.12	0.32**	-0.12	0.18	-0.12
Registered unemployed	-0.34	-0.18	-0.34	-0.18	-0.34	-0.17	-0.33	-0.17	-0.36*	-0.16
Unemployed but not registered	-0.29	-0.39	-0.30	-0.39	-0.28	-0.38	-0.30	-0.38	-0.34	-0.36
Student/full-time education	-0.09	-0.15	-0.08	-0.15	-0.06	-0.15	-0.05	-0.15	-0.17	-0.14
Working status (other)	-0.45	-0.33	-0.48	-0.33	-0.33	-0.33	-0.35	-0.33	-0.34	-0.31
Housing situation (ref.: own property outright)										
Buying on mortgage	-0.11	-0.11	-0.12	-0.11	-0.14	-0.11	-0.17	-0.11	-0.09	-0.10
Rented from council	-0.15	-0.11	-0.19	-0.11	-0.10	-0.11	-0.17	-0.11	-0.07	-0.11
Rented from housing association	-0.26	-0.16	-0.29	-0.16	-0.28	-0.15	-0.35*	-0.15	-0.25	-0.15
Rented from private landlord	-0.12	-0.12	-0.13	-0.12	-0.10	-0.12	-0.14	-0.12	-0.13	-0.11
Tenure (other)	0.11	-0.27	0.10	-0.27	0.20	-0.27	0.18	-0.27	0.14	-0.26
Household access to a car	-0.05	-0.07	-0.02	-0.07	-0.08	-0.07	-0.04	-0.07	-0.01	-0.07
Number of kids	0.07	-0.08	0.08	-0.08	0.09	-0.08	0.09	-0.08	0.04	-0.07
Trust in police effectiveness									0.10***	-0.02
Trust in police fairness and intentions									0.39***	-0.02
Neighbourhood level (N = 881)										
Concentrated disadvantage			0.06	-0.06			0.19***	-0.05	0.18***	-0.05
Residential stability			0.06	-0.05			0.01	-0.05	-0.01	-0.04
Immigrant concentration			0.14**	-0.05			0.09*	-0.05	0.07	-0.04
Crime			-0.03	-0.06			0.01	-0.06	-0.02	-0.05
Collective efficacy					0.95***	-0.12	0.94***	-0.12	0.52***	-0.11
Perceived disorder					-0.46***	-0.06	-0.47***	-0.06	-0.48***	-0.05
Worry about crime					-0.05	-0.06	-0.10	-0.06	-0.06	-0.06

Variance components

	Model 1	Model 2	Model 3	Model 4	Model 5
Between neighbourhoods	1.21				
Within neighbourhoods	1.85				

Variance explained

Model 1	Model 2	Model 3	Model 4	Model 5
2%	4%	38%	40%	48%

Note: unstandardised coefficients,* significant at the 5% level, ** significant at the 1% level, *** significant at the 0.1% level.

of such neighbourhoods may view the law as having less legitimacy because the institution seems distant and they feel unprotected. Policing may be more aggressive in deprived areas, encouraging an 'us-and-them' atmosphere in which feelings of obligation and moral alignment decrease.

But contrary to expectations, we find that concentrated disadvantage is positively associated with both dimensions of police legitimacy in London. The more deprived an area, the more residents tended to feel obligated to obey the police and morally aligned with police values. Importantly these effects are not mediated by trust in the police.[2] What should we make of the positive association between deprivation and police legitimacy? One explanation is that people rely more on the police to regulate their deprived community and thus grant this authority greater legitimacy (irrespective of whether they believe that the police are fair or just) because they are dependent on police power (van der Toorn *et al.* 2011). There is certainly some evidence from social and political psychology that supports this idea. People are motivated to see institutions and social arrangements as legitimate: to do so satisfies various basic psychological needs and motivations (Jost and Banaji, 1994; Jost *et al.* 2004; Jost *et al.* 2008), in this case to reduce uncertainty and manage threat.

But a word of caution: the negative effects of neighbourhood disorder on police legitimacy (and negative effects of neighbourhood worry about crime on obligation to obey the police) seem to contradict this idea. Other research shows individual levels of worry about crime and perceived disorder are negatively associated with individual levels of public trust and police legitimacy (Jackson and Sunshine 2007; Jackson and Bradford 2009; Bradford and Jackson 2011). More research is needed to unpick why there might be a positive relationship between concentrated disadvantage and police legitimacy.

We also find an association between the ethnic composition of an area and feelings of obligation to obey the police: the more diverse the neighbourhood the higher the levels of consent to police power. This is consistent with recent work that challenges the pessimistic view of the effect of immigration on the social fabric (e.g. Sturgis *et al.* 2011).

What about the social characteristics of a neighbourhood? Two findings are notable. First, the more disorder in a locality the less legitimacy people confer on the police (and the more worry about crime in a locality the less felt obligation to obey the police), with people who live in orderly areas tending to hold the police to be more legitimate. Perhaps this is because the police represent apparently successful attempts to reproduce normative social order. Drawing upon Bourdieu's notions of field and habitus, we suggest that the police are an organisation located within the social field of policing (Bradford and Jackson 2011). Organisations that dominate their fields – the police certainly do dominate the general activity of policing in society – may be able to draw on sources of legitimacy that encompass the relational and symbolic aspects of their behaviour, as well as the extent to which they embody the activity of the field within which they are embedded.[3] In short, the police are seen as legitimate when the mechanisms of *policing*, which extend beyond formal policing, are seen to be strong.

Second, this idea is strengthened by the strong positive effect of collective efficacy on police legitimacy, especially on moral alignment. The public believe that the police share their moral values when the community is seen to be orderly and informally policed. Indeed, trust in police fairness and intentions is a strong mediator of the estimated effect of collective efficacy on legitimacy. The idea that the police represent and even embody the social group suggests one more reason why the social health of the neighbourhood is so strongly linked to people's sense of moral congruence with the police. One of the ways in which people come to a judgement on the concurrence between the values of the police and their own may be via inference from their assessments of the characteristics of the group the police represent. Perhaps, when people feel that others in their neighbourhood – that is, other group members – are trustworthy, share their values, and act accordingly, they are more likely to conclude that the police, as an embodiment of the group, will do the same. Feeling that other group members do not share their values points people toward different assessments of group representatives, undermining their sense that the moral values of the police are aligned with their own.

13 Procedural justice and contact with the police

Our analysis in the book has thus far provided empirical support for the idea that day-to-day aspects of neighbourhood social order are important in understanding individual-level and neighbourhood-level heterogeneity in public trust and police legitimacy. It matters where people live. Individuals who live in orderly areas, in areas that have a sense of shared values and a sense that local people can (and will) act upon those values to regulate behaviour and enforce social norms, also tend to believe that the police are trustworthy, and also tend to believe that the police are a legitimate authority. It is as if people evaluate the strength of formal social control mechanisms from the strength of informal social control mechanisms (Jackson and Sunshine 2007). Trust and legitimacy may emerge partly as the result of the strength of social control mechanisms. A sense that the community is able to protect itself against disruptive social behaviour may generate a sense that the police impose their authority and legitimacy on the community. A crucial justification for police power may be effective social regulation, and people seem to feel a loss of moral alignment or identification when the police are seen to be failing to impose themselves as a source of moral authority and discipline.

In this chapter we continue to build the model of legitimacy up further. We focus in particular on public encounters with the police. The procedural justice model predicts that contact with the police (specifically, judgements of the quality of the contact) shapes trust in the police, and in turn trust shapes legitimacy (and cooperation with the police, see Part 5). The work of Tyler and others suggests that the actions of officers, especially during interactions with the public, are vital in forming and influencing perceptions of police legitimacy, and through this, cooperation, compliance and readiness to obey the law. It follows that the legitimacy of the police may not simply be a given – or pre-ordained – but is in an important sense created and reproduced by the mundane actions of officers going about their daily business. How police treat people may matter not only on legal or ethical grounds, but in terms of influencing how people will interact with officers in the future, whether they will cooperate by providing information, and so on.

Thus far in this book we have addressed the effect of contact on trust. We next consider whether there is a knock-on effect on legitimacy via trust, as well as direct statistical effects of contact on legitimacy. If contact shapes legitimacy via trust, we might conclude that contact shapes people's sense that the police are competent, fair and share the motives and priorities of individuals. People, we might surmise, infer from the procedural justice of the police whether the police are reliable, dependable and are at least trying to impose mechanisms of formal social control. This sense of alignment and group connection may then activate legitimacy, whether obligation to obey the police or moral alignment with the police.

What about the direct effect of contact on legitimacy? To our knowledge only one study has examined direct effects of encounters with officers on police legitimacy. Drawing upon panel data, Tyler and Fagan (2008) found that contact explained a good deal of variation in police legitimacy in New York City. But what does it mean if we find direct effects of contact on legitimacy, separate to any indirect effect via trust? Consider the contrasting nature of trust and legitimacy. Trust is one's assessment of the trustworthiness of the police to do the things we want them to do, as well as one's sense that they have our interests at heart. By contrast, legitimacy refers to feelings of obligation to power and moral alignment with power. If dissatisfactory encounters – for example, stop-and-search incidents – are negatively associated with legitimacy (an effect not mediated by trust), then this is a kind of delegitimisation that does not flow through assessment of effectiveness, fairness and shared priorities. It is about the abuse of the authority of individual officers and how this damages the recognition and justification of institutional power; people withdraw consent to power when they experience an abuse of authority, and they feel less obligated to obey officers and less morally aligned with officers.

We also address the issue of symmetry (Skogan 2006; Tyler and Fagan 2008; Bradford *et al.* 2009a; Myhill and Bradford 2011). Do positive encounters have an equally *positive effect* on legitimacy compared to the *negative effect* of negative encounters? There is some empirical evidence, from some quarters, that contact which is found by citizens to be satisfactory can have an uplifting effect on trust and confidence (Tyler and Fagan 2008; Bradford *et al.* 2009a). But the magnitude of such effects is usually much smaller than any negative consequences from unsatisfactory contacts. This has led some to talk of an 'asymmetry' in impacts of contact on confidence (Skogan 2006). The implication is that schemes designed to improve the standing of police by improving the quality of contacts are destined to failure. This would be bad news for UK policing, which is firmly fixed on increasing the presence, visibility and activity of police in local areas, and which explicitly links these to improvements in both trust and confidence and feelings of reassurance (OPSR 2003; Dalgliesh and Myhill 2004; Tuffin *et al.* 2006; Quinton and Morris 2008).

Obligation to obey the police

We start by considering the role of contact with the police in people's feelings of consent to authority (the models build upon model 4 in Table 13.1).

Table 13.1 shows the following factors to be important in explaining variation in obligation:

- Neighbourhood characteristics, particularly concentrated disadvantage, immigrant concentration, disorder and worry about crime;
- Dissatisfactory contact with the police;
- Trust in police fairness and intentions.

A number of individual social characteristics are also associated with stronger feelings of obligation, most notably: older people; being 'Pakistani', 'Bangladeshi' or 'Chinese' and not being 'Black' or 'Black African British', all compared to being 'White British'; and being registered unemployed.

The entirely asymmetrical effect of personal encounters with the police is striking, especially in being stopped in the street or car by an officer or officers. Even after holding constant the large effect of trust in police fairness and/or intentions, being very or completely dissatisfied with the police during a stop encounter is associated with lower expected levels of obligation to police authority. Consider experience with the police as a result of criminal victimisation. Here the effect of being dissatisfied with police treatment is almost entirely mediated through trust in police fairness and/or shared priorities.

Table 13.1 Police-initiated contact and felt obligation to obey the police in London.

	Model 1		Model 2		Model 3	
	Coefficient	S.E.	Coefficient	S.E.	Coefficient	S.E.
Intercept	−1.23	−0.79	6.34***	−1.06	6.56***	−1.05
Person level (N=4,048)						
Female	−0.01	−0.07	−0.02	−0.07	−0.03	−0.07
Age	0.15***	−0.03	0.14***	−0.03	0.11***	−0.03
Ethnicity (reference: White – British)						
White – Irish	0.04	−0.20	0.04	−0.20	−0.02	−0.20
White – any other	0.23*	−0.11	0.24*	−0.11	0.19	−0.11
Mixed – White and Black Caribbean	−0.06	−0.24	−0.01	−0.24	0.07	−0.23
Mixed – White and Black African	−0.33	−0.30	−0.24	−0.30	−0.17	−0.29
Mixed – White and Asian	−0.21	−0.40	−0.09	−0.40	−0.08	−0.39
Other mixed	−0.04	−0.21	0.06	−0.21	0.11	−0.21
Indian	0.18	−0.16	0.17	−0.16	0.00	−0.15
Pakistani	0.59**	−0.20	0.57**	−0.20	0.46*	−0.19
Bangladeshi	1.23***	−0.19	1.23***	−0.19	1.15***	−0.18
Other Asian or Asian British	0.30	−0.24	0.30	−0.24	0.27	−0.23
Black or Black British – Caribbean	−0.40*	−0.17	−0.40*	−0.17	−0.40*	−0.16
Black or Black British – African	0.27	−0.14	0.30*	−0.14	0.22	−0.14
Other Black or Black British	−0.24	−0.31	−0.20	−0.31	−0.13	−0.30
Chinese	0.88*	−0.37	0.87*	−0.37	0.79*	−0.36
Other Chinese or other ethnic group	−0.06	−0.54	−0.05	−0.54	−0.31	−0.52
Work status (reference: working full-time)						
Working part time (8–29 hrs/wk)	−0.09	−0.13	−0.09	−0.13	−0.04	−0.12
Working part time (<8hrs/wk)	−0.44	−0.33	−0.46	−0.33	−0.46	−0.33

continued overleaf

	Model 1		Model 2		Model 3	
	Coefficient	*S.E.*	*Coefficient*	*S.E.*	*Coefficient*	*S.E.*
Not working	0.35*	−0.17	0.37*	−0.17	0.35*	−0.17
House person	0.29*	−0.13	0.31*	−0.13	0.24	−0.13
Retired	0.36**	−0.13	0.37**	−0.13	0.30*	−0.13
Registered unemployed	−0.32	−0.19	−0.34	−0.19	−0.38*	−0.18
Unemployed but not registered	0.25	−0.41	0.20	−0.41	0.23	−0.40
Student/full-time education	0.28	−0.16	0.26	−0.16	0.19	−0.15
Working status (other)	−0.19	−0.35	−0.17	−0.35	−0.18	−0.34
Housing situation (ref.: own property outright)						
Buying on mortgage	0.00	−0.12	0.00	−0.11	0.05	−0.11
Rented from council	0.13	−0.12	0.13	−0.12	0.20	−0.12
Rented from housing association	−0.13	−0.17	−0.10	−0.17	−0.04	−0.16
Rented from private landlord	0.03	−0.13	0.02	−0.13	0.05	−0.13
Tenure (other)	0.04	−0.29	0.03	−0.29	0.08	−0.28
Household access to a car	−0.13	−0.08	−0.13	−0.08	−0.13	−0.08
Number of kids	0.00	−0.08	0.00	−0.08	−0.03	−0.08
Very or completely dissatisfied with the police during a stop encounter (reference: no police-initiated contact)			−3.70***	−0.93	−3.13***	−0.91
Fairly dissatisfied with the police during a stop encounter			−1.13	−0.78	−0.72	−0.77
Fairly satisfied with the police during a stop encounter			−0.32	−0.36	−0.30	−0.35
Very satisfied with the police during a stop encounter			0.28	−0.30	0.18	−0.29
Satisfied with police treatment when reporting the crime (No contact is the reference category)			0.14	−0.18	−0.05	−0.17
Neither satisfied nor dissatisfied with police treatment when reporting the crime			0.23	−0.40	0.46	−0.39
Dissatisfied with police treatment when reporting the crime			−0.75**	−0.28	−0.25	−0.28
Trust in police fairness and intentions					0.30***	−0.02
Trust in police effectiveness					0.01	−0.03
Neighbourhood level (N=881)						
Concentrated disadvantage	0.30***	−0.06	0.30***	−0.06	0.29***	−0.06
Residential stability	0.02	−0.05	0.02	−0.05	0.02	−0.05
Immigrant concentration	0.22***	−0.05	0.22***	−0.05	0.20***	−0.05
Crime	0.02	−0.06	0.02	−0.06	−0.01	−0.06
Collective efficacy	0.28*	−0.14	0.28*	−0.14	−0.04	−0.14
Perceived disorder	−0.47***	−0.06	−0.47***	−0.06	−0.49***	−0.06
Worry about crime	−0.22**	−0.07	−0.21**	−0.07	−0.22**	−0.07

Note: unstandardised coefficients,* significant at the 5% level, ** significant at the 1% level, *** significant at the 0.1% level.

Being stopped by the police therefore seems to have a subtly different effect on felt obligation than approaching the police as a result of victimisation experience. The effect of negative experiences when people contact the police seems to flow entirely through trust in police fairness and interests. In such a situation, an individual who feels the police treated them badly seems to feel less inclination to consent to authority, perhaps because disrespectful treatment damages motive-based trust and identification with the group. Tyler and Blader (2003: 356) refer to this as: 'thinking of themselves and the group in similar terms and defining themselves in terms of their group membership'. Motive-based trust places less emphasis on predictability and perceived willingness or ability to keep promises, and more on estimates of character and mutual affect – that is, the perception that those who are trusted have the best interests of the truster at heart.

Yet, although unsatisfactory encounters resulting from stop and search are also negatively associated with this aspect of legitimacy, none of this association is mediated by trust. Here, de-legitimisation of authority does not flow through assessments of effectiveness, fairness and shared priorities. Instead, it is about the apparent abuse of power of individual officers and the way in which people withdraw consent to power when they experience what may seem to be an abuse of power. This is not through a separation of interests and shared identity, but through a direct effect on the internalisation of a set of moral values that is consonant with the aims of the police as an institution. Reflecting the idea that a person authorises an authority to determine appropriate behaviour within some situation, Kelman and Hamilton (1989) refer to legitimacy as 'authorisation.' A person feels obligated to follow the directives or rules that authority establishes; he or she *internalises* the value that it is morally just to obey the police; and authorisation obviates the necessity of making judgements or choices.

Moral alignment with the police

What about the other aspect of legitimacy? Table 13.2 shows a similar pattern. Four factors are again important. First, being 'very or completely' dissatisfied with the police during a stop encounter is associated with significantly lower expected legitimacy, even after holding constant an indirect effect through trust in police fairness and/or intentions. Second, there is an important effect of being dissatisfied with police treatment, half of which is mediated through trust in police fairness and/or shared priorities. Third, trust (especially trust in police fairness and intentions) is an important predictor. Fourth, neighbourhood characteristics are significant, particularly concentrated disadvantage, collective efficacy and disorder.

The experience of negative stop-and-search contact has a direct effect on moral alignment while the experience of negative public-initiated contact has a direct and indirect effect. It follows that procedural injustice damages a sense of shared moral purpose that is to some extent separate to the effect of damaged social connections to the police via a sense of trustworthiness.

Table 13.2 Police-initiated contact and moral alignment with the police in London.

	Model 1		Model 2		Model 3	
	Coefficient	*S.E.*	*Coefficient*	*S.E.*	*Coefficient*	*S.E.*
Intercept	3.06***	−0.93	3.07***	−0.93	2.38**	−0.88
Person level (N=4,048)						
Female	−0.05	−0.07	−0.06	−0.07	−0.08	−0.06
Age	0.07**	−0.03	0.06*	−0.03	0.03	−0.03
Ethnicity (reference: White – British)						
White – Irish	−0.19	−0.19	−0.20	−0.19	−0.27	−0.18
White – any other	0.18	−0.11	0.21*	−0.11	0.13	−0.10
Mixed – White and Black Caribbean	−0.19	−0.22	−0.12	−0.22	0.02	−0.21
Mixed – White and Black African	−0.61*	−0.28	−0.49	−0.28	−0.38	−0.26
Mixed – White and Asian	−0.80*	−0.37	−0.65	−0.37	−0.63	−0.35
Other mixed	−0.22	−0.20	−0.07	−0.20	−0.02	−0.19
Indian	0.70***	−0.15	0.68***	−0.15	0.44**	−0.14
Pakistani	0.61***	−0.18	0.58**	−0.18	0.42*	−0.17
Bangladeshi	0.86***	−0.18	0.86***	−0.17	0.79***	−0.17
Other Asian or Asian British	0.03	−0.22	0.02	−0.22	−0.03	−0.21
Black or Black British – Caribbean	−0.16	−0.16	−0.17	−0.16	−0.15	−0.15
Black or Black British – African	0.17	−0.13	0.20	−0.13	0.12	−0.13
Other Black or Black British	−0.20	−0.29	−0.14	−0.29	−0.02	−0.27
Chinese	0.34	−0.35	0.32	−0.35	0.26	−0.33
Other Chinese or other ethnic group	0.10	−0.50	0.13	−0.50	−0.17	−0.48
Work status (reference: working full time)						
Working part-time (8–29 hrs/wk)	−0.07	−0.12	−0.08	−0.12	−0.03	−0.11
Working part-time (<8hrs/wk)	−0.29	−0.31	−0.32	−0.31	−0.33	−0.29
Not working	0.11	−0.16	0.14	−0.16	0.1	−0.15
House person	0.30*	−0.12	0.33**	−0.12	0.23*	−0.12
Retired	0.32**	−0.12	0.34**	−0.12	0.22	−0.12
Registered unemployed	−0.32	−0.17	−0.35*	−0.17	−0.4*	−0.16
Unemployed but not registered	−0.30	−0.38	−0.37	−0.38	−0.32	−0.36
Student/full-time education	−0.05	−0.15	−0.08	−0.15	−0.17	−0.14
Working status (other)	−0.35	−0.33	−0.30	−0.32	−0.31	−0.31
Housing situation (reference: own property outright)						
Buying on mortgage	−0.17	−0.11	−0.17	−0.11	−0.09	−0.10
Rented from council	−0.17	−0.11	−0.18	−0.11	−0.08	−0.11
Rented from housing association	−0.35*	−0.15	−0.32*	−0.15	−0.24	−0.15
Rented from private landlord	−0.14	−0.12	−0.15	−0.12	−0.14	−0.11
Tenure (other)	0.18	−0.27	0.16	−0.27	0.16	−0.26
Household access to a car	−0.04	−0.07	−0.05	−0.07	−0.04	−0.07
Number of kids	0.09	−0.08	0.09	−0.07	0.05	−0.07
Very or completely dissatisfied with the police during a stop encounter (No police-initiated contact is the reference category)			−4.94***	−0.87	−4.09***	−0.83

	Model 1		Model 2		Model 3	
	Coefficient	*S.E.*	*Coefficient*	*S.E.*	*Coefficient*	*S.E.*
Fairly dissatisfied with the police during a stop encounter			−1.52*	−0.73	−0.95	−0.69
Fairly satisfied with the police during a stop encounter			−0.31	−0.33	−0.25	−0.32
Very satisfied with the police during a stop encounter			0.39	−0.27	0.22	−0.26
Satisfied with police treatment when reporting the crime (No contact is the reference category)			0.23	−0.17	0.03	−0.16
Neither satisfied nor dissatisfied with police treatment when reporting the crime			0.07	−0.37	0.4	−0.35
Dissatisfied with police treatment when reporting the crime			−1.46***	−0.26	−0.72**	−0.25
Trust in police fairness and intentions					0.35***	−0.02
Trust in police effectiveness					0.13***	−0.02
Neighbourhood level (N=881)						
Concentrated disadvantage	0.19***	−0.05	0.18***	−0.05	0.18***	−0.05
Residential stability	0.00	−0.05	0.00	−0.05	−0.01	−0.04
Immigrant concentration	0.09*	−0.05	0.10*	−0.05	0.05	−0.04
Crime	0.01	−0.06	0.01	−0.05	−0.02	−0.05
Collective efficacy	0.94***	−0.12	0.93***	−0.12	0.57***	−0.11
Perceived disorder	−0.48***	−0.06	−0.47***	−0.06	−0.48***	−0.05
Worry about crime	−0.10	−0.06	−0.08	−0.06	−0.04	−0.06

Note: unstandardised coefficients,* significant at the 5% level, ** significant at the 1% level, *** significant at the 0.1% level.

The sense of a shared moral position thus seems to be partly communicated to citizens by the police when there is a quality of their behaviour in specific interactions, and in particular when there is a lack of procedural fairness. If shared moral values are central to legitimate authority, and if contact is an important moment in the erosion of moral alignment, then this is further evidence that legitimacy is a fluid and active process, that public experience of police actions and interpersonal encounters interact in ways that compromise and undermine police legitimacy.

A focus on young males from Black and Minority Ethnic groups

What about our special population, the BME booster? We should raise, at the outset, one complication. The survey includes measures of trust in police fairness that are comparable to those in the METPAS. But it also includes more specific measures of trust in police procedural justice. As outlined in Chapter 5, measures of trust in police fairness constitute agreement or disagreement to sentiments like 'the police in this area treat everyone fairly regardless of who they are', and 'they would treat you with respect if you had contact with them for any reason'. Measures of trust in police procedural justice constitute agreement or disagreement to sentiments like 'the police use rules and procedures that are fair to everyone', and 'the police clearly explain reasons for their action'. Another feature of the BME survey is the separation between being stopped by the police and being searched by the police. There is a further focus on whether individuals had personally seen the police use unjustified violence or whether someone in their household had seen the police use unjustified violence.

Starting with obligation to obey the police, Table 13.3 shows asymmetry of contact once more. Experiencing procedural injustice and witnessing police violence is associated with less obligation, and most if not all of this estimated effect flows through trust. Models 5 and 6 differentiate between trust in police fairness and trust in police procedural justice. Moving to moral alignment with the police, we find a similar pattern to the METPAS: negative encounters with the police seem to have direct and indirect effects on moral alignment. Again asymmetry is evident. Even controlling for trust in fairness or trust in procedural justice, negative contacts are associated with lower expected levels of moral alignment. We should note, before we move to Part 5, that we also fitted these models using ordinal logistic regression, and the findings were similar to linear models.

Summary

In Part 3 of this book we found that contact with the police is an important predictor of trust in the police. Negative encounters were linked to much lower levels of trust, while positive encounters were linked to moderately higher levels of trust. As Tyler *et al.* (2007: 24) state:

> People react favourably when they believe that the authorities are sincerely trying to do what is best for the people in their communities. Authorities communicate this type of concern when they listen to people's accounts and explain their actions in ways that show an awareness of and concern about people's needs and interests.

In Part 4 we then highlighted the robust associations between trust and legitimacy. Procedural justice seems to justify the power of the police in the eyes of those they serve. But in this chapter we examined the empirical links between contact and legitimacy, finding total asymmetry in the effect of contact on legitimacy. In the case of being stopped by the police, very little of the effect seems to be mediated by trust. When it comes to the justifiability of police power, then, encounters in which officers wield their authority in fair ways may be treated as a given. People may question police authority only after experiencing bad encounters (Weitzer and Tuch 2004), and because the police patrol the inclusion–exclusion boundaries, contact with them may be inherently status challenging (Waddington 1999). The best that might be expected of any encounter – in the

Table 13.3 Police-initiated contact and felt obligation to obey the police in the booster sample.

	Model 1		Model 2		Model 3		Model 4		Model 5		Model 6	
	Coefficient	S.E.	Coefficient	S.E.	Coefficient	S.E.	Coefficient	S.E.	Coefficient	S.E.	Coefficient	S.E.
Intercept	0.37	−0.32	0.22	−0.32	0.61	−0.32	0.65*	−0.32	−0.58	−0.31	−0.47	−0.92
Ethnicity (White and Black Caribbean is the reference category):												
White and Black African	−0.57	−0.36	−0.57	−0.37	−0.51	−0.36	−0.53	−0.36	−0.25	−0.33	−0.43	−0.34
White and Asian	−0.29	−0.33	−0.35	−0.34	−0.32	−0.33	−0.21	−0.33	−0.07	−0.30	−0.03	−0.32
Any other mixed background	−0.37	−0.29	−0.35	−0.30	−0.32	−0.29	−0.33	−0.29	−0.28	−0.26	−0.26	−0.28
Indian	0.25	−0.21	0.22	−0.22	0.30	−0.21	0.30	−0.21	0.09	−0.19	0.30	−0.20
Pakistan	0.18	−0.22	0.16	−0.23	0.24	−0.22	0.25	−0.22	0.16	−0.20	0.27	−0.21
Bangladeshi	−0.06	−0.21	−0.08	−0.22	0.03	−0.21	0.02	−0.21	−0.04	−0.19	0.06	−0.20
Any other Asian background	0.10	−0.23	0.05	−0.24	0.11	−0.23	0.12	−0.23	0.02	−0.21	0.18	−0.22
Caribbean	−0.20	−0.22	−0.26	−0.22	−0.19	−0.22	−0.15	−0.22	−0.08	−0.20	−0.01	−0.21
African	0.05	−0.21	0.01	−0.21	0.04	−0.21	0.08	−0.20	0.04	−0.19	0.10	−0.19
Any other Black background	0.07	−0.38	0.12	−0.39	0.05	−0.38	0.05	−0.38	0.08	−0.34	0.11	−0.36
Chinese	0.11	−0.28	0.10	−0.28	0.15	−0.28	0.14	−0.27	0.00	−0.25	0.14	−0.26
Any other ethnic group	0.03	−0.27	−0.03	−0.28	−0.04	−0.27	0.01	−0.27	−0.07	−0.25	0.09	−0.26
Stopped by the police, experienced no procedural justice	−0.78***	−0.12					−0.64***	−0.13	−0.40**	−0.12	−0.49***	−0.13
Stopped by the police, experienced some procedural justice	−0.24*	−0.11					−0.11	−0.12	−0.06	−0.11	−0.03	−0.11
Stopped by the police, experienced strong procedural justice	−0.01	−0.11					0.07	−0.13	0.04	−0.12	0.06	−0.12
Searched by the police, experienced no procedural justice			−0.49**	−0.17			0.09	−0.18	0.26	−0.17	0.12	−0.18
Searched by the police, experienced some procedural justice			−0.42*	−0.18			−0.20	−0.19	−0.01	−0.17	−0.11	−0.18
Searched by the police, experienced strong procedural justice			−0.13	−0.16			−0.05	−0.18	0.02	−0.17	0.00	−0.17
Seen a police officer act in a violent manner					−0.26***	−0.04	−0.21***	−0.04	−0.09*	−0.04	−0.13***	−0.04
Someone in the household seen a police officer act in a violent manner					0.04*	−0.02	0.05*	−0.02	0.07***	−0.02		
Trust in police effectiveness									0.04**	−0.02	0.06**	−0.02
Trust in police procedural fairness (new)									0.16***	−0.02		
Trust in police procedural fairness (old)											v0.13***	−0.02
N	869		869		869		869		869		869	

Note: unstandardised coefficients; * significant at the 5% level, ** significant at the 1% level, *** significant at the 0.1% level.

Table 13.4 Police-initiated contact and moral alignment with the police in the booster sample.

	Model 1		Model 2		Model 3		Model 4		Model 5		Model 6	
	Coefficient	S.E.	Coefficient	S.E.	Coefficient	S.E.	Coefficient	S.E.	Coefficient	S.E.	Coefficient	S.E.
Intercept	-1.23	0.79	-1.36	0.80	-0.99	0.80	-0.91	0.79	-2.40**	0.68	-1.93	0.73
Ethnicity (White and Black Caribbean is the reference category):												
White and Black African	-0.44*	0.27	-0.55	0.28	-0.46	0.28	-0.51	0.27	-0.29	0.23	-0.42	0.25
White and Asian	-0.45	0.29	-0.54	0.29	-0.48	0.29	-0.49	0.29	-0.37	0.25	-0.27	0.26
Any other mixed background	-0.34	0.23	-0.40	0.23	-0.34	0.23	-0.41*	0.23	-0.39	0.20	-0.40	0.21
Indian	-0.19	0.17	-0.29	0.18	-0.20	0.18	-0.23**	0.17	-0.45	0.15	-0.23	0.16
Pakistan	-0.21	0.19	-0.31	0.19	-0.21	0.19	-0.25*	0.19	-0.35	0.16	-0.20	0.17
Bangladeshi	-0.31*	0.18	-0.42	0.18	-0.30*	0.18	-0.36**	0.17	-0.45	0.15	-0.29	0.16
Any other Asian background	-0.24	0.20	-0.36	0.20	-0.27	0.20	-0.32**	0.19	-0.45	0.17	-0.26	0.18
Caribbean	-0.37**	0.18	-0.48*	0.18	-0.39*	0.18	-0.38*	0.18	-0.34	0.16	-0.23	0.17
African	-0.31*	0.17	-0.40*	0.17	-0.35*	0.17	-0.36**	0.17	-0.41*	0.14	-0.32	0.16
Any other Black background	-0.15	0.32	-0.17	0.32	-0.26	0.32	-0.22	0.31	-0.20	0.27	-0.13	0.29
Chinese	-0.03	0.24	-0.12	0.24	-0.05	0.24	-0.10	0.24	-0.27	0.21	-0.08	0.22
Any other ethnic group	-0.17	0.23	-0.28	0.23	-0.23	0.23	-0.23	0.22	-0.24	0.19	-0.16	0.21
Stopped by the police, experienced no procedural justice	-0.63	0.10					-0.39	0.11	-0.16*	0.10	-0.22	0.10
Stopped by the police, experienced some procedural justice	-0.33	0.09					-0.19*	0.10	-0.18	0.09	-0.12	0.09
Stopped by the police, experienced strong procedural justice	0.03	0.09					0.07	0.11	0.02	0.09	0.04	0.10
Searched by the police, experienced no procedural justice			-0.70	0.14			-0.31	0.15	-0.14*	0.13	-0.28	0.14
Searched by the police, experienced some procedural justice			-0.44	0.14			-0.25	0.15	-0.03	0.13	-0.16	0.14
Searched by the police, experienced strong procedural justice			0.00	0.13			0.04	0.15	0.12	0.13	0.08	0.14
Seen a police officer act in a violent manner					-0.17***	0.03	-0.12	0.03	0.00	0.03	-0.04	0.03
Someone in the household seen a police officer act in a violent manner					-0.03	0.02	-0.02	0.02	-0.01	0.02	-0.01	0.02
Trust in police effectiveness							**		0.04***	0.01	0.05	0.01
Trust in police procedural fairness (new)			***		***		***		0.17***	0.01		
Trust in police procedural fairness (old)											0.15	0.02
N	869		869		869		869		869		869	

Note: unstandardised coefficients,* significant at the 5% level, ** significant at the 1% level, *** significant at the 0.1% level.

effect on people's sense of legitimacy of police power – may be the confirmation of an individual's social standing and the status quo in police legitimacy. But there are many possibilities for police behaviour to undermine this status, resulting in resentment, damaged opinions of the police and the corrosion of the authority of officers.

Part 5

Why do people cooperate with the police?

To call the police, to report crime or suspicious activities, to provide information to help police identify a criminal – these are acts of 'the community to regulate itself and the behavior of residents and visitors' (Bursik and Gramsik 2003: 15). Linking formal and informal mechanisms of social control, cooperative acts help to constitute a certain kind of normative order. But they also imply recognition of the police role in maintaining order and 'fighting crime'. Active cooperation with the police acknowledges and expresses police legitimacy.

Acts of cooperation are central also to the effective and equitable day-to-day functioning of the criminal justice system. Many criminal offences become known to the police through being identified first by a member of the public. Cooperation from citizens – whether as witnesses, jurors or in other roles – is then required throughout the criminal justice process. An absence of cooperation impairs the efficiency of the police and other criminal justice agencies and erodes the fairness of their operations (Goudriaan *et al.* 2006). If crimes are less likely to be reported by people living in certain areas, then police resources will be allocated in ways that do not reflect the 'true' distribution of crime, favouring those areas where people are more likely to report (even if the incidence of crime is lower).

In the final empirical part of the book, we turn to people's willingness to cooperate with legal authorities. In the following few pages we complete our examination of the links between neighbourhood, contact, trust, legitimacy and cooperation with the police. In Chapter 14 we consider the picture across London. In Chapter 15 we turn to our special population of young males from certain ethnic minority groups.

14 Cooperation and the portability of procedural justice

Individuals make contact with the police for many reasons, from the most serious life-or-death situation, to the most mundane everyday circumstance. In this chapter we examine the calls that citizens imagine they might make to the police to report crimes or anti-social behaviour, and the situations in which they could assist the police through the provision of information. These are types of cooperation that may not involve matters of personal concern to those involved. But they are nonetheless of great practical benefit to the police, as well as an active recognition of the propriety of the police remit over matters of crime and disorder.

The legal system benefits when people voluntarily defer to regulations and continue to defer over time. In the context of personal experiences with police officers or judges, the legal system is more effective if people voluntarily accept the decisions made by legal authorities. Absent such acceptance, and legal authorities must engage in a continuing effort to create a credible threat of punishment to assure long-term rule-following and/or decision acceptance. These types of voluntary activity are not effectively motivated by the risk of punishment; threats can sometimes compel obedience, but they do not motivate voluntary deference.

Our data speak to the perceptual and cognitive factors that influence decisions by citizens to invoke the police as agents of formal social control. Such acts of informal social control are responses to 'conduct regarded as undesirable from a normative viewpoint, that is … *conduct which ought not to occur*' (Black 1993: 22, emphasis added; see also Bursik and Gramsik 1993: 14). We examine whether individuals' willingness to contact and cooperate with the police are related to (a) the legitimacy of the police, (b) their trust in the police, (c) their contact with the police and (d) their normative assessments of the area in which they live and those they share it with (what ought or ought not to occur, what should be done about deviancy and whether it is worth getting involved).

Following the same analytical strategy as in prior sections on trust (Part 3) and legitimacy (Part 4), we begin by partitioning individual and neighbourhood level variance. After testing compositional and neighbourhood-characteristic models, we then factor in (a) contact and instrumental and/or relational concerns, (b) trust in the police and (c) legitimacy. We also examine whether the model generalises across social groups and contexts. Is the effect of contact or trust stronger for some individuals than for other individuals? Is the importance of legitimacy greater in some sorts of neighbourhoods than other sorts of neighbourhoods?

Does neighbourhood matter?

We begin by examining whether cooperation clusters in neighbourhoods (Table 14.1). Strikingly, we found that 23 per cent of variation in willingness to cooperate with the police occurs between neighbourhoods (the rest is individual, that is, within-neighbourhood variation, plus random error). Adding in individual-level factors – including age, gender, ethnicity and work status – shows that 10 per cent of the between-neighbourhood variation can be explained by certain compositional aspects. Introducing structural and social characteristics indicates the relative importance of collective efficacy, disorder and worry about crime over ethnic diversity, for example, or residential stability. Finally, adding in individual-level trust and legitimacy does not help explain neighbourhood variation: the composition of trust and legitimacy in the sampled individuals within each neighbourhood does not help us account for between-neighbourhood differences.

Table 14.2 builds up the model of cooperation in four incremental steps. Model 1 includes socio-demographic factors and social and structural neighbourhood characteristics. Model 2 adds contact with the police. Model 3 adds trust. Model 4 adds legitimacy. This structure reflects the assumed patterns of mediations. First, where someone lives (and who they are) is expected to influence the contact they have with officers. Second, the contact people have with the police is expected to shape levels of trust. Third, trust may then shape legitimacy. And all may have an effect on people's willingness to cooperate with the police.

We begin with socio-demographic predictors. According to the first fitted model, older people are more likely to report being willing to cooperate with the police, renters are less likely to cooperate (compared to people who own outright their property) and people who identify as 'White – Irish', 'Mixed – White and Black Caribbean' and 'Mixed – White and Asian' are less likely to cooperate than 'White British'. The effects do not change much as we move from model 1 to model 4, when we successively add contact, trust and legitimacy.

Of the neighbourhood characteristics, social aspects are more important than structural aspects. The stronger the level of collective efficacy, the more residents will be likely to cooperate with the police. Individuals who feel they live in

Table 14.1 Neighbourhood variation in cooperation with the police in London.

	ICC	Variance explained (%)
Empty model	0.23	
Compositional	0.20	10
Structural characteristics	0.20	11
Social characteristics	0.18	22
Structural and social characteristics	0.17	23
Structural and social characteristics and trust in the police	0.17	25
Structural and social characteristics, trust and legitimacy	0.17	25

Table 14.2 Explaining individual and neighbourhood variation in willingness to cooperate with the police in London.

	Model 1		Model 2		Model 3		Model 4	
	Coefficient	S.E.	Coefficient	S.E.	Coefficient	S.E.	Coefficient	S.E.
Intercept	2.90**	-1.05	2.97**	-1.04	4.01***	-1.06	2.53*	-1.02
Person level (N = 4,048)								
Female	0.06	-0.08	0.06	-0.08	0.07	-0.08	0.08	-0.07
Age	0.17***	-0.03	0.17***	-0.03	0.15***	-0.03	0.13***	-0.03
Ethnicity (reference: White British)								
White – Irish	-0.74***	-0.22	-0.74***	-0.22	-0.78***	-0.21	-0.72***	-0.21
White – any other	-0.08	-0.12	-0.08	-0.12	-0.12	-0.12	-0.17	-0.12
Mixed – White and Black Caribbean	-0.83**	-0.25	-0.81**	-0.25	-0.79**	-0.25	-0.79**	-0.24
Mixed – White and Black African	-0.40	-0.32	-0.32	-0.32	-0.28	-0.31	-0.17	-0.30
Mixed – White and Asian	-0.92*	-0.43	-0.81	-0.43	-0.83*	-0.42	-0.67	-0.41
Other mixed	-0.17	-0.23	-0.12	-0.23	-0.08	-0.22	-0.08	-0.22
Indian	0.00	-0.17	0.02	-0.17	-0.10	-0.17	-0.20	-0.16
Pakistani	0.07	-0.21	0.08	-0.21	-0.03	-0.20	-0.18	-0.20
Bangladeshi	0.46*	-0.20	0.47*	-0.20	0.38	-0.20	0.06	-0.19
Other Asian or Asian British	-0.14	-0.25	-0.13	-0.25	-0.15	-0.25	-0.17	-0.24
Black or Black British – Caribbean	-0.32	-0.18	-0.31	-0.18	-0.33	-0.18	-0.24	-0.17
Black or Black British – African	-0.02	-0.15	0.01	-0.15	-0.08	-0.15	-0.13	-0.14
Other Black or Black British	-0.19	-0.33	-0.16	-0.33	-0.10	-0.33	-0.08	-0.31
Chinese	-0.54	-0.40	-0.53	-0.40	-0.63	-0.39	-0.77*	-0.38
Other Chinese or other ethnic group	-0.14	-0.57	-0.17	-0.57	-0.39	-0.56	-0.30	-0.54
Work status (reference: working full-time)								
Working part-time (8–29 hrs/wk)	-0.17	-0.14	-0.19	-0.14	-0.15	-0.13	-0.14	-0.13
Working part-time (<8hrs/wk)	-0.27	-0.35	-0.25	-0.35	-0.22	-0.35	-0.09	-0.34

Continued overleaf

	Model 1		Model 2		Model 3		Model 4	
	Coefficient	S.E.	Coefficient	S.E.	Coefficient	S.E.	Coefficient	S.E.
Not working	0.17	-0.18	0.17	-0.18	0.15	-0.18	0.09	-0.17
House person	-0.04	-0.14	-0.04	-0.14	-0.11	-0.14	-0.18	-0.13
Retired	0.01	-0.14	0.03	-0.14	-0.03	-0.14	-0.11	-0.13
Registered unemployed	-0.31	-0.20	-0.33	-0.20	-0.34	-0.19	-0.22	-0.19
Unemployed but not registered	-0.23	-0.43	-0.27	-0.43	-0.30	-0.42	-0.23	-0.41
Student/full-time education	0.11	-0.17	0.11	-0.17	0.05	-0.16	0.07	-0.16
Working status (other)	-0.54	-0.37	-0.61	-0.37	-0.65	-0.36	-0.54	-0.35
Housing situation (ref.: own property outright)								
Buying on mortgage	-0.14	-0.12	-0.12	-0.12	-0.07	-0.12	-0.06	-0.12
Rented from council	-0.49***	-0.13	-0.47***	-0.13	-0.41***	-0.12	-0.42***	-0.12
Rented from housing association	-0.66***	-0.18	-0.64***	-0.18	-0.58***	-0.17	-0.53**	-0.17
Rented from private landlord	-0.44**	-0.14	-0.41**	-0.14	-0.38**	-0.14	-0.36**	-0.13
Tenure (other)	-0.43	-0.31	-0.39	-0.31	-0.36	-0.30	-0.40	-0.29
Household access to a car	0.21*	-0.08	0.19*	-0.08	0.19*	-0.08	0.21**	-0.08
Number of kids	0.20*	-0.09	0.18*	-0.09	0.15	-0.08	0.15	-0.08
Very or completely dissatisfied with the police during a stop encounter (No police-initiated contact is the reference category)			-2.74**	-0.99	-2.40*	-0.98	-1.06	-0.95
Fairly dissatisfied with the police during a stop encounter			-0.14	-0.83	0.09	-0.82	0.42	-0.79
Fairly satisfied with the police during a stop encounter			0.45	-0.38	0.42	-0.38	0.53	-0.36
Very satisfied with the police during a stop encounter			0.47	-0.31	0.42	-0.31	0.35	-0.30
Satisfied with police treatment when reporting the crime (No contact is the reference category)			0.79***	-0.19	0.63***	-0.19	0.63***	-0.18
Neither satisfied nor dissatisfied with police treatment when reporting the crime			0.70	-0.42	0.91*	-0.41	0.74	-0.40
Dissatisfied with police treatment when reporting the crime			0.27	-0.30	0.61*	-0.30	0.80**	-0.29

	Model 1		Model 2		Model 3		Model 4	
	Coefficient	S.E.	Coefficient	S.E.	Coefficient	S.E.	Coefficient	S.E.
Trust in police fairness and intentions					-0.08**	-0.03	-0.09***	-0.03
Trust in police effectiveness					0.27***	-0.03	0.15***	-0.03
Obligation to obey the police							0.12***	-0.02
Moral alignment with the police							0.23***	-0.02
Neighbourhood level (N=881)								
Concentrated disadvantage	0.16**	-0.06	0.16**	-0.06	0.15**	-0.06	0.07	-0.05
Residential stability	0.00	-0.05	0.00	-0.05	0.00	-0.05	0.00	-0.05
Immigrant concentration	0.01	-0.05	0.01	-0.05	0.02	-0.05	-0.02	-0.05
Crime	-0.08	-0.06	-0.07	-0.06	-0.09	-0.06	-0.09	-0.06
Collective efficacy	0.61***	-0.14	0.59***	-0.14	0.30*	-0.14	0.18	-0.13
Perceived disorder	-0.23***	-0.06	-0.25***	-0.06	-0.28***	-0.06	-0.11	-0.06
Worry about crime	0.35***	-0.07	0.35***	-0.07	0.32***	-0.07	0.36***	-0.07

Note: unstandardised coefficients, * significant at the 5% level, ** significant at the 1% level, *** significant at the 0.1% level.

communities where other citizens will intercede when children are misbehaving (for example) may be on average more likely to cooperate with the police (Girling *et al.* 2000; Jackson and Bradford 2009). The British police – as important group representatives – seem to garner support when local communities are seen to be cohesive, efficacious and 'pulling in the same direction'. Because the police is an organisation so strongly associated with the maintenance of social order (with the activity of policing), it is possible that individual-level cooperation with the police is fostered in part by a sense of community cohesion and collective efficacy based on a view that social order is, in fact, being maintained.

We also find that the less the amount of disorder in a given neighbourhood, the more willing people are to cooperate with the police. Table 14.3 shows that these effects are not dependent on the other social characteristics being in the fitted regression equation. At the neighbourhood level, collective efficacy and disorder are strongly correlated ($r=-0.49$) but holding each factor constant has no effect on the other coefficients. We find additive effects, whereby the more disorderly and the less cohesive the neighbourhood, the less willing local people are to cooperate with the police.

One might imagine that neighbourhoods with high levels of disorder and low levels of collective efficacy have a greater need for the police. According to this perspective, when people think that informal mechanisms of social control have been attenuated – and when they judge local order to be under threat – they would be more likely to require the assistance of the police and more ready to say they would cooperate.. With collective efficacy and disorder, we find the opposite: greater cooperation is linked with more collective efficacy and lower disorder. With worry about crime we do find some evidence for this idea: the greater the level of worry about crime in a neighbourhood, the more willing residents are to call the police and give evidence in court. It may be that lower-level social bonds and cues of order–disorder have one effect on cooperation (the more cohesive a community the greater the cooperation) while specific concerns about crime and victimisation have the opposite effect (the less fearful a community the less readiness there is to cooperate).

Looking at models 3 and 4 (Table 14.2), we can see whether these neighbourhood effects seem to work via trust and/or legitimacy. According to model 3, we find that the effect of collective efficacy is halved once trust is factored into the equation. As with legitimacy, this means that neighbourhoods with low levels of

Table 14.3 Adding neighbourhood social characteristics separately to the fitted model.

	Model 1	*Model 2*	*Model 3*	*Model 4*
	Coefficient	*Coefficient*	*Coefficient*	*Coefficient*
Collective efficacy	0.66***			0.61***
Disorder		−0.32***		−0.28***
Worry about crime			0.22***	0.43***

Note: unstandardised coefficients,* significant at the 5% level, ** significant at the 1% level, *** significant at the 0.1% level.

Table 14.4 Does the effect of satisfaction with contact vary across gender, age and ethnic status?

	Model 1		Model 2		Model 3		Model 4	
	Coefficient	S.E.	Coefficient	S.E.	Coefficient	S.E.	Coefficient	S.E.
Female	0.01	−0.02	0.01	−0.02	0.01	−0.02	0.01	−0.02
Under 25	0.03***	−0.01	0.03***	−0.01	0.03***	−0.01	0.03***	−0.01
White, British/Irish	−0.10***	−0.02	−0.10***	−0.02	−0.10***	−0.02	−0.10***	−0.02
Very or completely dissatisfied with the police during the encounter	−2.45***	−0.17	−2.81***	−0.29	−2.47***	−0.19	−2.76***	−0.21
Fairly dissatisfied with the police during the encounter	−1.14***	−0.21	−1.89***	−0.40	−1.11***	−0.24	−1.39***	−0.25
Fairly satisfied with the police during the encounter	0.01	−0.11	−0.25	−0.23	−0.04	−0.13	0.06	−0.15
Very satisfied with the police during the encounter	0.70***	−0.10	1.19***	−0.22	0.73***	−0.12	0.88***	−0.15
Female*Very or completely dissatisfied with the police during the encounter			0.13	−0.08				
Female*Fairly dissatisfied with the police during the encounter			0.27*	−0.12				
Female*Fairly satisfied with the police during the encounter			0.08	−0.06				
Female*Very satisfied with the police during the encounter			−0.13*	−0.05				
Under25*Very or completely dissatisfied with the police during the encounter					0.06	−0.40		
Under25*Fairly dissatisfied with the police during the encounter					−0.11	−0.54		
Under25*Fairly satisfied with the police during the encounter					0.18	−0.26		
Under25*Very satisfied with the police during the encounter					−0.10	−0.21		
White, British/Irish*Very or completely dissatisfied with the police during the encounter							0.85*	−0.35
White, British/Irish*Fairly dissatisfied with the police during the encounter							0.89	−0.47
White, British/Irish*Fairly satisfied with the police during the encounter							−0.13	−0.23
White, British/Irish*Very satisfied with the police during the encounter							−0.31	−0.20
N	37584		37584		37584		37584	

Note: unstandardised coefficients; * significant at the 5% level, ** significant at the 1% level, *** significant at the 0.1% level.

collective efficacy also include residents with typically lower levels of trust in the police; in turn, lower levels of trust help explain lower levels of cooperation. For disorder and worry about crime, however, effects on cooperation do not appear to work via trust. According to model 4, the effect of collective efficacy is no longer statistically significant, suggesting that both trust and legitimacy are mediating factors. Similarly, the effect of disorder is also no longer statistically significant. Finally, the effect of worry about crime does not change.

Worry about crime seems to have a direct effect on cooperation. Net of many other factors in the model, the more fearful a neighbourhood, the more the residents are willing to cooperate with the police. This may reflect a greater need for the police and legal authorities more generally. By contrast, the more cohesive and orderly a neighbourhood, the more people are willing to cooperate. And these effects run entirely thorough both trust and legitimacy. Orderly neighbourhoods tend to contain trusting residents who confer legitimacy to the police. Such trust and legitimacy may then have a knock-on effect on cooperation.

What about contact with the police? Recall that earlier in the book we showed that negative contacts are associated with lower levels of trust and legitimacy, and positive contacts are associated with higher levels of trust. The effect of contact on legitimacy was entirely asymmetrical. We find the same with cooperation: people who had been stopped by the police over the past 12 months, and had felt 'very or completely' dissatisfied with the police, were much less likely to cooperate with the police than those who had not experienced a stop (and those who felt satisfied with the police during a stop). By contrast, people who had been a victim of crime, who had reported the crime to the police, and who had felt satisfied with the police, were more likely to cooperate with the police than those who had not been a victim and reported it to the police.

We thus find asymmetry for both types of contact, but the direction is reversed. For police-initiated contact (being stopped by the police) negative contact has a strong estimated negative effect on cooperation. For public-initiated contact (reporting a crime to the police) positive contact has an estimated positive effect on cooperation. Adding trust (model 3) and legitimacy (model 4) has no effect on the estimated effect of public-initiated contact, suggesting that such positive experience makes people more willing to cooperate with the police, not because the experience raises their feelings of trust and legitimacy, but rather perhaps, because of the interpersonal nature of the encounter itself. By contrast, adding legitimacy (model 4) renders the estimated effect of police-initiated contact no longer significant. This suggests that such negative experience makes people less willing to cooperate with the police, because perhaps the experience delegitimizes the police.

What about the last aspect of the procedural justice model? Consistent with Tyler's framework, we find that trust in police fairness and/or intentions is a more important predictor of cooperation than trust in police effectiveness (model 3). Just under half of the effect of trust in police fairness and/or intentions works via legitimacy (model 4). Of the two aspects of legitimacy, moral alignment is a more powerful predictor of cooperation than obligation to obey.

The portability of procedural justice

Thus far we have tested models on either the entire London sample or the booster sample of young males from various ethnic minority communities. The METPAS involves data from a variety of heterogeneous groups. But might there be important variation between key social groups that is masked by our analyses thus far?

Does the procedural justice model work differently for different social groups or in different neighbourhood contexts? We examine the portability of the procedural justice model across key social groups and contexts. We start with the impact of contact on trust in police fairness and/or interests among different groups of people. Table 14.4 successively adds interactions between stop experiences and gender (model 2), age (model 3) and ethnic group (model 4; because of sample size issues, we differentiate between 'White British'/'White Irish' and the rest). The evidence suggests that:

- The effect of stop-and-search is slightly weaker for females compared to males;
- The effect of stop-and-search is the same for over-25s and under-25s;
- The negative effect of very dissatisfactory stop-and-search contact is slightly stronger for people who are not 'White British' or 'White Irish'.

Tables 14.5 and 14.6 turn to interaction effects involving neighbourhood characteristics. Does the effect of contact on trust to some extent depend upon the social or structural context? With respect to structural characteristics we find no significant interactions. With respect to social characteristics we find only one small interaction effect: the positive effect of positive contact is slightly smaller in neighbourhoods with high levels of worry about crime and disorder.

We ran the same models for being searched by the police. For reasons of space we do not include the full findings (please contact the first author), but to summarise, we find no interaction effects involving gender and ethnicity yet a slightly stronger positive effect of positive contact among under-25s. By contrast, we find more positive effects of contact deemed to convey some (but not total) procedural justice in neighbourhoods that are disadvantaged, disorderly and fearful.

We next turn to interactions between trust in police fairness and/or intentions and a range of other factors, each predicting police legitimacy. For this we move to the first quarter of the 2009/2010 METPAS sweep. Starting with obligation to obey the police, we find no interactions involving age, gender and ethnicity, nor with having been stopped by the police in the past 12 months or having been a victim of crime in the past 12 months. The effect of trust on obligation also did not differ across neighbourhoods: none of the structural or social characteristics had significant interaction effects with trust.

The effect of trust on moral alignment also does not seem to differ much across social groups and neighbourhood contexts. Two exceptions are small interaction effects involving ethnicity (the effect of trust on moral alignment was slightly smaller for 'White British'/'White Irish') and immigrant concentration (the effect

Table 14.5 Does the effect of satisfaction with contact vary according to social characteristics of the neighbourhood?

	Model 1		Model 2		Model 3		Model 4	
	Coefficient	S.E.	Coefficient	S.E.	Coefficient	S.E.	Coefficient	S.E.
Concentrated disadvantage	0.01	-0.01	0.01	-0.01	0.01	-0.01	0.01	-0.01
Residential stability	0.03*	-0.01	0.03*	-0.01	0.03*	-0.01	0.03*	-0.01
Immigrant concentration	-0.03*	-0.01	-0.03*	-0.01	-0.03*	-0.01	-0.03*	-0.01
Crime	-0.01	-0.01	-0.01	-0.01	-0.01	-0.01	-0.01	-0.01
Collective efficacy	1.02***	-0.03	1.02***	-0.03	1.02***	-0.03	1.02***	-0.03
Perceived disorder	0.20***	-0.01	0.20***	-0.01	0.20***	-0.01	0.20***	-0.01
Worry about crime	-0.04**	-0.02	-0.04**	-0.02	-0.04**	-0.02	-0.04*	-0.02
Very or completely dissatisfied with the police during the encounter	-2.46***	-0.17	-2.48***	-0.17	-2.48***	-0.17	-2.45***	-0.17
Fairly dissatisfied with the police during the encounter	-1.14***	-0.21	-0.97***	-0.24	-1.08***	-0.23	-1.04***	-0.23
Fairly satisfied with the police during the encounter	0.00	-0.11	0.00	-0.11	-0.06	-0.14	0.02	-0.12
Very satisfied with the police during the encounter	0.70***	-0.10	0.69***	-0.10	0.74***	-0.10	0.74***	-0.10
Collective efficacy*Very or completely dissatisfied with the police during the encounter			-0.23	-0.49				
Collective efficacy*Fairly dissatisfied with the police during the encounter			0.88	-0.52				
Collective efficacy*Fairly satisfied with the police during the encounter			0.01	-0.30				
Collective efficacy*Very satisfied with the police during the encounter			0.25	-0.22				
Disorder*Very or completely dissatisfied with the police during the encounter					-0.32	-0.23		
Disorder*Fairly dissatisfied with the police during the encounter					-0.27	-0.32		
Disorder*Fairly satisfied with the police during the encounter					0.15	-0.20		
Disorder*Very satisfied with the police during the encounter					-0.36*	-0.16		
Worry about crime*Very or completely dissatisfied with the police during the encounter							-0.17	-0.18
Worry about crime*Fairly dissatisfied with the police during the encounter							-0.25	-0.17
Worry about crime*Fairly satisfied with the police during the encounter							-0.08	-0.12
Worry about crime*Very satisfied with the police during the encounter							-0.26	-0.11

Note: unstandardised coefficients, * significant at the 5% level, ** significant at the 1% level, *** significant at the 0.1% level.

Table 14.6 Does the effect of satisfaction with contact vary according to structural characteristics of the neighbourhood?

	Model 1		Model 2		Model 3		Model 4		Model 5	
	Coefficient	S.E.	Coefficient	S.E.	Coefficient	S.E.	Coefficient	S.E.	Coefficient	S.E.
Concentrated disadvantage	0.01	-0.01	0.02	-0.01	0.01	-0.01	0.01	-0.01	0.01	-0.01
Residential stability	0.03*	-0.01	0.03**	-0.01	0.03**	-0.01	0.03*	-0.01	0.03*	-0.01
Immigrant concentration	-0.03*	-0.01	-0.03*	-0.01	-0.03*	-0.01	-0.03*	-0.01	-0.03*	-0.01
Crime	-0.01	-0.01	-0.01	-0.01	-0.01	-0.01	-0.01	-0.01	-0.01	-0.01
Collective efficacy	1.02***	-0.03	1.02***	-0.03	1.02***	-0.03	1.02***	-0.03	1.02***	-0.03
Perceived disorder	0.20***	-0.01	0.20***	-0.01	0.20***	-0.01	0.20***	-0.01	0.20***	-0.01
Worry about crime	-0.04**	-0.02	-0.04**	-0.02	-0.04**	-0.02	-0.04**	-0.02	-0.04**	-0.02
Very or completely dissatisfied with the police during the encounter	-2.46***	-0.17	-2.42***	-0.18	-2.46***	-0.17	-2.48***	-0.17	-2.43***	-0.20
Fairly dissatisfied with the police during the encounter	-1.14***	-0.21	-1.13***	-0.22	-1.10***	-0.21	-1.11***	-0.22	-1.18***	-0.24
Fairly satisfied with the police during the encounter	0.00	-0.11	0.01	-0.11	0.00	-0.11	0.00	-0.11	-0.03	-0.14
Very satisfied with the police during the encounter	0.70***	-0.10	0.69***	-0.10	0.70***	-0.10	0.68***	-0.10	0.71***	-0.10
Concentrated disadvantage*Very or completely dissatisfied with the police during the encounter			-0.14	-0.15						
Concentrated disadvantage*Fairly dissatisfied with the police during the encounter			-0.09	-0.20						
Concentrated disadvantage*Fairly satisfied with the police during the encounter			-0.23	-0.12						
Concentrated disadvantage*Very satisfied with the police during the encounter			-0.12	-0.10						
Residential stability*Very or completely dissatisfied with the police during the encounter					-0.06	-0.18				
Residential stability*Fairly dissatisfied with the police during the encounter					-0.48	-0.25				

Continued overleaf

	Model 1		Model 2		Model 3		Model 4		Model 5	
	Coefficient	S.E.	Coefficient	S.E.	Coefficient	S.E.	Coefficient	S.E.	Coefficient	S.E.
Residential stability*Fairly satisfied with the police during the encounter					-0.12	-0.14				
Residential stability*Very satisfied with the police during the encounter					-0.10	-0.08				
Immigrant concentration*Very or completely dissatisfied with the police during the encounter							-0.24	-0.17		
Immigrant concentration*Fairly dissatisfied with the police during the encounter							-0.23	-0.20		
Immigrant concentration*Fairly satisfied with the police during the encounter							-0.05	-0.12		
Immigrant concentration*Very satisfied with the police during the encounter							-0.10	-0.10		
Crime*Very or completely dissatisfied with the police during the encounter									-0.06	-0.22
Crime*Fairly dissatisfied with the police during the encounter									0.10	-0.29
Crime*Fairly satisfied with the police during the encounter									0.05	-0.16
Crime*Very satisfied with the police during the encounter									-0.03	-0.13

Note: unstandardised coefficients,* significant at the 5% level, ** significant at the 1% level, *** significant at the 0.1% level.

of trust on moral alignment was slightly bigger in neighbourhoods with greater ethnic diversity).

Moving finally to interaction effects where the outcome variable is cooperation, we again find very few moderations. Four exceptions are:

1 The effect of moral alignment on cooperation is slightly weaker in neighbourhoods with high levels of worry about crime;
2 The effect of obligation to obey on cooperation is slightly weaker in neighbourhoods with high levels of worry about crime;
3 The effect of obligation to obey on cooperation is slightly weaker for females compared to males;
4 The effect of trust in police fairness and/or interests on cooperation is slightly weaker for 'White British'/'White Irish' than for other ethnic groups.

Summary

Four findings emerge from the analyses in this penultimate empirical chapter. First, a good deal of variation in cooperation clusters at the neighbourhood level. Around one-fifth of this variation can be explained by the social characteristics and composition of the neighbourhood. At the neighbourhood level, high collective efficacy (shared values and the willingness to act upon those shared values to achieve collective goods) and low disorder are associated with higher individual levels of cooperation.

One way to interpret these findings is to consider Bursik and Gramsik's (1993) three types of 'informal' social control (see also Warner 2007). First is the private social control that is embedded in the relationships between family and close friends. Second is the parochial social control exerted by more diffuse networks of people usually imagined to be operating within a geographically and/or socially bounded area. Third is the indirect informal social control, or what Warner (2007: 101) calls public control, that is bound up in the ability of individuals and social networks to 'secure public goods and services that are allocated by agencies located outside the area' (Bursik and Gramsik 1993: 17; quoted in Warner 2007: 101). We find that people who live in an area with strong levels of parochial social control are more likely to act in ways that 'bridge' to formal social control mechanisms. Conversely, we find that people are less willing to get personally involved if they do not feel that others around them share similar concerns and would support them. People who live in a neighbourhood with high levels of worry about crime are also more likely to get involved. If high levels of cohesion and order are associated with greater cooperation, high levels of worry about crime are also associated with greater cooperation. This reflects the idea that fearful neighbourhoods contain problems that lead to a greater need to involve the police: our London respondents may see a greater need for the police, so they report being more likely to call the police.

Second, contact with the police is linked directly to cooperation. Negative police-initiated encounters (being stopped by the police) are associated with lower levels of cooperation, and positive public-initiated encounters (reporting a crime) are associated with higher levels of cooperation. These effects are entirely asymmetrical: in the case of police-initiated encounters, a bad encounter seems to have a strong negative effect while a good encounter seems to have no effect; in the case of public-initiated encounters, a good encounter seems to have a positive effect while a bad encounter seems to have no effect.

Third, trust in police fairness and/or intentions is a more important predictor of cooperation than trust in police effectiveness. This is consistent with Tyler's procedural justice model: fairness activates people's connections with authorities, thus increasing their propensity to cooperate. Fourth, legitimacy explains a good deal of variation in cooperation. But moral alignment is more important than obligation to obey. The value of cultivating people's feeling of obligation to the police lies in the fact that such legitimacy enables the effective exercise of social authority. While authorities can exercise power directly through the promise of rewards or the threat of punishment, such approaches to deterrence are expensive, inefficient and psychologically naive. They may be especially problematic during instability or crisis, when authorities need the support of the people at a time in which they lack control over resources. An organisation or society whose governance is motivated only by incentives and sanctions is at risk of disintegrating during times of trouble or change. If a system enjoys widespread authority, institutions can appeal to members based upon their shared purposes and values, providing the system with much-needed stability.

Finally, we find that the procedural justice model generalises across social groups and contexts. Testing interaction effects involving contact, trust, legitimacy and cooperation, we show that most of the associations do not depend on aspects like gender, age and ethnicity nor on neighbourhood characteristics such as crime rates, deprivation and collective efficacy.

15 Revisiting a special population

A focus on young males from Black and Minority Ethnic groups

In this final empirical chapter we test the full model of cooperation on our special population. Young males from various ethnic minority groups are more likely than the general population to be 'police property', to have a more adversarial and tense relationship with police officers, and to see the police as a source of social regulation. In Chapter 14 we examined whether the model generalises across gender, age and ethnic groups. But we did not focus on one particular group that combines categories of these three different variables: young males who belong to ethnic minority groups. In this chapter we test the model on 1,000 such individuals.

Testing the procedural justice model

We use structural equation modelling to investigate the layered associations between a series of latent variables. In order to deal with missing values, we implement full information maximum likelihood estimation. Because our models contain both categorical and continuous manifest and latest variables, different types of regression are used in different parts of the model. Figure 15.1 presents the findings. Since the model places few constraints on paths between latent constructs, the adequate fit of the model (CFI >0.95; TLI >0.95; RMSEA = 0.06, see Hu and Bentler 1999) refers mostly to the measurement models (Mulaik *et al.* 1989; McDonald and Ho 2002). Factor loadings are high in every case.

First, trust in police procedural justice is a strong predictor of obligation to obey and moral alignment. Second, obligation to obey is a strong predictor of cooperation. But strikingly, moral alignment is a weaker predictor of cooperation. Among this special population, then, cooperation seems to be more responsive to feelings of obligation than to feelings of moral alignment. Figure 15.1 does not include the effects of contact: these are summarised instead in Table 15.1. Having seen an officer act in a violent manner, or having someone in the household having seen an officer act in a violent manner, is associated with lower levels of trust in police effectiveness and procedural justice. Personal encounters with the police are also predictive of trust in procedural justice, with evidence of asymmetry: negative encounters are associated with lower levels of trust while positive encounters seem to have no effect.

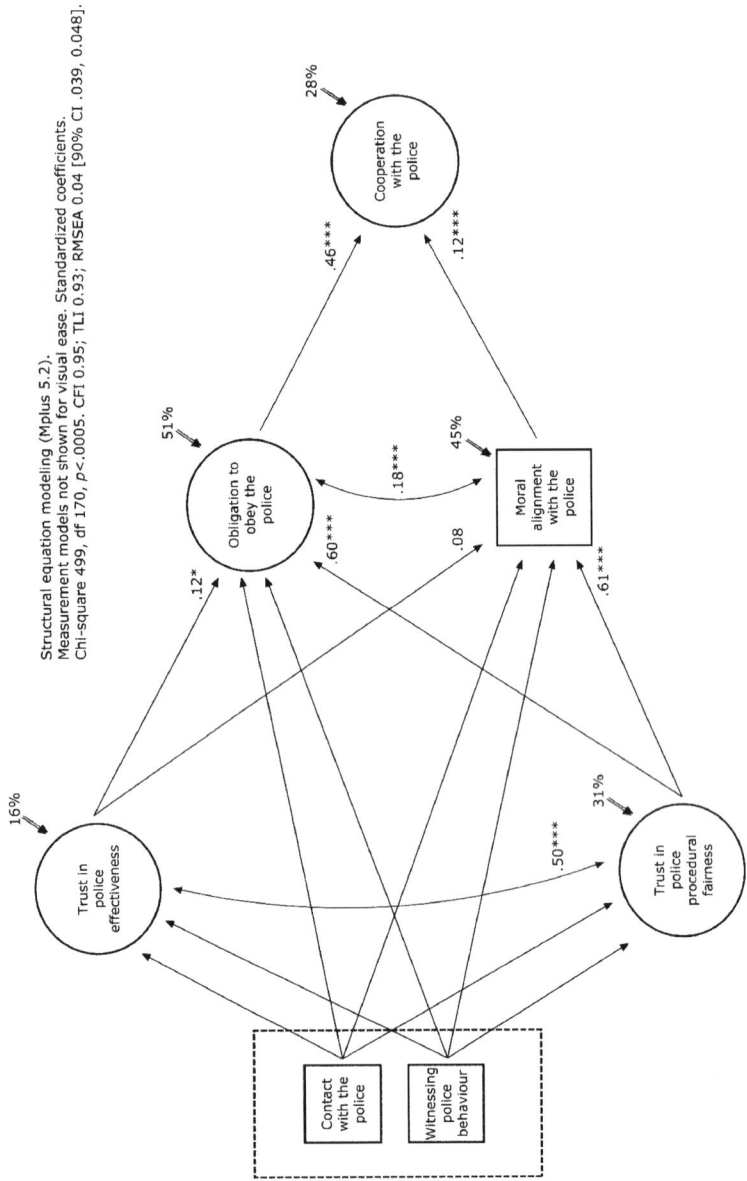

Structural equation modeling (Mplus 5.2).
Measurement models not shown for visual ease. Standardized coefficients.
Chi-square 499, df 170, p<.0005. CFI 0.95; TLI 0.93; RMSEA 0.04 [90% CI .039, 0.048].

Figure 15.1 Explaining cooperation with the police: structural equation model from the booster sample (1).

Table 15.1 Summary of the statistical effects of contact from the structural equation model.

	Effectiveness		Procedural justice		Obligation to obey		Moral alignment	
	Coefficient	S.E.	Coefficient	S.E.	Coefficient	S.E.	Coefficient	S.E.
Stopped by the police, experienced no procedural justice	−0.06	0.04	−0.10**	0.04	−0.08	0.04	0.01	0.03
Stopped by the police, experienced some procedural justice	−0.07	0.04	−0.08*	0.03	−0.01	0.03	0.01	0.03
Stopped by the police, experienced strong procedural justice	−0.02	0.04	−0.03	0.04	−0.02	0.04	0.03	0.03
Searched by the police, experienced no procedural justice	−0.11**	0.04	−0.19***	0.04	−0.07	0.04	−0.02	0.03
Searched by the police, experienced some procedural justice	−0.04	0.04	−0.03	0.03	−0.04	0.03	−0.07*	0.03
Searched by the police, experienced strong procedural justice	−0.01	0.04	0.00	0.04	−0.03	0.04	−0.01	0.03
Seen a police officer act in a violent manner	−0.24***	0.04	−0.29***	0.03	−0.10**	0.04	0.02	0.03
Someone in the household seen a police officer act in a violent manner	−0.11**	0.04	−0.14***	0.03	−0.12***	0.03	0.02	0.03

Note: unstandardised coefficients,* significant at the 5% level, ** significant at the 1% level, *** significant at the 0.1% level.

What about indirect effects of contact on cooperation? We do not show this here, but a test of indirect effects showed that none of the search variables have indirect effects on cooperation. Only those who were stopped and experienced no procedural justice had lower expected levels of cooperation, with half the estimated effect going via procedural justice and obligation, and one-third of the effect going via procedural justice and moral alignment. Having personally seen an officer acting in a violent manner also had a significant indirect effect, with half of the effect going via procedural justice and obligation.

We finish our analysis with a tentative reformulation of the model. In the model above we treat our concepts as reflective. Each concept is regarded as a latent construct that is the cause of its appropriate measures and which exists independent of those measures (Borsboom *et al.* 2003). Variation in the obligation to obey is thus assumed to precede variation in the indicators. The measurement model specifies that its indicators are independent after conditioning on the latent variable.

We have considered two dimensions of legitimacy – obligation to obey and moral alignment – and we have assumed that these two legitimising beliefs have separate (orthogonal) effects on cooperation. But might we think about legitimacy as being a formative concept, more specifically formed out of different dimensions of legitimacy? Levels of obligation and moral alignment may, in other words, cause (or define) some overall level of the concept. In this final analysis we bring into the fold people's perceptions of the legality of the police. We consider whether legitimacy is built up from its three constituent parts (obligation to obey, moral alignment and perceived legality), and we assume that each of these constituent parts cause – exist independently to – higher-level legitimacy.

Figure 15.2 shows the findings of a model in which 'legitimacy' is treated as a linear combination of the three aspects of legitimacy (as well as a linear combination of the variables specified further back in the model). The new 'formative concept' stands in for the idea that an individual recognises police power and believes that this power is justified. Part of this is compliance and obligation. Part of this is the belief that the police follow the rule of law (that is, they follow their own rules and the rules that they impose on people). And part of this is the belief that the police have an appropriate sense of right and wrong. We have no expectation about the correlations between the sub-dimensions; we are entirely pragmatic about them summing together to indicate something important.

Testing this model, we find that police legitimacy is a strong predictor of cooperation, explaining just over one-quarter of the variation. Most of this effect comes via obligation to obey and trust in police procedural fairness, again showing support for Tyler's framework. Then, by examining indirect effects of contact and witnessing police behaviour, we find a large indirect pathway from experiencing no procedural justice during a stop-and-search to cooperate, via procedural justice, obligation to obey, and legitimacy as a formative concept.

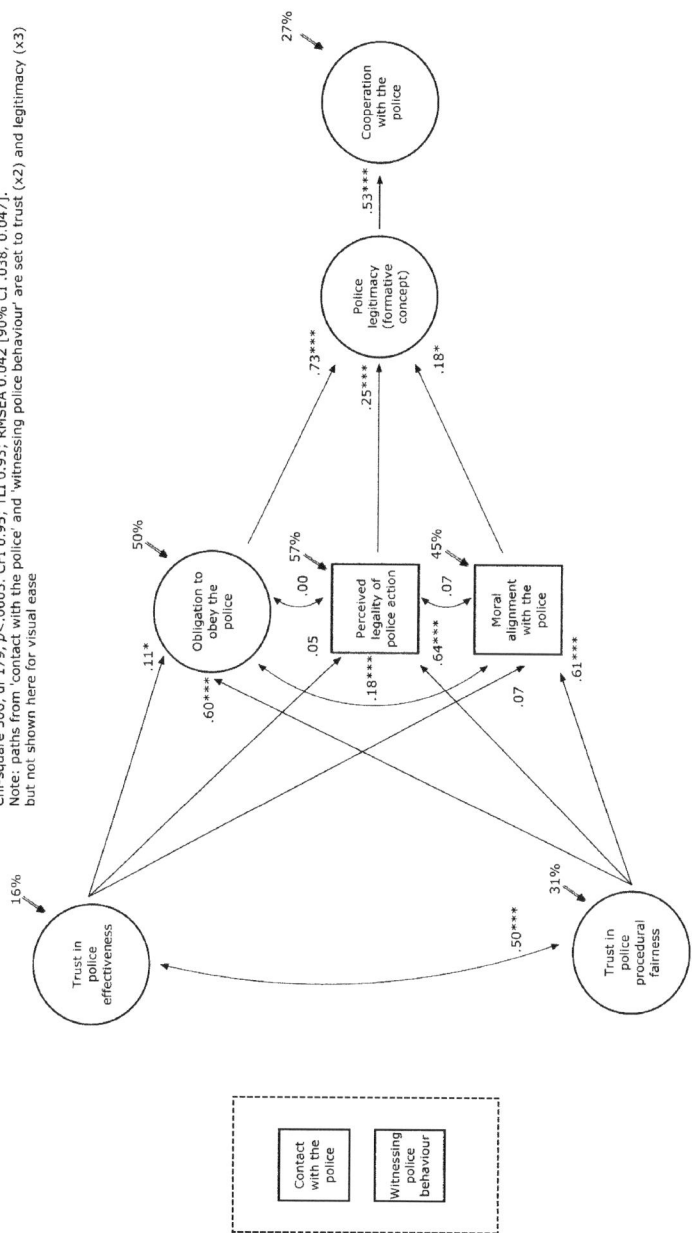

Structural equation modeling (Mplus 5.2).
Measurement models not shown for visual ease. Standardized coefficients.
Chi-square 506, df 179, p <.0005. CFI 0.95; TLI 0.93; RMSEA 0.042 [90% CI .038, 0.047].
Note: paths from 'contact with the police' and 'witnessing police behaviour' are set to trust (x2) and legitimacy (x3)
but not shown here for visual ease

Figure 15.2 Explaining cooperation with the police: structural equation model from the booster sample (2).

Summary

Our findings in this chapter again support Tyler's procedural justice model, this time with a group of individuals who have a more complex relationship with the police. Of significance, however, is the particular aspect of legitimacy that seems to be most important in explaining willingness to cooperate. In Chapter 14 we showed that moral alignment is a more powerful predictor of cooperation than obligation to obey. But in this chapter we found the opposite. Obligation to obey is most important. It may be that people with a more conflicted relationship with the police base their connection with authorities less on shared moral purpose, and more on notions of obligation, consent and regulation.

Part 6

Conclusions

Policing in its contemporary forms affects the lives of everyone living in states with functioning police services. While this influence manifests in many different ways – largely negatively in repressive or excessively corrupt environments – social scientists studying mature democracies have made claims, based on empirical data, about the influence of police on citizens' propensities to commit crime, engage in informal social control and generally cooperate in the co-production of social order (Tyler 2006a, 2011a, 2011b). These claims are founded upon specific notions of trust, legitimacy and the nature of the relationship between police and public – in particular, that the police represent and embody a social group most people want to, need to and indeed do feel part of. Such claims imply a role for policing that extends far beyond simply apprehending individuals who break the law.

It is still a common notion that police fight crime by enforcing the law. Yet we have shown that the police can influence the policed in more consensual and less confrontational ways. By enhancing legitimacy through justified and procedurally fair action, they can engender in citizens the belief that it is morally just to obey the law (Tyler and Huo 2002). Compared to a deterrence model of legal authority, advocating procedural justice as an appeal to improvement for policing in mature democracies promotes normative modes of compliance and cooperation that are both more stable and more sustainable in the long run (Schulhofer *et al.* 2010). The evidence presented in this book supports many of these claims. In this concluding part we highlight the main points raised, and we note some of their practical and theoretical implications.

16   Conclusions

Trust

The public police have been the focus of this book, and both 'public' and 'police' provide important markers of delimitation. We have examined the nature and extent of the trust citizens place in what most still consider as 'the police': uniformed protectors, peacekeepers or enforcers, paid for by the public purse and with a stated mission to serve – or govern – all members of society. We recognise that this is a limited vision of policing. It pays little attention to either private and other forms of police organisation or to the fact that some members of the public may be well aware that these other forms exist. Public ideas about private policing, and an empirical investigation into the legitimacy of private or quasi-state police, would be a fascinating topic for another book.

But provisos aside, concentrating on the public police allows us to focus on those forms and sources of trust that are most relevant to the topic at hand. These concern the relationship between citizens, as individuals and as members of communities, and a key state agency. The police is an agency for which citizens pay in a collective manner and therefore of which, at least in a technical sense else, they have joint ownership.

As might be expected, we find the trust relationship between police and public to be a complicated one. On the one hand, trust is a practical matter (O'Neill 2005), relating closely to notions of accountability. Trust in the police should be warranted by its ability to act fairly, effectively and on the basis of shared values and interests, as well as the extent to which it is accountable to the public it serves and to the rule of law. In an important, indeed necessary sense, trust needs to be realistic and specific. We do not want people to trust an untrustworthy institution; we want people to trust an institution that is worthy of the faith they put in it. We should therefore not underestimate the importance of making intelligent and discriminatory judgements about police actions and activities; nor should we underestimate people's ability to do this. Trust in these terms is a *tool of accountability*. When trust is an intelligent and discriminating attitude, when citizens actively and realistically assess the trustworthiness of the police, then this in itself holds the police to account for its actions and position in society.

Of prime concern, therefore, is where trust comes from. Consistent with Tyler's process-based model of policing, we find that fair and respectful treatment and decision-making is key. Modelling within-neighbourhood variation and incorporating ecological effects, we show that contact with the police and the procedural justice demonstrated by officers is critical. There is thus strong evidence that people base their trust judgements in part on what the police actually do (and how people make sense and interpret police actions); they withdraw trust when they see police behaving in what they think are unfair or morally unjustifiable ways.

Yet, it would be naive to suggest that trust is always conscious and discriminatory. Concerning the acceptance of risk and vulnerability, trust is placed without guarantees. We do not have a guarantee that the police will always do what they are asked or tasked to do. The police have the choice not to act in our interests but in ways that benefit themselves and/or their political masters. While it may be based on personal experience and even cold calculation, trust also always involves a 'leap of faith' (Mollering 1994; c.f. Smith 2007). To trust in the police is to believe that officers have appropriate motives, are technically competent in the roles assigned to them, and will carry out their fiduciary obligations (that is, in certain situations place our interests above their own). People look to officers to deal with crime and disorder in terms of prevention, of apprehending those who disobey the law, to be impartial and fair and restrained in their use of authority. And while their experience of police and policing are critical to whether they find the police to be trustworthy, many other factors influence the judgements they make.

Our investigation of the social connection between police and public suggests, then, that individuals judge the police not only on the encounters they have with officers, but also in part on the strength of subtle, informal social controls in their immediate social environment. The extent of policing by local residents (or levels of collective efficacy) is linked to evaluations of the success of policing by legal authorities. The police seem more successful the less they are needed, as Reiner (2000: xi) insightfully notes. When order is being maintained in the community, by subtle, informal social controls, the police get some of the credit, and their moral authority seems to be enhanced. But when disorder is evident, when incivilities are present and residents do not act upon shared values in order to regulate behaviour for the collective good, the police seem weak and disengaged.

These effects are likely to be multiplicative. Meares and Kahan (1998: 806) argue that:

> Individuals [do not] decide to obey or break the law in isolation; rather their decisions interact with and reinforce each other, creating norms of order or disorder within their communities. By shaping preferences for crime, accentuating the perceived status of law-breaking, and enfeebling the institutions that normally hold criminal propensities in check, disorderly norms create crime.

If the police are not presenting a visible and accessible source of moral authority, in a community that already lacks strong norms to regulate daily life, people not only conclude that the community is unable or unwilling to enforce basic norms of civility: they also infer that the police are powerless to impose sanction on those who violate basic norms. People identify less with the police, and a police force that is seen to be failing to regulate social behaviour is a police force that lacks the legitimacy that its position in society requires.

Legitimacy

A multi-dimensional notion of legitimacy guided our empirical work. Based in large part on recognition and consent (Beetham 1991), police legitimacy is the normative basis of police authority. Legitimacy is a recognition of, or orientation toward, power which often involves a 'largely unquestioned' acceptance of authority (Barker 2001: 33), but there is also *justification* in legitimacy. Given the specific symbolism and the foundational legitimation of the police in England and Wales, including moral alignment in any definition of police legitimacy makes sense. The cultural symbolism of the police is rooted in the myth of the 'British bobby'. Robert Peel's principles of policing operation for the London Metropolitan Police remain ideologically important. Phrases like 'the police are the public and the public are the police' and 'the ability of the police to perform their duties is dependent upon public approval of police actions' (for example, Reith 1952: 154) speak to a close social connection between what were then 'subjects of the crown' and the police.

Our framework is premised on the idea that the justice system is considered legitimate by the public when individuals governed by it feel (a) an obligation to obey the authority (a special case of Beetham's notion of expressed consent) and (b) that the authority expresses shared morals (people justify the existence of legal authorities when those authorities are believed to enact, defend and strengthen shared moral values). Assessments of the extent of 'moral alignment' between citizen and authority provide a metric for assessing whether those authorities operate in a normatively justifiable manner. A sense of value alignment provides the police with the *moral authority* to act as a source of guidance or an exemplar of proper conduct. On this account the moral authority of the police stems from the beliefs people have about it and the intentions they impute to it. Individuals confer on the police a right to dictate appropriate behaviour when they believe it is legitimate in the authority it possesses, and when it represents and defends moral values they share with it. People may obey the police, even if they disagree with the specific context of the instructions, because of the authority it possess and because it embodies a sense of shared moral purpose.

But how does this play out on an empirical level? In the eyes of many citizens, the continued justification of the existence and moral authority of the police may rest on the idea that it reflects and defends this common moral purpose. People look to the police to defend and typify shared values and they assess its right to determine appropriate behaviour partly on the basis of its success in doing so. When people 'wrap up' the inferred strength of formal social controls, that is, the police, with the strength of informal social controls, as we argue they do, failures in informal social controls mean the police are seen to be failing in their core justifying functions – keeping the peace, imposing their authority and working with the community to achieve adherence to shared norms. When people perceive a lack of shared purpose in their communities they are less likely to feel a sense of moral congruence with the police. And as with trust, we find that an important component of police legitimacy is bound up with the strength and condition of the social fabric. There is a significant element of social ecology in police legitimacy that warrants further study. We have shown that the legitimacy of the police is bound up with factors beyond its immediate behaviour, and that people draw on a diverse range of ideas and experiences when assessing the nature and quality of police authority.[1]

The evidence presented in the preceding chapters concurs with Tyler and colleagues' work on procedural justice. Public perceptions of fairness, equitability and transparency of procedure play a key role in securing support for and cooperation with authorities such as the police. Fair and decent treatment fosters satisfaction with the authority, enhances its legitimacy and increases cooperation. According to the broader procedural justice model, if that authority is the police, this enhanced legitimacy will boost compliance with the law and encourage self-regulation. In contrast, if the police are perceived to be illegitimate not only will cooperation decline but people will be less likely to obey the law, encouraging or forcing authorities to take a more punitive and/or aggressive stance – which is likely to be perceived as procedurally unfair by members of the public. A downward spiral of increasing distance and antagonism between police and public is therefore one possible outcome from widespread perceptions that police are procedurally unfair or unjust.

We did not have measures of compliance available for this study. So a definitive test of Tyler's model of legal compliance was beyond us (but see Hough *et al.* 2010; Jackson *et al.* 2011, 2012a). But the evidence we have presented is so overwhelmingly in favour of a 'procedural justice effect' it would be surprising if, in future UK studies, strong links between perceptions of police fairness, legitimacy and compliance were not to be found. Be that as it may, the potential of downward spirals in police–public relations are in any case indicated by the strong links we find between procedural justice, legitimacy and cooperation (as well, of course, by a long series of previous studies stretching back at least as far as the first *Policing for London* report and right up to the present day – e.g. Clayman and Skinns 2011). When local communities feel they can no longer rely on the police then the police can no longer rely on the support and cooperation it would otherwise receive when policing those communities. This implies either a withdrawal from those communities, as solving crimes becomes more difficult, or a ramping up of aggressive or coercive tactics to compensate for the absence of more consensual policing tools. In either case, the implications for the community involved would be profoundly negative, and would likely serve to exacerbate existing tensions with the police.

Final words

Our final thoughts pick up this last point. Why is trust in the police and the legitimacy granted to it by citizens so important? First, ethically justifiable criminal justice policy relies on their active and willing cooperation. Absent such cooperation, and the most likely alternative is aggressive interventions from police and other criminal justice agents in the face of public opposition, rapidly leading to confrontation and, eventually, violence. The alternative, withdrawal of the police to leave the community to maintain itself, carries significant long-term costs for both the community and the criminal justice system itself, costs it is unlikely either would be willing to bear in the long run. Second, and in a much broader sense, modes of social regulation not based on concepts of fairness and justified legitimacy are not only ethically undesirable but also unstable and, in the long run, unviable. It is simply not possible for a democratic state to control its citizens against their will, or via simple 'dull compulsion'. An active, positive relationship between the people and state agencies is required and, when it comes to the police at least, it seems that this relationship is founded most strongly in trust and legitimacy. We might also note that trust and legitimacy inspire normative motivations in relation to crime and crime control that are both in contrast to dominant 'command and control' models and likely to more effective and cheaper than these alternative models in the long run (Sunshine and Tyler 2003a; Tyler 2006a, 2006b, 2011a, 2011b; Schulhofer *et al.* 2011; Tyler *et al.* in press).

Given this second point, we return to the issue of accountability. Institutions such as the police need to be held accountable for their performance, power and position in society. While there are many ways in which such accountability can be 'done', procedural justice theory offers some useful ways of moving beyond the New Public Management of the 1990s (Hough 2003) and the one-dimensional confidence model of the last Labour government. Do people hold the police to be legitimate? Do they cooperate with officers? Do all groups in society trust the police, and if not, why not? These and similar questions might usefully be asked across the United Kingdom, and the answers generated would provide invaluable insight into the performance of the police and the nature of its relationship with those it serves. Given the strength of the associations we find between contact with officers, trust, legitimacy and cooperation, perhaps police managers should care a little less about how many arrests their officers are making, or how much intelligence they are gathering, and a little bit more about how those officers are treating the citizens they encounter and the way in which they are exercising their authority.

We have shown in this book that police authority must be just, and that the procedural fairness of the police lies at the heart of people's connections with legal authorities. A sense of shared purpose lies at the heart of justified police power and action, and there is early evidence that this idea pertains not only in the UK but also across Europe (European Social Survey 2011). Fairness seems to be a universal criterion. It is critical to people's connections and commitment to institutions. Legitimacy finds practical expression in people's sense that they are under a moral obligation to defer to police officers and to comply with the law. When the justice system enjoys legitimacy, people believe that they should comply with the law and that it is unacceptable to use violence to achieve their own social or political goals.

Sceptics may say that our findings do not speak to the real dilemmas that the police face. Are they really to ignore crime and antisocial behaviour, for fear of damaging this abstract idea of police legitimacy? Surely the key factor in keeping the lid on crime is ensuring that the police offer a credible deterrent threat to would-be offenders. But the argument is less about *what* police do than about *how* they do it. It is the quality rather than quantity of policing that is the critical ingredient securing public order. Crime and antisocial behaviour should not be ignored, but in all their work police should strive to treat those they encounter fairly and respectfully. Failure to do so undermines people's sense that police are themselves worthy of respect and that the law defines acceptable behaviour.

Police unfairness makes the task of dealing with crime and disorder more difficult in the long run; fairness, on the other hand, helps secure long-term commitment to institutions and the rule of law. Adversarial tactics such as stop-and-search represent a significant risk to police legitimacy. This is not to say they should never be deployed. But their costs in terms of trust and legitimacy must always be weighed against their gains. Our research lends support to the Danish adage that trust arrives on foot and leaves on horseback. The negative effect of one poorly handled stop-and-search may have implications far beyond an immediate sense of annoyance. Once police have lost the trust of the policed, it may be very hard to regain not just trust, but also the legitimacy that binds police to the public.

Notes

1 Social and moral connections

1   In this, we build upon Hough *et al.* 2010; Jackson *et al.* 2011, 2011a. But police legitimacy may have a further empirical property (Jackson 2012b). A recent study of 1,000 young males from various ethnic minority groups in London found that people's belief in the legitimacy of the state was negatively associated with their approval of the use of violence to achieve certain goals. This is consistent with the idea that legitimacy entails not only recognition (and justification) of state power, but also recognition of the state's monopoly of power. To the extent that the state's use of power and violence loses legitimacy, private violence may gain legitimacy.

2   The empirical evidence suggests that people care about having 'voice' less because of narrow self-interest (because they can exert greater influence over the outcomes of decisions) and more because of concern about their social connection to groups and group authorities. Procedural justice is then linked to group pride and feelings of respect within the group (Tyler *et al.* 1996).

3   Further work by Huo, Tyler and colleagues (Huo *et al.* 1996; Smith and Tyler 1996; Tyler and Degoey 1995) suggests that when people identify with the superordinate group (e.g. the nation and the procedural protections that the US affords to its citizens) they accept decisions and obey rules when they view the authorities and institutions involved as making decisions in fair ways. But when they have strong subgroup identification (e.g. to their specific ethnic group) and weak superordinate-group identification, individuals focus more on instrumental rather than relational issues when evaluating a superordinate-group authority (Huo *et al.* 1996). Smith and Tyler (1996: 192) reported similar findings when explaining variation in the perceived legitimacy and feelings of obligation towards Congress.

4   In this study we treat trust as a construct quite separate from legitimacy (c.f. Gau 2011). For us, there is a tendency in the literature to measure legitimacy using solely a set of questions about trust and confidence in the police (e.g. in Australian research, Hinds and Murphy 2007: 42; Hinds 2007: 209; Murphy *et al.* 2009: 155; Hinds 2009: 20; Murphy and Cherney 2010: 20; in Israeli research, Jonathan-Zamir and Weisburd 2011: 21). Given the analytical centrality of legitimacy in a psychological model of authorisation, this approach may be problematic (c.f. Reisig *et al.* 2007; Gau 2011). While finding authorities to be trustworthy *is* related to believing that authorities have the right to dictate appropriate behaviour and exert power, they are not the same thing. In particular, the underlying psychological mechanisms linking legitimacy and cooperation seem to be quite different to those linking trust and cooperation.

5   Identification reflects an emotional connection based upon perceived shared values and purposes and a common definition of social roles and expectations. When people feel aligned with the moral values of an authority in a group setting, they act in ways that support the group that the authority represents: moral alignment activates a group-based morality. Triggering the ethical motivations that lead people to adhere

to group rules, moral norms become particularly strong guidelines for individual behaviour. Enacting shared moral values may also be an important way of receiving or maintaining in-group respect and acceptance (Pagliaro *et al.* 2011). People identify with the expectations of the police, strengthening moral identity and influencing moral action (Aquino *et al.* 2009; Hardy and Carlo 2005; Aquino and Reed 2002, Reed and Aquino 2003; c.f. Blasi 1984; Lapsley and Narvaez 2005). Adherence to moral group norms can be an important source of group pride, earning respect from other in-group members (Pagliaro *et al.* 2011) because it shows that one is willing to act in ways that are approved by the group (Barreto and Ellemers 2000).

6　van der Toorn *et al.* (2011: 128) raise an intriguing possibility They argue that 'dependence on authorities for desired resources activates system justification motivation, and this contributes to the legitimation of powerholders. The idea is that when an individual is dependent on a powerful other, he or she is motivated to perceive the powerholder as relatively legitimate in order to rationalize the system of authority relations and to feel better about the status quo.' The data they present support their hypothesis. For example, when people felt that crime was a big problem in their neighbourhood, they also tended to view the police as a relatively legitimate authority. Applying this reasoning to the current study, it may be that people in deprived areas feel a stronger sense of reliance on the police to regulate the streets; they grant greater authority to the police because they feel dependent upon an important outcome of police action, i.e. regulation. But further analysis of our METPAS data shows that people's perceptions of the crime problem in their area and their sense of safety in the street are associated with legitimacy, but in the opposite direction expected (not presented here, see xxx). The more an individual believes that crime is on the rise in their neighbourhood, the less likely they are to feel obligated to the police. So this is not yet settled. Indeed, it is for future research to explore outcome dependency and police legitimacy.

7　The effect of neighbourhood levels of collective efficacy on legitimacy is particular strong on moral alignment with the police, suggesting that public legitimation of the police is founded in both procedural justice and informal social control processes. The public believe that the police share their moral values – that they are justified in holding the power to regulate social behaviour – when the community is seen to be orderly and informally policed.

8　The problem here is that prior studies have not incorporated area-level analysis within the assessment of individual level processes. Are trust, legitimacy, cooperation and compliance mutually determined by social context? Neighbourhood characteristics may simultaneously explain joint individual-level covariation in contact with the police, trust in the police, the legitimacy of legal authorities, and cooperative intentions. And once context is adjusted for, we may find that individual-level psychological and experiential variables are not correlated.

2　Design of the study

1　The 1982 BCS was omitted from this process because it contained only very few questions directly comparable with those of later years. The initial file obtained contained socio-demographic variables as well as those concerning victimisation, fear of crime, and perceptions of disorder. To this we added variables concerning contact with the police and opinions of the police and the criminal justice system.

2　As is common elsewhere (Skogan 2006; Bradford *et al.* 2009b), we divide contact with the police into those that were initiated by the member of the public involved (self-initiated) and those that were initiated by the police. Comparable and comprehensive questions about personal contacts began to be asked in 1988.

3　At what level does 'neighbourhood' operate? Kearns and Parkinson (2001) identify three general spatial scales: the home area, the locality and the urban region. Defined in general terms, in reality the spatial scales are more flexible, varying considerably depending on the type of person and the characteristics of the natural environment.

The home area is typically defined as the area within a 5–10 minute walk of the individual's home. This is a small neighbourhood classified as the most inclusive residential grouping with boundaries primarily defined by interactions with others and the friendship networks that this fosters. If the home area is the most important for engendering a sense of belonging and community, the second neighbourhood layer reflects the wider area in which residential activities take place. This is typically defined by the structure of the housing market and the level of local service provision. The physical structure is generally taken as more important for delineating the boundaries of this wider neighbourhood. Broader still is the final layer. Described as the urban region, this is defined primarily by the individual's employment connections and the location of leisure interests, incorporating the wider social networks that are relevant to individuals. Qualitative studies also focus on the importance of the relations between places in determining how neighbourhoods are defined by residents. Therefore, the way that people define their local neighbourhood can be thought of as partially a reflection of comparisons with the areas that surround them, and their beliefs about how the neighbourhood is perceived by others (Chaskin 1998).

4   Postcode sectors (which are generally the primary sampling units (PSU) in national surveys) have been used to assess area-based variations, although PSU boundaries cover fairly broad areas that have no real meaning beyond their postcode classification. And like wards, there is considerable variation in the size of postcode sectors. This makes it difficult to argue that they all refer to a similar neighbourhood definition.

3 Twenty-five years of public confidence in the police

1   We think of confidence as a single overall summary statement of the job that the police are doing. The assumption that 'overall confidence in police' is revealed by answers to overall job-rating questions is in line with the UK policy debate, as well as the current trend in US criminology to think of public satisfaction as overall summaries of police performance. The definition of confidence is also in line with some sociological thinking on the nature of trust and confidence. Earle (2010a) sees trust as intention, driven by indicators of value similarity and related matters, while confidence is a kind of calculative and/or instrumental trust concerning ability. Driven by indicators of past expertise and track record, confidence is a function 'to control future behaviour through knowledge of the past or constraints on the future' (ibid: 544). If one believes that the police have been competent in the past, one has confidence (or calculative trust) in the ability of the police to perform its roles in the future. We should note, however, that there is recent empirical evidence that confidence condenses not just assessments of police effectiveness, but also (and more acutely) a motive-based trust that is rooted in procedural fairness and a sense of shared priorities and joint interests (Jackson and Bradford 2010). This work suggests that intentions and shared values may be more important to people than instrumental abilities, with confidence more relational than calculative, to borrow Rousseau *et al.*'s (1998) terminology (see also Earle 2010a; Seigrist 2010; and Earle 2010b). Or put more simply, people think a large part of the job that the police do is to act fairly and to be response to people's needs, interests and priorities.

2   Note that small sample sizes for the Black and Asian groups in 1984 and 1992 mean that estimates for those years should be treated with caution.

5 What is trust in the police?

1   In Tyler's work, procedural justice also includes motive-based trust in the authority. People are influenced by their inferences about the motivations of the authorities with whom they are dealing. If people feel that authorities are acting out of a sincere desire to do what is right, then they view the authorities as acting more fairly. If people think

that an authority is not concerned about their well-being then they react negatively to its actions. How can authorities communicate trust? They can give people a chance to explain their concerns, show that what people say is being considered, and explain why and how decisions are made. In this study we do not treat motive-based trust as part of our measure of trust in the fairness or procedural justice of the police.

6 Mass media

1 www.esds.ac.uk/findingData/snDescription.asp?sn=6627
2 See Chapter 5 for more details. But briefly, the score is based on eight survey items, where respondents were asked to rate on a 5-point scale the extent to which the they feel the police listen to the concerns of the local people, understand the issues that affect the community, are dealing with things that matter to the community and can be relied upon to be there when you need them, treat everyone fairly regardless of who they are, would treat the respondent with respect if they had contact with them for any reason, are friendly and approachable, and are helpful. The latent score has a range of 6.57.
3 Note that the media variables in Table 6.5 are measured as proportions of articles rather than percentages of articles (proportions and percentages out of the total number of articles). The regression coefficients in the table are interpreted as follows: for *The Times* readers, a 1-point increase in the proportion of articles mentioning community engagement (range 0 to 1) is equivalent to a 100-point increase in the percentage of articles mentioning community engagement and associated with a 3.71 point increase in confidence (range 1 to 5).

7 The social ecology of trust in the police

1 See MacDonald *et al.* (2007) for a study that found ethnic different in perceptions of police injustice and racial bias, which survived even when one accounted for neighbourhood contact.
2 The measures are (1=strongly disagree, 5=strongly agree): 'People in this neighbourhood can be trusted', 'People act with courtesy to each other in public space in this area', 'You can see from the public space here in the area that people take pride in their environment', 'If I sensed trouble whilst in this area, I could get help from people who live here', 'The people who live here can be relied upon to call the police if someone is acting suspiciously', and 'If any of the children or young people around here are causing trouble, local people will tell them off'.
3 The measures are (1=not a problem at all, 4=very big problem): 'Noisy neighbours or loud parties', 'Teenagers hanging around on the streets', 'Rubbish or litter lying around', 'Vandalism, graffiti and other deliberate damage to property or vehicles' and 'People being drunk or rowdy in public places'.
4 The measures are (1=not at all worried, 5=very worried): Overall, how worried are you about ... 'having your home broken into and something stolen', 'being mugged or robbed', 'being physically attacked by strangers' and 'being insulted or pestered by anybody while in the street or any other public space'. For discussion on the strengths and weaknesses of these measures, see Gray *et al.* (2011), Jackson and Kuha (2011) and Farrall *et al.* (2009).
5 Comparison and context can, of course, be confounded by self-selection of individuals into certain neighbourhoods.
6 Recall that Sampson and Bartusch (1998) found that ethnicity was a strong predictor of satisfaction with the police in Chicago. This effect dropped away once one took into account the neighbourhood context. In the London data we do not find this. When we fit a linear model without conditioning on neighbourhood – not shown here – the estimated effect of ethnicity is not very different to that found in model 1 of Table 7.3. In general, all of the effects shrink a little bit towards zero. Moreover,

'Other Asian or Asian British' and 'Other Black or Black British' become not statistically significant. But the effects are small in the linear model which does not condition on neighbourhood.

7   Again, we added the structural and social characteristics one at a time. The only interesting effect was that the effect of neighbourhood-levels of worry about crime decreased significantly once one added in neighbourhood level perceived disorder and collective efficacy.

8 One type of contact

1   The survey itself may exert a strong contextual effect on respondents. Perhaps an intensive period of thinking about the police while completing the questionnaire results in people reporting only what they feel to be meaningful contact with the police, and in a kind of discounting of more ephemeral experiences. Respondents may be thinking about what the police do in a formal, professional sense, and thus omit contacts (such as asking officers for directions, exchanging small-talk at a demonstration, or even being approached informally by an officer in the street) they feel do not involve 'real' policing. On the other hand, there is the equally plausible suggestion that the context of the survey primes respondents to recall many more contacts with the police than would otherwise be the case.

2   One characteristic that predicts a higher chance of being stopped in one's local area, namely economic activity status, is much less predictive at the level of 'elsewhere in London'. But ethnicity, while being moderately important in relation to local stops, is more strongly predictive of experiencing a stop outside the area in which people live. We can only conjecture on the reason for this. Perhaps policing in inner London – presumably the modal location of 'elsewhere in London' – is different. People from most ethnic minority groups are not more likely to be stopped in their own areas, but are more likely to be stopped when outside them, suggesting perhaps that ethnic minority groups are targeted more by the police in the centre of the capital.

3   Please note: we also fitted four other models. Each included just one of the neighbourhood-level structural characteristics. The findings were similar to the model presented here, which includes all four characteristics.

10 Another type of contact

1   Note that a small number of these contacts will have been initiated by someone other than the victim, such as a family member or witness.

11 What is police legitimacy?

1   Although some political philosophers would argue that legitimacy must involve some 'objective' criteria or requirements of justice and rationality (see Habermas 1979; Rawls 1993).

2   There are two more aspects of legitimacy in policing also worth mentioning. The first is the legitimacy granted by the public (and by the political system) to specific *spheres of police action and power.* In which areas of social life are the police allowed to wield their authority? What legal powers are the police granted? Will the public support empowerment such as detention without trial, and the mandate to deal with anti-social behaviour? The second is the *internal legitimacy* of the police organisation that governs officer behaviour and police culture (Tyler 2008; Tankebe 2009).

3   But they also found that combining trust in the police and obligation to obey (into one overall measure of legitimacy) was problematic. The combined scales were predictive of cooperation and compliance. But when they were disaggregated and entered in as separate variables, only trust in the police was statistically significant.

12 The social ecology of police legitimacy

1   We also took an intermediate step briefly worth reporting upon. In order to assess the effect of conditioning on a neighbourhood in estimating the predictive role of an individual's ethnicity on obligation to obey, we fitted a linear model without random intercepts. As with trust in the police, modelling within-neighbourhood variation made little effect on ethnicity as a predictor. Again in contrast to Sampson and Bartusch (1998), we did not find that ethnicity effects drop away once the neighbourhood context is taken into account. In particular, the estimated effect of ethnicity was not very different to that found in model 1 of Table 12.4. In general, all of the effects shrank a little bit towards zero, and none dropped any level of statistical significance.

2   This is consistent with our analyses in Part 3 of the book, which shows that concentrated disadvantage is *negatively associated* with trust in the police.

3   The legitimacy of institutionalised organisations – like the police – may be affected by processes that relate to the socio-structural position of the institution itself. Bradford and Jackson (2011) argue that the legitimacy of the police may be premised in part on what *it is*, namely, the physical embodiment of social control activities. Understanding the social place of the police allows insight into processes by which police legitimacy is simultaneously challenged and reinforced: day-to-day disorder and the breakdown of shared values generate contest over the role of the police.

16 Conclusions

1   The notion of expressed consent implies that the legitimacy of an authority resides not only in the beliefs of those it governs but also in their actions. The legitimacy of the police resides not only in what people think about it but also in the ways they act in relation to it. It is also actualised or instantiated in specific acts of deference, compliance or cooperation. Calling upon or assisting the police are thus not simply outcomes arising from its legitimacy: they are acts that *constitute* its legitimacy, defining and delimiting the roles of police and public and articulating the relationship between the police and policed (Bradford and Jackson 2010). Such acts place obligations on both officer and citizen that are expressive of underlying moral values and beliefs.

References

Alesina, A. and la Ferrara, E. (2000) 'Participation in heterogeneous communities', *Quarterly Journal of Economics*, August, 847–904.

Allen, J., Edmonds, S., Patterson, A. and Smith, D. (2006) *Policing and the Criminal Justice System. Public confidence and perceptions: Findings from the 2004/05 British Crime Survey.* Home Office Online Report 2006/2007: http://library.npia.police.uk/docs/hordsolr/rdsolr0706.pdf.

Anderson, E. (1990) *Streetwise: Race, Class, and Change in an Urban Community.* Chicago: University of Chicago Press.

Anderson, E. (1997) 'Violence and the inner city street code', in J. McCord (ed.) *Violence and Childhood in the Inner City.* New York: Cambridge University Press.

Anderson, E. (1999) *Code of the Streets: Decency, Violence, and the Moral Life of the Inner-city.* New York: Norton.

Aquino, K. F. and Reed, A. II. (2002) 'The self-importance of moral identity', *Journal of Personality and Social Psychology, 83,* 1423–40.

Aquino, K., Freeman, D., Reed, A. II, Lim, V. K. G. and Felps, W. (2009) 'Testing a social-cognitive model of moral behavior: The interaction of situational factors and moral identity centrality', *Journal of Personality and Social Psychology, 97,* 123–41.

Banton, M. (1964) *The Policeman in the Community.* London: Tavistock.

Barber, B. (1983) *The Logic and Limits of Trust.* New Brunswick: Rutgers University Press.

Barker, M. and Petley, J. (1996) *Ill Effects: The Media Violence Debate,* 2nd edn. London: Routledge.

Barker, R. (2001) *Legitimating Identities: The Self-Presentation of Rulers and Subjects.* Cambridge: Cambridge University Press.

Barreto, M. and Ellemers, N. (2000) 'You can't always do what you want: Social identity and self-presentational determinants of the choice to work for a low status group', *Personality and Social Psychology Bulletin, 26,* 891–906.

Bauman, Z. (2002) *Society under Siege.* Cambridge: Polity Press.

Baumann, Z. (2005) *Liquid Life.* Cambridge: Polity Press.

Baumann, Z. (2007) *Liquid Times: Living in an Age of Uncertainty.* Cambridge: Polity Press.

Beck, U. (1992) *Risk Society: Toward a New Modernity.* London: Sage.

Beck, U. and Beck-Gernsheim, E. (2002) *Individualization: Institutionalized Individualism and Its Social and Political Consequences.* London: Sage.

Beckett, K. (1997) *Making Crime Pay: Law and Order in Contemporary American Politics.* New York: Oxford University Press.

Beetham, D. (1991) *The Legitimation of Power.* London: Macmillan.

Belson, W. A. (1975) *The Public and the Police: An Extended Summary of the Aims, Methods and Findings of a Three-Part Enquiry Into the Relations Between the London Public and its Metropolitan Police Force*. London: Harper and Row.

Belvedere, K., Worrall, J. L. and Tibbetts. S. G. (2005) 'Explaining suspect resistance in police-citizen encounters', *Criminal Justice Review* 30(1): 30–44.

Benesh, S. C. and Howell, S. (2001) 'Confidence in the courts: A comparison of users and non-users', *Behavioral Sciences and the Law*, 19: 199–214.

Bittner, E. (1974) 'Florence Nightingale in pursuit of Willie Sutton: A theory of the police', in H. Jacobs (ed.) *The Potential for Reform of Criminal Justice*, Vol. 3. Beverly Hills, CA: Sage.

Bittner, E. (1975) *The Functions of the Police in Modern Society*. New York: Aronson.

Black, D. (1993) *The Social Structure of Right and Wrong*. San Diego: Academic Press.

Blader, S. and Tyler, T. R. (2009) 'Testing and expanding the group engagement model', *Journal of Applied Psychology*, 94, 445–64.

Blasi, A. (1984) 'Moral identity: Its role in moral functioning', in W. Kurtines and J. Gewirtz (eds), *Morality, moral behaviour and moral development*. New York: Wiley.

Blumler, J. and Katz, E. (1974) *The Uses of Communications*. Beverly Hills, CA: Sage.

Bollen, K. A. (1989) *Structural Equations with Latent Variables*. New York: Wiley.

Borsboom, D., Mellenbergh, G. J. and van Heerden, J. (2003) 'The theoretical status of latent variables', *Psychological Review, 110,* 203–19.

Bottoms, A. and Tankebe, J. (2012) 'Beyond procedural justice: A dialogic approach to legitimacy in criminal justice', *Journal of Criminal Law and Criminology*, 102: 119—70.

Bourdieu, P. (1993) *The Field of Cultural Production*. Cambridge: Polity Press.

Bowling, B. and Philips, C. (2002) *Racism, Crime and Justice*. Harlow: Pearson Education.

Bowling, B. and Philips, C. (2007) 'Disproportionate and discriminatory: Reviewing the evidence on police stop and search', *The Modern Law Review*, 70: 936–61.

Bradford, B. (2011a) 'Voice neutrality and respect: Use of victim support services procedural fairness and confidence in the Criminal Justice System', *Criminology and Criminal Justice*, 11, 4, 345–66.

Bradford, B. (2011b) 'Convergence, not divergence?: Trends and trajectories in public contact and confidence in the police', *British Journal of Criminology*, 51(1): 179–200.

Bradford, B. and Jackson, J. (2011) 'Legitimacy and the social field of policing', available at SSRN: http://ssrn.com/abstract=1914458 or doi:10.2139/ssrn.1914458.

Bradford, B. and Jackson, J. (2010) *Trust and Confidence in the Police: A Conceptual Review*. National Policing Improvement Agency Wiki, available at SSRN: http://papers.ssrn.com/sol3/papers.cfm?abstract_id=1684508.

Bradford, B., Jackson, J. and Stanko, E. (2009a) 'Contact and Confidence: Revisiting the impact of public encounters with the police', *Policing and Society*, 19(1): 20–46.

Bradford, B., Stanko, E. and Jackson, J. (2009b) 'Using research to inform policy: The role of public attitude surveys in understanding public confidence and police contact', *Policing: A Journal of Policy and Practice*, 3(2): 139–48.

Brandl, S., Frank, J., Wooldredge, J. and Watkins, R. C. (1997) 'On the measurement of public support for the police: a research note', *Policing: An International Journal of Police Strategy and Management* 20(3): 473–80.

Brandl, S., Frank, J., Worden, R. and Bynum, T. (1994) 'Global and specific attitudes toward the police: disentangling the relationship', *Justice Quarterly* 11: 119–34.

Brodeur, J-P. (2010) *The Policing Web*. Oxford: Oxford University Press.

Brooks, R. and Jeon-Slaughter, H. (2001) 'Race, income and perceptions of the U.S. court system', *Behavioral Sciences and the Law* 19: 249–64.

Brunson, R. (2007) '"Police don't like Black People": African-American young men's accumulated police experiences', *Criminology and Public Policy*, 6(1): 71–102.

Brunson, R. and Miller, J. (2006) 'Young Black men and urban policing in the United States', *British Journal of Criminology* 46(6): 13–40.

Brunton-Smith, I. (2008) *Local Areas and Fear of Criminal Victimisation: Applying Multilevel Models to the British Crime Survey*. Doctoral thesis, University of Surrey.

Brunton-Smith, I. and Sturgis, P. (2011) 'Do neighbourhoods generate fear of crime?: An empirical test using the British Crime Survey', *Criminology*, 49(2): 331–69.

Bureau of Justice Statistics (2007) Sourcebook of criminal justice statistics online. www.albany.edu/sourcebook/

Bursik, R. J. and Gramsik, H. G. (1993) *Neighborhoods and Crime: The Dimensions of Effective Community Control*. New York: Lexington Books.

Callanan, V. and Rosenberger, J. (2011) 'Media and public perceptions of the police: the impact of race and personal experience', *Policing and Society*, 21(2): 167–89.

Cao, L. (2001) 'A problem in no-problem-policing in Germany: Confidence in the police, Germany and USA', *European Journal of Crime, Criminal Law, and Criminal Justice*, 9(3): 167–79.

Carr, P., Napolitano, L. and Keating, J. (2007) 'We never call the cops and here is why: A qualitative examination of legal cynicism in three Philadelphia neighbourhoods', *Criminology*, 45: 445–80.

Cavender, G. (2004) 'Media and crime policy. A reconsideration of David Garland's The culture of control', *Punishment and Society*, 6(3): 335–48.

Chaskin, R. J. (1998) 'Neighborhood as a unit of planning and action: A heuristic approach', *Journal of Planning Literature*, 13(1): 11–30.

Cherney, A. and Murphy, K. (2011) 'Understanding the contingency of procedural justice outcomes', *Policing: A Journal of Policy and Practice*, 5(3): 228–35.

Chibnall, S. (1977) *Law-and-Order News: An Analysis of Crime Reporting in the British Press*. London: Tavistock Publishing.

Choongh, S. (1997) *Policing as Social Discipline*. Oxford: Clarendon Press.

Clayman, S. and Skinns, L. (2012) 'To snitch or not to snitch? An exploratory study of the factors affecting active youth co-operation with the police', *Policing and Society*, 22(1): 1–21.

Cohen, S. (1987) *Folk Devils and Moral Panics. The Creation of the Mods and Rockers*. Oxford: Blackwell Publishers.

Coicaud, J. (2002) *Legitimacy and Politics: A Contribution to the Study of Political Right and Political Responsibility*. Cambridge: Cambridge University Press.

Cooke, C. A. (2005) 'Issues concerning visibility and reassurance provided by the new "policing family"', *Journal of Community and Applied Social Psychology*, 15: 229–40.

Costa, D. and Kahn, M. (2003) 'Civic engagement and community heterogeneity: An economist's perspective', *Perspective on Politics* 1(1): 103–11.

Côté-Lussier, C. (in press) 'Narratives of legitimacy: Police expansionism and the contest over policing', *Policing and Society*.

van Craen, M. (2012) 'Explaining majority and minority trust in the police', *Justice Quarterly*, Advance Online Access.

Crawford, A. (2003) 'The pattern of policing in the UK: policing beyond the police', in T. Newburn (ed.) *Handbook of Policing*. Cullompton: Willan Publishing.

Critchley, T. A. (1978) *A History of Police in England and Wales*. London: Constable.

Dalgliesh, D. and Myhill, A. (2004) *Reassuring the Public: A Review of International Policing Interventions*. Home Office Research Study 284. London: Home Office.

Davis, A. (2006) 'Media effects and the question of the rational audience: lessons from the financial markets', *Media, Culture and Society* 28(4): 603–25.

DCLG (2010) *Citizenship Survey: 2009–10* (April 2009–March 2010). London: Department for Communities and Local Government.

de Cremer, D., van de Dijke, M. H. and Mayer, D. M. (2010) 'Cooperating when "you" and "I" are treated fairly: The moderating role of leader prototypicality', *Journal of Applied Psychology,* 95(6): 1121–33.

de Cremer, D. and Tyler, T. R. (2005) 'Am I respected or not?: Inclusion and reputation as issues in group membership', *Social Justice Research*, 18(2): 121–53.

Dixon, A. and LeGrand, J. (2006) 'Is greater patient choice consistent with equity? The case of the English NHS', *Journal of Health Services Research and Policy*; 11: 161–6.

Dobbs, J., Green, H. and Zealey, L. (eds), (2006) *Focus on Ethnicity and Religion, Office for National Statistics*. Basingstoke: Palgrave MacMillan.

Dowler, K. (2002) 'Media influence on citizen attitudes toward police effectiveness', *Policing and Society,* 12(3): 227–38.

Dowler, K. and Zawilski, V. (2007) 'Public perceptions of police misconduct and discrimination: Examining the impact of media consumption', *Journal of Criminal Justice,* 35(2): 193–203.

Earle, T. and Cvetkovich, G. (1995) *Social trust: toward a cosmopolitan society.* Westport, CT: Prager.

Earle, T. C. (2010a) 'Trust in risk management: A model-based review of empirical research', *Risk Analysis*, 30: 541–74.

Earle, T. C. (2010b) 'Distinguishing trust from confidence: Manageable difficulties, worth the effort', *Risk Analysis,* 30(7): 1025–7.

Edwards, J. R. and Bagozzi, R. P. (2000) 'On the nature and direction of relationships between constructs and measures',. *Psychological Methods*, 5: 155–74.

Elliott, I., Thomas, S. D., Ogloff, M. and James, R. P. (2011) 'Procedural justice in contacts with the police: Testing a relational model of authority in a mixed methods study', *Psychology, Public Policy, and Law*, 17(4): 592–610.

Emirbayer, M. and Johnson, V. (2008) 'Bourdieu and Institutional Analysis', *Theoretical Sociology*, 37: 1–44.

Emsley, C. (1996) *The English Police: Apolitical and Social History* (2nd edn). Longman: London.

Emsley, C. (2003) 'The birth and development of the police', in T. Newburn, Tim (ed.) *Handbook of Policing.* Cullompton: Willan Publishing.

Emsley, C. (2007) 'Community policing/policing and communities: Some historical perspectives', *Policing: A Journal of Policy and Practice*, 1(2): 235–43.

Engel, R. S. (2005) 'Citizens' perceptions of procedural and distributional injustice during traffic stops with police', *Journal of Research in Crime and Delinquency*, 42(4): 445–81.

Equality and Human Rights Commission (2010) *Stop and Think: A Critical Review of the Use of Stop and Search Powers in England and Wales*. London: EHRC.

Eschholz, S., Blackwell, B., Gertz, M. and Chiricos, T. (2002) 'Race and attitudes toward the police: Assessing the effects of watching "reality" police programs', *Journal of Criminal Justice,* 30(4): 327–41.

European Social Survey (2011) 'Trust in justice: Topline findings from the European Social Survey', *ESS Topline Results Series Issue 1,* by Jackson, J., Hough, M., Bradford, B., Pooler, T. M., Hohl, K. and Kuha, J. URL: www.europeansocialsurvey.org/index.php?option=com_docman&task=doc_download&gid=902&itemid=80.

Farrall, S., Jackson, J. and Gray, E. (2009) *Social Order and the Fear of Crime in Contemporary Times.* Oxford: Oxford University Press.

Fitzgerald, M., Hough, M., Joseph, I. and Qureshi, T. (2002) *Policing for London.* Cullompton: Willan Publishing.

Flatley, J., Kershaw, C., Smith, K., Chaplin, R. and Moon, D. (eds), (2010) *Crime in England and Wales 2009/10.* Home Office Statistical Bulletin 12/10 London: Home Office.

French, J. R. P. and Raven, B. (1959) 'The bases of social power', in D. Cartwright (ed.) *Studies in social power.* Ann Arbor: University of Michigan Press.

Garland, D. (2001) *The Culture of Control. Crime and Social Order in Contemporary Society.* Oxford: Oxford University Press.

Gau, J. M (2010) 'A longitudinal analysis of citizens' attitudes about police', *Policing: An International Journal of Police Strategies and Management*, 33(2): 236–52.

Gau, J. M. (2011) 'The convergent and discriminant validity of procedural justice and police legitimacy: An empirical test of core theoretical propositions', *Journal of Criminal Justice*, 39: 489–98.

Gau, J. M. and Brunson, R. K. (2010) 'Procedural justice and order maintenance policing: A study of inner-city young men's perceptions of police legitimacy', *Justice Quarterly* 27(2): 255–79.

Gauntlett, D. (1998) 'Ten things wrong with the Effects Model', in R. Dickinson, R. Havindranath and O. Linne (eds), *Approaches to Audiences: A Reader.* London: Arnold.

Gauntlett, D. (2001) 'The Worrying Influence of "Media Effects" Studies', in M. Barker and J. Petley (eds), *Ill Effects: The Media/Violence Debate.* London: Routledge.

Gelman, A., and Hill, J. (2007) *Data Analysis Using Regression and Multilevel/ Hierarchical Models.* Cambridge: Cambridge University Press.

Gerbner, G. and Gross, L. (1976) 'Living with television: the violence profile', *Journal of Communication*, 26(2): 172–94.

Gibbons, S., Green, A., Gregg, P. and Machin, S. (2005) *Is Britain Pulling Apart? Area Disparities in Employment, Education and Crime.* CMPO Working Paper Series, 5.

Giddens, A. (1991) *Modernity and Self-Identity.* Cambridge: Polity Press.

Gilroy, P. (1987) *There Ain't No Black in the Union Jack: The Cultural Politics of Race and Nation.* London: Hutchinson.

Girling, E., Loader, I. and Sparks, R. 2000. *Crime and Social Control in Middle England: Questions of Order in an English Town.* London: Routledge.

Goodhart, D. (2004) 'Too diverse?', *Prospect*, 95.

Gorringe, H. and Rosie, M. (2009) 'What a difference a death makes: Protest, policing and the press at the G20', *Sociological Research Online* 14: 5.

Goudriaan, H., Wittebrood, K. and Nieuwbeerta, P. (2006) 'Neighbourhood characteristics and reporting crime', *English Journal of Criminology*, 46: 719–42.

Gray, E., Jackson, J. and Farral, S. (2011) 'Feelings and functions in the fear of crime: Applying a new approach to victimisation insecurity', *British Journal of Criminology*, 51(1): 79–94.

Greer, C. and McLaughlin, E. (2010) 'We predict a riot: Public order policing, news coverage and the rise of the citizen journalist', *British Journal of Criminology*, 50(6): 1041–59.

Greer, C. and McLaughlin, E. (2011) '"Trial by media": Policing, the 24–7 news media sphere and the "politics of outrage"', *Theoretical Criminology,* 15(1): 23–46.

Habermas, J. (1979) *Communication and the Evolution of Society.* Boston: Beacon Press.

Hadfield, P. (2007) 'A hard act to follow: Assessing the consequences of licensing reform in England and Wales', Editorial, *Addiction*, 102: 177–80.

Hall, S., Crichter, C. and Jefferson, T. (1978) *Policing the Crisis: Mugging, the State and Law and Order*. London: Macmillan.

Hardin, R. (2002) *Trust and Trustworthiness*. New York: Russell Sage Foundation.

Hardy, S. A. and Carlo, G. (2005) 'Identity as a source of moral motivation', *Human Development*, 48: 232–56.

Harvey, D. (1990) *The Condition of Postmodernity: An Enquiry into the Origins of Cultural Change*. Oxford: Blackwell.

Hasisi, B. and Weisburd, D. (2011) 'Going beyond ascribed identities: The importance of procedural justice in airport security screening in Israel', *Law and Society Review*, 45(4): 867–92.

Hinds, L. (2007) 'Building police–youth relationships: The importance of procedural justice', *Youth Justice* 7(3): 195–209.

Hinds, L. (2009) 'Youth, police legitimacy and informal contact', *Journal of Police and Criminal Psychology*, 24: 10–21.

Hinds, L. and Murphy, K. (2007) 'Public satisfaction with the police: Using procedural justice to improve police legitimacy', *Australian and New Zealand Journal of Criminology* 40(1): 27–42.

Hinsch, W. (2008) 'Legitimacy and justice', in J. Kuhnelt (ed.) *Political Legitimation without Morality?* London: Springer.

Hirschman, A. O. (1970) *Exit, Voice, and Loyalty: Responses to Decline in Firms, Organizations, and States*. Cambridge, MA: Harvard University Press.

Hohl, K., Bradford, B. and Stanko, E. (2010) 'Influencing trust and confidence in the Metropolitan Police: results from an experiment testing the effect of leaflet-drops on public opinion', *British Journal of Criminology*, 50(3):491–513.

Hough, M. (2003) 'Modernization and public opinion: Some criminal justice paradoxes', *Contemporary Politics*, 9: 143–55.

Hough, M. (2007a) 'Policing, new public management and legitimacy in Britain', in T. R. Tyler (ed.) *Legitimacy and Criminal justice: International Perspectives*. New York: Russell Sage Foundation.

Hough, M. (2007b) 'Policing London, 20 years on', in A. Henry and D. Smith (eds), *Transformations of Policing*. Aldershot: Ashgate Publishing.

Hough, M., Jackson, J., Bradford, B., Myhill, A. and Quinton, P. (2010) 'Procedural justice, trust and institutional legitimacy', *Policing: A Journal of Policy and Practice*, 4(3): 203–10.

Howitt, D. (1998) *Crime, the Media, and the Law*. Wiley: West Sussex.

Hu, Li-Tze and Bentler, P. M. (1999) 'Cutoff criteria for fit indexes in covariance structure analysis: Conventional criteria versus new alternatives', *Structural Equation Modeling*, 6: 1–55.

Huo, Y. J., Smith, H. J., Tyler, T. R. and Lind, E. A. (1996) 'Superordinate identification, subgroup identification and justice concerns: Is separatism the problem; is assimilation the answer?', *Psychological Science*, 7(1): 40–5.

Huq, A. Z., Tyler, T. R. and Schulhofer, S. J. (2011) 'Mechanisms for eliciting cooperation in counter-terrorism policing: The case of Muslims in London', *Journal of Empirical Legal Studies*, 8(4): 728–61.

Innes, M. (2004) 'Signal crimes and signal disorders: notes on deviance as communicative action', *British Journal of Sociology*, 55(3): 335–55.

Innes, M. (2007) 'The reassurance function', *Policing: A Journal of Policy and Practise*, 1(2): 132–41.

Jackson, J. and Bradford, B. (2009) 'Crime, policing and social order: On the expressive nature of public confidence in policing', *British Journal of Sociology*, 60(3): 493–521.

Jackson, J. and Bradford, B. (2010) 'What is trust and confidence in the police?', *Policing: A Journal of Policy and Practice*, 4(3): 241–48.

Jackson, J. and Kuha, J. (2012) 'Worry about crime among European citizens: A latent class analysis of cross-national data', available at SSRN: http://ssrn.com/abstract=1603465 or http://dx.doi.org/10.2139/ssrn.1603465.

Jackson, J. and Sunshine, J. (2007) 'Public confidence in policing: A neo-Durkheimian perspective', *British Journal of Criminology*, 47(2): 214–33.

Jackson, J., Bradford, B., Hohl, K. and Farrall, S. (2009) 'Does the fear of crime erode public confidence in policing?', *Policing: A Journal of Policy and Practice*, 3(1): 100–1.

Jackson, J., Bradford, B., Hough, M. and Murray, K. H. (in press) 'Compliance with the law and policing by consent: Notes on police and legal legitimacy', chapter in A. Crawford and A. Hucklesby, A. (eds), *Legitimacy and Compliance in Criminal Justice*. London: Routledge. Available at SSRN: http://ssrn.com/abstract=1717812.

Jackson, J., Bradford, B., Hough, M., Kuha, J., Stares, S. R., Widdop, S., Fitzgerald, R., Yordanova, M. and Galev, T. (2011) 'Developing European indicators of trust in justice', *European Journal of Criminology*, 8(4): 267–85.

Jackson, J., Bradford, B., Hough, M., Myhill, A., Quinton, P. and Tyler, T. R. (2012a) 'Why do people comply with the law? Legitimacy and the influence of legal institutions', forthcoming in *British Journal of Criminology*.

Jackson, J., Huq, A. Z., Bradford, B. and Tyler, T. R. (2012b) 'Police legitimacy and public attitudes to private acts of violence', *University of Chicago, Public Law Working Paper No. 372*. Available at SSRN: http://ssrn.com/abstract=1984957 or doi:10.2139/ssrn.1984957.

Jansson, K. (2008) *British Crime Survey: Measuring Crime Over 25 Years*. London: Home Office.

Jansson, K., Budd, S., Lovbakke, J., Moley, S. and Thorpe, K. (2007) *Attitudes, Perceptions and Risks of Crime: Supplementary Volume 1 to Crime in England and Wales 2006/07*. London: Home Office.

Jefferson, T. (2002) 'Subordinating hegemonic masculinity', *Theoretical Criminology* 6(1): 63–88.

Jefferson, T. (1992) 'The racism of criminalization: Policing and the reproduction of the criminal other', in L. R. Gelsthorpe (ed.) *Minority Ethnic Groups in the Criminal Justice System*. Cambridge: University of Cambridge Press.

Jewkes, Y. (2004) *Media and Crime*. Sage: London.

Johnston, L. (1992) *The Rebirth of Private Policing*. London: Routledge.

Johnston, R., Jones, K., Burgess, S., Propper, C., Sarker, R., and Bolster, A. (2005a) *Fractal Factors? Scale, Factor Analyses and Neighbourhood Effects*. ESRC Research Methods Programme Working Paper, 2.

Johnston, R., Propper, C., Sarker, R. and Jones, K. (2005b) 'Neighbourhood social capital and neighbourhood effects', *Environment and Planning A*, 37 (8), 1143–59.

Jonathan-Zamir, T. and Weisburd, D. (2011) 'The effects of security threats on antecedents of police legitimacy: Findings from a quasi-experiment in Israel', *Journal of Research in Crime and Delinquency, Online First*.

Jones, T. and Newburn, T. (2002) 'The transformation of policing? Understanding current trends in policing systems', *British Journal of Criminology*, 41(1): 129–46.

Jost, J. T. and Banaji, M. R. (1994) 'The role of stereotyping in system-justification and the production of false consciousness', *British Journal of Social Psychology*, 33: 1–27.

Jost, J. T., Banaji, M. R. and Nosek, B. A. (2004) 'A decade of system justification theory: Accumulated evidence of conscious and unconscious bolstering of the status quo', *Political Psychology*, 25: 881–919.

Jost, J. T., Ledgerwood, A. and Hardin, C. D. (2008) 'Shared reality, system justification, and the relational basis of ideological beliefs', *Social and Personality Psychology Compass*, 2: 171–86.

Kahan, D. (1999) 'The secret ambition of deterrence', *Harvard Law Review*, 113: 413–500.

Kearns, A. and Parkinson, M. (2001) 'The significance of neighbourhood', *Urban Studies*, 38(12), 2103–10.

Keith, M. (1993) *Race, Riots and Policing: Lore and Disorder in a Multi-Racist Society*. London: UCL Press.

Kelman, H. C. (2006) 'Interests, relationships, identities: Three central issues for individuals and groups in negotiating their social environment', *Annual Review of Psychology*, 57: 1–26.

Kelman, H. C. and Hamilton, V. L. (1989) *Crimes of Obedience*. New Haven: Yale.

Kirk, D. S. and Matsuda, M. (2011) 'Legal cynicism, collective efficacy, and the ecology of arrest', *Criminology*, 49(2): 443–72.

Kirk, D. S. and Papachristos, A. V. (2011) 'Cultural mechanisms and the persistence of neighborhood violence', *American Journal of Sociology* 116(4): 1190–233.

Klinger, D. A. (1997) 'Negotiating order in patrol work: An ecological theory of police response to deviance', *Criminology*. 35(2): 277–306.

Kochel, T. R. (2011) 'Can police legitimacy promote collective efficacy?', *Justice Quarterly*, Online First.

Kuha, J., Skrondal, A. and Fisher, S. (2011) *Group Means as Explanatory Variables in Multilevel Models*. Paper presented at the Conference in honour of Professor Emeritus David J. Bartholomew, London School of Economics, London.

Lapsley, D. K. and Narvaez, D. (2005) 'Moral psychology at the crossroads', in D. K. Lapsley and F.C. Power (eds), *Character Psychology and Character Education*. Notre Dame, IN: University of Notre Dame Press.

Lasley, L. (1994) 'The impact of the Rodney King incident on citizen attitudes toward police', *Policing and Society*, 3(4): 245–55.

Lee, M. and McGovern, A. (2012) 'Force to sell: Policing the image and manufacturing public confidence', *Policing and Society*, iFirst DOI: 10.1080/10439463.2011. 647913.

Leishman, F. and Mason, P. (2003) *Policing and the Media: Facts, Fictions and Factions*. Cullompton: Willan Publishing.

Lentz, S. A. and Chaires, R. H. (2007) 'The invention of Peel's principles: A study of policing "textbook" history', *Journal of Criminal Justice*, 35: 69–79.

Lind, E. and Tyler, T. R. (1988) *The Social Psychology of Procedural Justice*. New York, Plenum Press.

Livingstone, S. (1996) 'The scope and context of media effects research', in J. Curran and M. Gurevitch *Mass Media and Society*, 2nd edn. London: Edward Arnold.

Loader, I. (1996) *Youth, Policing and Democracy*. Basingstoke: Palgrave Macmillan.

Loader, I. (1999) 'Consumer culture and the commodification of policing and security', *Sociology*, 33(2): 373–92.

Loader, I. (2006) 'Fall of the platonic guardians', *British Journal of Criminology*, 46: 561–86.

Loader, I. and Mulcahy, A. (2003) *Policing and the Condition of England: Memory, Politics and Culture*. Oxford: Oxford University Press.

Loader, I. and Walker, N. (2007) *Civilising Security*. Cambridge University Press.

Lofthouse, M. (1996) 'The core mandate of policing', in C. Critcher and D. Waddington (eds), *Policing Public Order: Theoretical and Practical Issues*. Avebury.

Luhmann, N. (1979) *Trust and Power*. Chichester: John Wiley and Sons.

MacAllister, I., Johnston, R. J., Pattie, C. J., Tunstall, H., Dorling, D. F. L. and Rossiter, D. J. (2001) 'Class dealignment and the neighbourhood effect: Miller revisited', *British Journal of Political Science*, 31: 41–60.

MacDonald, J. and Stokes, R. J. (2006) 'Race, social capital, and trust in the police', *Urban Affairs*, 41(3): 358–75.

MacDonald, J., Stokes, R. J., Ridgeway, G. and Riley, K. J. (2007) 'Race, neighborhood context, and perceptions of injustice by the police in Cincinnati', *Urban Studies*, 13: 2567–85.

Macpherson, Sir W. (1999) *The Stephen Lawrence Inquiry: The Report of an Inquiry.* London: HMSO.

Manning, P. (2003) *Policing Contingencies.* Chicago: The University of Chicago Press.

Manning, P. (2010) *Democratic Policing in a Changing World.* Boulder: Paradigm Publishers.

Martin, S. (2003) 'On public management reform', *British Journal of Management*, 14: 79–81.

Mastrofski, S., Reisig, M. D. and McCluskey, J. D (2002) 'Police disrespect toward the public: an encounter-based analysis', *Criminology*, 39: 519–52.

Mastrofski, S., Snipes, J. B. and Supina, A. E. (1996) 'Compliance on demand: The public's response to specific police requests', *Journal of Research in Crime and Delinquency* 33(3): 269–305.

Mawby, R. (2002) *Policing Images: Policing, Communication and Legitimacy.* Cullompton: Willan Publishing.

Mawby, R. (2010) 'Police corporate communication, crime reporting and the shaping of policing news', *Policing and Society,* 20(1): 124–39.

Mazerolle, L., Bennett, S., Manning, M., Ferguson, P. and Sargeant, E. (2012) *Legitimacy in Policing: A Systematic Review of Procedural Justice.* Campbell Crime and Justice Group.

McAra, L. and McVie, S. (2005) 'The usual suspects: Street-life, young people and the police', *Criminal Justice*, 5(1): 3–36.

McCabe, S., Wallington, P., with Alderson, J., Gostin, L. and Mason, C. (1988) *The Police, Public Order and Civil Liberties: Legacies of the Miners' Strike.* London: Routledge.

McCluskey, J. D. (2003) *Police Requests for Compliance: Coercive and Procedurally Just Tactics.* New York: LFB.

McCluskey, J. D., Mastrofski, S. and Parks, R. (1999) 'To acquiesce or rebel: predicting citizen compliance with police requests', *Police Quarterly*, 2: 389–416.

McDonald, R. P. and Ho, M.-H.R. (2002) 'Principles and practice in reporting statistical equation analyses', *Psychological Methods*, 7(1): 64–82.

McGovern, S. and Lee, M. (2012) 'Police communications in the social media age', in P. Keyzer, J. Johnston, and M. Pearson (eds), *Courts and the Media in the Digital Era.* Sydney: Halstead Press.

Meares, T. L. and Kahan, D. M. (1998) 'Law and norms of order in the inner city', *Law and Society Review*, 324: 805–31.

Miliband, R. (1978) 'A state of desubordination', *British Journal of Sociology*, 29(4): 399–409.

Miller, J. (2010) 'Stop and search in England: A reformed tactic or business as usual?', *British Journal of Criminology*, 50(5): 954–74.

Miller, J., Bland, N. and Quinton, P. (2000) *The Impact of Stops and Searches on Crime and the Community.* Police Research Series paper 127. London: Home Office.

Miller, J., Bland, N. and Quinton, P. (2001) 'A challenge for police-community relations: rethinking stop and search in England and Wales', *European Journal on Criminal Police and Research*, 9: 71–93.

Miller, J., Davies, R., Henderson, N., Markovic, J. and Ortiz, C. (2004) *Public Opinion of the Police: The Influence of Friends, Family and New Media*. New York: Vera Foundation.

Misztal, B. (1996) *Trust in Modern Societies*. Cambridge: Polity Press.

Morenoff, J. and Sampson, R. J. (1997) 'Violent crime and the spatial dynamics of neighborhood transition: Chicago, 1970–1990', *Social Forces*, 76: 31–64.

Morenoff, J. R., Sampson, R. J. and Raudenbush, S. W. (2001) 'Neighborhood inequality, collective efficacy, and the spatial dynamics of urban violence', *Criminology*, 39: 517–60.

Morgan, R. and Newburn, T. (1997) *The Future of Policing*. Oxford: Clarendon Press.

Morgan, S. and Winship, C. (2007) *Counterfactuals and Causal Inference*. New York: Cambridge University Press.

Mulaik, S. A., James, L. R., van Alstine, J., Bennet, N., Lind, S. and Stilwell, C. D. (1989) 'Evaluation of goodness-of-fit indices for structural equation models', *Psychological Bulletin*, 105(3): 430–45.

Mulford, M., Jackson, J. and Svedsater, H. (2008) 'Encouraging cooperation: Revisiting group identity and cooperative norm effects in prisoners' dilemma games', *Journal of Applied Social Psychology*, 38(12): 2964–89.

Murphy, K. and Cherney, A. (2010) *Policing Ethnic Minority Groups with Procedural Justice*. Geelong: Alfred Deakin Research Institute.

Murphy, K. and Cherney, A. (2012) 'Understanding cooperation with police in a diverse society', *British Journal of Criminology*, 52: 181–201.

Murphy, K., Hinds, L. and Fleming, J. (2008) 'Encouraging public cooperation and support for police', *Policing and Society*, 18: 136–55.

Murphy, K., Tyler, T. R. and Curtis, A. (2009) 'Nurturing regulatory compliance: Is procedural justice effective when people question the legitimacy of the law?', *Regulation and Governance*, 3(1):1–26.

Myhill, A. and Bradford, B. (2011) 'Can police enhance public confidence by improving quality of service? Results from two surveys in England and Wales', *Policing and Society*, iFirst.

Nagin, D. S. (1998) 'Criminal deterrence research at the outset of the twenty-first century', *Crime and Justice: a Review of Research,* 23: 1–42.

Newburn, T. (2003) 'Policing since 1945', in T. Newburn (ed.) *Handbook of Policing*. Cullompton: Willan Publishing.

Newburn, T. (2001) 'The commodification of policing: security networks in the late modern city', *Urban Studies*, 38(5–6): 829–48.

Newburn, T. and Reiner, R. (2004) 'From PC Dixon to Dixon plc: policing and police powers since 1954', *Criminal Law Review*: 601–18.

O'Neill, O. (2002) *A Question of Trust: The BBC Reith Lectures 2002*. Cambridge: Cambridge University Press.

Office for National Statistics (2003) *Ethnic Group Statistics: A Guide for the Collection and Classification of Ethnicity Data*. London: Office for National Statistics.

OPSR (2003) *Citizen Focused Policing*. Office of Public Services Reform.

Pagliaro, S., Ellemers, N. and Barreto, M. (2011) 'Sharing moral values: Anticipated ingroup respect as a determinant of adherence to morality-based (but not competence-based) group norms', *Personality and Social Psychology Bulletin*, 37(8): 1117–29.

Phillips, C. (2005) 'Ethnic inequalities under New Labour: Progress or entrenchment?', in J. Hills and K. Stewart (eds), *A More Equal Society? New Labour, Poverty, Inequality and Exclusion*. Bristol: Policy Press.

Pollitt, C. (2000) 'Is the emperor in his underwear? An analysis of the impact of public management reform', *Public Management*, 2(2): 181–99.

Putnam, R. D. (2007) *E Pluribus Unum: Diversity and Community in the Twenty-first Century.* The 2006 Johan Skytte Prize Lecture.

Quinton, P. and Morris, J. (2008) *Neighbourhood Policing: The Impact of Piloting and Early National Implementation.* London: Home Office.

Rao, J. N. K. (2003) *Small Area Estimation.* Hoboken, New Jersey: John Wiley & Sons.

Rawlings, P. (2002) *Policing: A Short History.* Cullompton: Willan Publishing.

Rawls, J. (1993) *Political Liberalism.* New York: Columbia University Press.

Rawls, J. (1995) 'Reply to Habermas', *Journal of Philosophy* XCII: 132–80.

Reed, A. II and Aquino, K. (2003) 'Moral identity and the circle of moral regard towards out-groups', *Journal of Personality and Social Psychology*, 84: 1270–86.

Reiner, R. (1992) 'Fin de siècle blues: the police face the millennium', *Public Opinion Quarterly,* 63(1): 37–49.

Reiner, R. (1997) 'Mass media criminality: The representation of crime', in M. Maguire, R. Morgan, and R. Reiner (eds), *The Oxford Handbook of Criminology.* Oxford: Oxford University Press.

Reiner, R. (2000) *The Politics of the Police*, 3rd edn. Oxford: Oxford University Press.

Reiner, R. (2003) 'Policing and the media', in T. Newburn (ed.) *Handbook of Policing.* Cullompton: Willan Publishing.

Reiner, R. (2010) *The Politics of Policing*, 4th edn. Hemel Hempstead: Prentice Hall/ Harvester Wheatsheaf.

Reiner, R., Livingstone, S. and Allen, J. (2000) 'No more happy endings? The media and popular concern about crime since the Second World War', in T. Hope and R. Sparks (eds), *Crime, Risk and Insecurity.* London: Routledge.

Reiner, R., Livingstone, S. and Allen, J. (2001) 'Casino culture: Crime and media in a winner-loser society', in K. Stenson and R. Sullivan (eds), *Crime, Risk and Justice: the politics of crime control in liberal democracies.* Cullompton: Willan Publishing.

Reisig, M. and Chandek, M. (2001) 'The effects of expectancy disconfirmation on outcome satisfaction in police-citizen encounters', *Policing: An International Journal of Police Strategies and Management*, 24(1): 88–99.

Reisig, M. D. and Lloyd, C. (2009) 'Procedural justice, police legitimacy, and helping the police fight crime: Results from a survey of Jamaican adolescents', *Police Quarterly*, 12(1): 42–62.

Reisig, M. D. and Parks, R. B. (2000) 'Experience, quality of life, and neighbourhood context: A hierarchical analysis of satisfaction with the police', *Justice Quarterly* 17(3). 607–30.

Reisig, M. D. and Parks, R. B. (2004) 'Can community policing help the truly disadvantaged?', *Crime and Delinquency*, 50(2) , 139–67.

Reisig, M. D., Bratton, J. and Gertz, M. G. (2007) 'The construct validity and refinement of process-based policing measures', *Criminal Justice and Behaviour*, 34: 1005–27.

Reith, C. (1948) *A Short History of the British Police.* Oxford: Oxford University Press.

Reith, C. (1952) *The Blind Eye of History: A Study of the Origins of the Present Police Era.* London: Faber & Faber.

Roberts, J. and Hough, M. (2005) *Understanding Public Attitudes to Criminal Justice.* Maidenhead: Open University Press.

Robinson, C., Scaglion, R. and Olivero, J. (1994) *Police in Contradiction: The Evolution of the Police Function in Society.* Westport, CT: Greenwood Press.

Rosenbaum, D., Schuck, A., Costebllo, S., Hawkins, D. and Ring, M. (2005) 'Attitudes toward the police: The effects of direct and vicarious experience', *Police Quarterly*, 83: 343–65.

Rousseau, D. M., Sitkin, S. B., Burt, R. S. and Camerer, C. (1998) 'Not so different after all: A cross-discipline view of trust', *Academy of Management Review*, 23: 393–404.

Rowe, M. (2004) *Policing, Race and Racism*. Cullompton: Willan Publishing.

Royal Commission on the Police (1962) *Final Report* Cmnd 1728, London: HMSO.

Sampson, R. J. and Bartusch, D. J. (1998) 'Legal cynicism and (subcultural?) tolerance of deviance: The neighbourhood context of racial differences', *Law and Society Review*, 32(4): 777–804.

Sampson, R. J. and Groves, W. B. (1989) 'Community structure and crime: testing social-disorganization theory', *American Journal of Sociology*, 94: 774–802.

Sampson, R. J. and Raudenbush, R. (2004) 'Seeing disorder: Neighborhood stigma and the social construction of "broken windows"', *Social Psychology Quarterly*, 67: 319–42.

Sampson, R. and Wilson, W. (1995) 'Toward a theory of race, crime, and urban inequality', in J. Hagan and R. Peterson (eds), *Crime and Inequality*. Stanford, CA: Stanford University Press.

Sampson, R. J., Morenoff, J. D. and Gannon-Rowley, T. (2002) 'Assessing "neighborhood effects": Social processes and new directions in research', *Annual Review of Sociology*, 28: 443–78.

Sampson, R. J., Raudenbush, S. W. and Earls, F. E. (1997) 'Neighborhoods and violent crime', *Science*, 277: 918–24.

Scarman, Lord (1982) *The Brixton Disorders 10–12 April 1981: Report of an Inquiry by Lord Scarman*. London: HMSO.

Schafer, J. A., Huebner, B. M. and Bynum, T. S. (2003) 'Citizen perceptions of police services: Race, neighbourhood context and community policing', *Police Quarterly*, 6: 440–68.

Schuck, A. M. and Rosenbaum, D. P. (2005) 'Global and neighbourhood attitudes toward the police: differentiation by race, ethnicity and type of contact', *Journal of Quantitative Criminology*, 21 (4), 391–418.

Schuck, A. M., Rosenbaum, D. P. and Hawkins, D. F. (2008) 'The influence of race/ethnicity, social class, and neighbourhood context on residents' attitudes toward the police', *Police Quarterly*, 11: 496–519.

Schulhofer, S. J., Tyler, T. R. and Huq, A. Z. (2011) 'American policing at a crossroads: Unsustainable policies and the procedural justice alternative', *Journal of Criminal Law and Criminology*, 101(2): 335–74.

Scott, W. R. (2001) *Institutions and Organizations,* 2nd edn. Thousand Oaks: Sage Publications.

Sharp, D. and Atherton, S. (2007) 'To Serve and protect? The experiences of policing in the community of young people from Black and other ethnic minority groups', *British Journal of Criminology*, 47: 746–63.

Shearing, C. and Stenning, P. (1981) 'Modern private security: Its gGrowth and implications', in M. Tonry and N. Morris (eds), *Crime and Justice: An Annual Review of Research* Vol. 3. Chicago: University of Chicago Press.

Shiner, M. (2006) *National Implementation of the Recording of Police Stops*. London: Home Office.

Siegrist, M. (2010) 'Trust and confidence: The difficulties in distinguishing the two concepts in research', *Risk Analysis* 30(7): 1022–4.

Siegrist, M., Cvetkovich, G. and Roth, C. (2000) 'Salient values similarity, social trust, and risk/benefit perceptions', *Risk Analysis*, 20: 353–62.

Silver, E. and Miller, L. L. (2004) 'Sources of informal social control in Chicago neighbourhoods', *Criminology*, 42(3): 551–83.

Sindall, J., Sturgis, P. and Jennings, W. (2012) 'Public confidence in the police: A time series analysis', *British Journal of Criminology*, 52: 744–64.

Skogan, W. (1994) *Contacts Between Police and Public: Findings From the 1992 British Crime Survey*. London: Home Office.

Skogan, W. (2006) 'Asymmetry in the impact of encounters with the police', *Policing and Society*, 162: 99–126.

Smith, D. (1983) *Police and People in London 1: A Survey of Londoners*. London: Policy Studies Institute.

Smith, D. (2007) 'New challenges to police legitimacy', in A. Henry and D. Smith (eds), *Transformations of Policing*. Aldershot: Ashgate.

Smith, D. and Gray, J. (1985) *Police and People in London: The PSI Report*. London: Gower.

Smith, H. J. and Tyler, T. R. (1997) 'Choosing the right pond: The influence of the status of one's group and one's status in that group on self-esteem and group-oriented behaviors', *Journal of Experimental Social Psychology*, 33: 146–70.

Smith, S. J. (1986) *Crime, Space and Society*. Cambridge: Cambridge University Press.

Spalek, B. (2008) *Reader in Ethnicity and Crime*. London: Open University Press.

Sparks, R. (1992) *Television and the Drama of Crime: Moral Tales and the Place of Crime in Public Life*. Buckingham: Open University Press.

Stanko, E. A. and Bradford, B. (2009) 'Beyond measuring "how good a job" police are doing: The MPS model of confidence in policing', *Policing: A Journal of Policy and Practice*, 4(3): 322–30.

Stott, C., Hoggett, J. and Pearson, G. (2012) '"Keeping the peace": Social identity, procedural justice and the policing of football crowds', *British Journal of Criminology*, 52(2): 381–99.

Stoutland, S. (2001) 'The multiple dimensions of trust in resident/police relations in Boston', *Journal of Research in Crime and Delinquency*, 38(3): 226–56.

Sturgis, P., Brunton-Smith, I., Jackson, J. and Kuha, J. (2012) 'Ethnic diversity, intergroup contact and the social cohesion of neighbourhoods', working paper.

Sturgis, P., Brunton-Smith, I., Read, S. and Allum, N. (2011) 'Does ethnic diversity erode trust? Putnam's "hunkering down" thesis reconsidered', *British Journal of Political Sociology*, 41(1): 57–82.

Sunshine, J. and Tyler, T. R. (2003a) 'Moral solidarity, identification with the community, and the importance of procedural justice: The police as prototypical representatives of a group's moral values', *Social Psychology Quarterly*, 66(2): 153–65.

Sunshine, J. and Tyler, T. R. (2003b) 'The role of procedural justice and legitimacy in public support for policing', *Law and Society Review*, 37(3): 513–48.

Surette, R. (1998) *Media, Crime, and Criminal Justice: Images and Realities,* 2nd edn. Belmont, CA: Wadsworth.

Sustainable Development Commission (2011) *Fairness in a Car Dependent Society*. Available at: www.sd-commission.org.uk/publications.php?id=1184.

Tajfel, H. and Turner, J. C. (1986) 'The social identity theory of inter-group behaviour', in S. Worchel and L. W. Austin (eds), *Psychology of Intergroup Relations*. Chicago: Nelson-Hall.

Tankebe, J. (2009) 'Public cooperation with the police in Ghana: Does procedural fairness matter?'*Criminology* 47(4): 1265–93.

Tankebe, J. (2010) 'Legitimation and resistance: police reform in the (un)making', in L. K. Cheliotis (ed.) *Roots, Rites and Sites of Resistance: The Banality of Good*. Basingstoke: Palgrave Macmillan.

Terrill, W. and Reisig, M. (2003) 'Neighborhood context and police use of force', *Journal of Research in Crime and Delinquency*, 40: 291–321.

Tuffin, R., Morris, J. and Poole, A. (2006) *An Evaluation of the Impact of the National Reassurance Policing Programme*. Home Office Research Report 296. London: Home Office Research, Development and Statistics Directorate.

Turner, J. C., Brown, R. J. and Tajfel, H. (1979) 'Social comparison and group interest in ingroup favoritism', *European Journal of Social Psychology*, 9: 187–204.

Turner, V. (1974) *Dramas, Fields, and Metaphors: Symbolic Action in Human Society*. Ithaca, NY: Cornell University Press.

Tyler, T. R. (1990) *Why People Obey the Law*. New Haven: Yale University Press.

Tyler, T. R. (1999) 'Why do people help organizations?: Social identity and pro-organizational behaviour', in B. Staw and R. Sutton (eds), *Research on Organizational Behavior* Vol. 21. Greenwich, CT: JAI.

Tyler, T. R. (2001) 'Public trust and confidence in legal authorities: what do majority and minority group members want from the law and legal institutions?', *Behavioural Sciences and the Law*, 19: 215–35.

Tyler, T. R. (2003) 'Procedural justice, legitimacy, and the effective rule of law', in M. Tonry (ed.), *Crime and Justice*, 30, 431–505.

Tyler, T. R. (2004) 'Enhancing police legitimacy', *Annals of the American Academy*, 593: 84–99.

Tyler, T. R. (2006a) 'Psychological perspectives on legitimacy and legitimation', *Annual Review of Psychology*, 57: 375–400.

Tyler, T. R. (2006b) *Why People Obey the Law*. Princeton: Princeton University Press.

Tyler, T. R. (2007) *Psychology and the Design of Legal Institutions*. Nijmegen: Wolf.

Tyler, T. R. (2008) 'Psychology and institutional design', *Review of Law and Economics*, 4(3): 801–87.

Tyler, T. R. (2011a) *Why People Cooperate: The Role of Social Motivations*. Princeton: Princeton University Press.

Tyler, T. R. (2011b) 'Trust and legitimacy: policing in the US and Europe', *European Journal of Criminology*, 8(4): 254–66.

Tyler, T. R. and Blader, S. L. (2003) 'The group engagement model: Procedural justice, social identity, and cooperative behaviour', *Personality and Social Psychology Review*, 7: 349–61.

Tyler, T. R. and Blader, S. L. (2005) 'Can businesses effectively regulate employee conduct?: The antecedents of rule-following in work settings', *Academy of Management Journal*, 48(6): 1143–58.

Tyler, T. R. and Boeckmann, R. (1997) 'Three strikes and you are out, but why? The psychology of public support for punishing rule breakers', *Law and Society Review*, 31(2): 237–65.

Tyler, T. R. and DeGoey, P. (1995) 'Collective restraint in social dilemmas: Procedural justice and social identification effects on support for authorities', *Journal of Personality and Social Psychology*, 69, 482–97.

Tyler, T. R. and Fagan, J. (2006) *Legitimacy and Cooperation: Why Do People Help the Police Fight Crime in Their Communities?*, Paper Number 06–99. Public Law and Legal Theory Working Paper Group, Columbia Law School.

Tyler, T. R. and Fagan, J. (2008) 'Legitimacy and cooperation: Why do people help the police fight crime in their communities?', *Ohio State Journal of Criminal Law*, 6: 231–75.

Tyler, T. R. and Huo, Y. (2002) *Trust in the Law: Encouraging Public Cooperation with the Police and Courts*. New York: Russell Sage Foundation.

Tyler, T. R. and Lind, E. A. (1992) 'A relational model of authority in groups', in M. P. Zanna (ed.), *Advances in Experimental Social Psychology*. San Diego: Academic Press.

Tyler, T. R. and Wakslak, C. J. (2004) 'Profiling and police legitimacy: Procedural justice, attributions of motive, and acceptance of police authority', *Criminology*, 42(2): 253–81.

Tyler, T. R., Braga, A., Fagan, J., Meares, T., Sampson, R. and Winship, C. (eds), (2007) *Legitimacy and Criminal Justice: International Perspectives.* N.Y.: Russell-Sage Foundation.

Tyler, T. R., DeGoey, P. and Smith, H. (1996) 'Understanding why the justice of group procedures matters: A test of the psychological dynamics of the group-value model', *Journal of Personality and Social Psychology*, 70: 913–30.

Tyler, T. R., Jackson, J. and Bradford, B. (in press) 'Social connections and material interests: On the relational basis of cooperation with legal authorities', *Encyclopedia of Criminology and Criminal Justice*, N. Harris (ed.), Springer-Verlag.

van der Toorn, J., Tyler, T. R. and Jost, J. (2011) 'More than fair: Outcome dependence, system justification, and the perceived legitimacy of authority figures', *Journal of Experimental Psychology*, 47(1): 127–38.

Van Dijke, M. H., de Cremer, D. and Mayer, D. (2010) 'The role of authority power in explaining procedural fairness effects', *Journal of Applied Psychology*, 95(3), 488–502.

Waddington, P. (1999) *Policing Citizens: Authority and Rights.* London: University College Press.

Waddington, P., Stenson, K. and Don, D. (2004) 'In proportion: Race, and police stop and search', *British Journal of Criminology*, 44: 889–914.

Walker, A., Kershaw, C. and Nicholas, S. (2006) *Crime in England and Wales 2005/06*, Home Office Statistical Bulletin 12/06. London: Home Office.

Ward, J. T., Nobles, M. R., Lanza-Kaduce, L. and Levett, L. (2011) 'Caught in their own speed trap: The intersections of speed enforcement policy, police legitimacy and decision acceptance', *Justice Quarterly*, DOI: 10.1177/1098611111413992.

Warner, B. D. (2007) 'Directly intervene or call the authorities? A study of forms of neighborhood social control within a social disorganization framework', *Criminology*, 45(1): 99–129.

Weber, M. (1978) *Economy and Society: Vol. 2.* Berkeley: University of California Press.

Webster, C. (2004) 'Policing British Asian communities', in R. Hopkins Burke (ed.), *Hard Cop, Soft Cop: Dilemmas and Debates in Contemporary Policing.* Cullompton: Willan Publishing.

Weinberger, B. (1995) *The Best Police in the World: An Oral History of English Policing from the 1930s to the 1960s.* Aldershot: Scholar Press.

Weiss, L. (2007) 'Defining neighbourhood boundaries for urban health research', *American Journal of Preventative Medicine*, 32(6):154–59.

Weitzer, R. (2000) 'Racialized policing: Residents' perceptions in three neighborhoods', *Law and Society Review*, 34:129–55.

Weitzer, R. (2002) 'Incidents of police misconduct and public opinion', *Journal of Criminal Justice*, 30: 397–408.

Weitzer, R. and Tuch, S. A. (2004) 'Race and perceptions of police misconduct', *Social Problems*, 51, 305–25.

Wells, H. (2008) 'The techno-fix versus the fair cop: Procedural (in)justice and automated speed limit enforcement', *British Journal of Criminology*, 48(6), 798–817.

Werthman, C., and Piliavin, I. (1967) 'Gang members and the police', in D. Bordua (ed.), *The Police: Six Sociological Essays.* New York: Wiley.

Williams, R. (1964) *The Long Revolution*. Harmondsworth: Penguin.

Wu, Y., Sun, I. Y. and Triplett, R. A. (2009) 'Race, class, or neighborhood context: Which matters more in measuring satisfaction with the police?', *Justice Quarterly*, 26 (1), 125–56.

Zelditch, M. (2001) 'Processes of legitimation: Recent developments and new directions', *Social Psychology Quarterly*, 64(1):4–17.

Index

Italic page numbers indicate relevant figures and tables.

22004893R00142

Printed in Great Britain
by Amazon